The Eighteenth Century Feminist Mind

The Eighteenth Century Feminist Mind

Alice Browne

Formerly Temporary Assistant Lecturer in the
History of the Classical Tradition,
Warburg Institute, London

WAYNE STATE UNIVERSITY PRESS   DETROIT   1987

Preassigned Library of Congress
Catalog Card Number 87-50710
ISBN 0-8143-1941-6

To my parents

Contents

Acknowledgements

I wish to thank the Fawcett Library, London, for their permission to quote from a manuscript in their possession, *The Female Protector*. I also wish to thank the Carl and Lily Pforzheimer Foundation, Inc., for permission to quote from manuscript letters from Mary Hays to William Godwin, located in the Carl H. Pforzheimer Library, New York.

Introduction

At the end of the eighteenth century, a reviewer commented on the number of women writers calling for an improvement in women's position, and summed up their perception of the three areas where change was needed. The first point on this feminist agenda was a call for women's education to be equal to men's, and a denial that men were intellectually superior to women. The second point concerned the legal and economic weaknesses of women's position, especially if they were married:

> They ask, in a masculine tone, by what pretence we make laws for them without their concurrence, exclude them from the acquisition of property, and from the possession of civil privileges, rendering them utterly dependent for comfort, for importance, even for existence in society, upon our caprices?

The third point was an attack on the double standard in sexual morality; for men to demand chastity of women, but not of themselves, was immoral, absurd and damaging to men as well as to women:

> They call upon us to relinquish our vices, to abandon our fallacies, to snap their chains, to disdain the brute argument of force, by which the many have too long been subjected by the worthless few, and to give future generations rational wives and mothers, who, by the dignity of their examples, shall teach their offspring to be virtuous and to be free.[1]

1

Much of this had been discussed throughout the eighteenth century and even earlier, but the combination of these three topics is characteristic of discussions of women's place at the end of the century. This agenda could lead to a wide range of practical recommendations, and it provides the framework both for feminist polemic and for some more or less conservative discussions of women's role in society. It can be recognised in nineteenth-century and modern feminisms, and so it is easy to overlook the fact that this unified, serious and secular way of discussing women's position was a new achievement at the time. Arguments in each of this agenda's areas of concern gain force from association with arguments in the other two, and are weakened by isolation. The history of the separate arguments which are brought together in this agenda makes this clear.

The first argument, that women are as rational as men and should be educated equally, has a long history and was put forcefully in the seventeenth century. However, if it is not coordinated with arguments about women's place in society and the way men should treat them, it lacks a secular account of the value of women's rationality or the point of educating them. Either educated women are mere curiosities, and learning is an occupation for the tiny minority of women who have no other responsibilities; or the value of education for women is a religious one, contributing to their spiritual welfare rather than their social usefulness. Religious motives for educating women can fit into the feminist agenda, but do not in themselves lead to feminism. They often lead to an ideal of women's behaviour which is too other-worldly to criticise the position of women in this world, and they are always vulnerable to the argument that intellectual activity is a very unimportant part of religious practice.

The career of Anna Maria van Schurman, one of the most famous learned women of the seventeenth century, and the author of a defence of women's right to learning, provides a symbol of these limitations.[2] Schurman achieved great fame as a young woman for her command of the learned languages; her greatest love was the study of Hebrew, and she saw all her studies as a means of learning more about God and the Bible. However, accounts of visits to her make it clear that much of her fame was not based on the quality of her achievements, but on the freakishness of a women knowing so many languages. Visiting dignitaries would put her through her paces, making her speak in all the languages she knew, and would admire her proficiency in the more feminine arts of paper-cutting and modelling in wax, as well as her linguistic skills.[3]

Frivolous displays of learning were not peculiar to women, but the impossibility of making a life out of learning was. When her mother died, Schurman had to take on the responsibility of running the household and caring for her two aunts, who were blind and infirm. In her autobiography, she describes this as a happy period in her life.[4] After her aunts died, she was disillusioned with her learned career, and saw it as a product of vanity and self-deception, which had been of no religious value. Her search for a deeper spiritual practice led her to a small mystical sect founded by Jean de Labadie, and the rest of her life was devoted to Labadie and his group. She shared in their persecutions, and left a detailed account of the sect's troubles in her autobiography.[5] Both her cultivation of learning and her mystical rejection of it belong to periods in her life when she was free of the responsibilities that occupied most women; they could have few implications for most women's lives.

The second type of argument, that about women's legal and social disabilities, represented something newer. Writers in earlier periods discuss these questions, but their discussions concern points of detail, or are exercises in paradox, rather than serious discussions of possible change. Texts which criticise the arbitrariness of men's power over women, or ask why women are excluded from certain professions, are not always about their ostensible subject-matter. Attacks on male tyranny may represent comments on the general unfairness of life, rather than calls to remedy particular injustices; texts which suggest women should engage in the professions or public life may be concerned with the nature of prejudice rather than with its content. Raising questions about the position of women is sometimes no more than a way of asking the reader to engage in the mental gymnastics of thinking about something paradoxical and absurd, and the fact that such questions could be read in this way created difficulties for writers trying to develop a feminist argument. Eighteenth-century works with a serious feminist intent could be misunderstood as exercises in paradox, or dismissed as perverse attempts to take absurd ideas seriously. Anti-feminist writing of the period often does not engage in serious argument, but in rhetoric designed to exclude feminist arguments from serious discourse altogether. Much of the achievement of eighteenth-century feminism is less in formulating new ideas than in developing serious discussion of ideas which were already familiar in frivolous contexts.

There is a similar development in discussions of the third problem, the sexual double standard. In the seventeenth century, some religious writers insisted that chastity was as important for men as for women, and secular writers suggested in comic contexts that it was unfair to impose a stricter sexual morality on women than on men. Secular arguments for chastity in both partners in a marriage developed during the eighteenth century, along with sentimental idealisation of marriage and parenthood, and male chastity ceased to be a purely religious ideal. At the end of the century, people argued about whether women should be excluded from good society for sexual misdemeanours that carried no penalties for men. This may be partly a response to standards growing stricter, but it also represents an increase in the possible area of serious secular discussion about women. Some writers argue that men with a bad reputation should suffer the same opprobrium as women. Respect for women as wives and mothers, and sympathy for women who did not conform to conventional standards of sexual morality, were not necessarily feminist positions, but could find a place in feminist arguments. These ideas could reinforce arguments about women's equal rationality and calls to give them greater independence, and could gain force from them in their turn.

Like later feminisms, the feminism of the late eighteenth century derives much of its energy from the tension between two apparently contradictory motives for improving women's position in society. The first is the idea that women are not fundamentally different from men, that, in the contemporary cliché, 'there is no sex in souls', and women's equal rationality entitles them to more control over their own lives. The weakness of a feminism built on this idea alone is that it implicitly identifies difference from men with inferiority to them; the best woman is only 'a softer man'.[6] The opposite motive for feminist arguments, the idea that women should have a more important role in society because of their difference from men and the unique importance of their role as mothers, could offer women a more satisfying sense of their own identity. However, without emphasis on women's and men's common rationality, this idea could lead to extremely oppressive views of women, which valued them only for their difference from men and their usefulness to men and children. The rational mother, who represents a common eighteenth-century feminist ideal, and the sort of women for whom feminists claimed greater independence in society, exemplifies both reasons for feminism; her rationality makes her man's equal, her role as mother is one he cannot fill.

In the eighteenth century, strictly feminist arguments which insist that women are rational beings, and that justice for women is desirable for its own sake, are often closely connected with instrumental feminist arguments. Instrumental feminist writers argue for improvements in women's education and women's position in society because such changes will benefit men, children, and society as a whole, rather than because justice to women demands them. Usually they are in sympathy with the strand in feminist thought which plays down differences between men and women, and argues that women can be improved by becoming more like men. Their tone is often patronising towards women, implying that they are passive objects of reform, rather than responsible moral beings.

A piece of dialogue from Robert Bage's novel *Hermsprong* shows how this tone can undermine an apparently strong expression of support for feminism:

'. . . if "a firm mind in a firm body" be supposed the best prayer of men to the gods, why not of women? Would they be worse mothers for it, or more helpless widows?'

'No,' said Sumelin, 'but they would be less charming figures.'

'Whilst they think of their charming figures, as much as you suppose them to do, Mrs. Wollstonecraft must write in vain.'

'And when,' the banker asked, 'will they think less of them?'

'When,' answered Hermsprong, 'they are better taught.'

'And when will that be?' again asked Sumelin.

'I know not,' his opponent returned. 'The change, if change there can be, must begin with men. Lovers must mix a little more wisdom with their adorations. Parents, in their mode of education, must make less distinction of sex.'[7]

A mild instrumental feminism, which argues that women should be better educated so as to make them more pleasing companions for men and more responsible wives and mothers, was a quite widely-held position. It appears in a great many educational and moralistic works addressed to women, and is part of Addison and Steele's message in their enormously influential *Spectator*. Feminists and their opponents could both use instrumentally feminist arguments. Feminists argue that justice for women is in everyone's interest; anti-feminists recognise women's oppression in other times and places, but argue that reform has gone as far as it can go without leading to women competing with men and neglecting their children. John Bennett's *Strictures on Female Education* begins with instrumentally feminist rhetoric criticising the neglect of women's education, and goes on to argue that women are not men's intellectual equals, and that they would lose their good qualities if they were over-educated.

> In that ardour of understanding, which rouses emulation, she would lose that soothing manner, which conciliates and endears. The world would be deprived of its fairest ornaments, life of its highest zest, and man of that gentle bosom, on which he can recline amidst the toils of labour, and the agonies of disappointment.[8]

Instrumental feminism helped to make possible feminism in the narrower sense; so did the intense eighteenth-century interest in women's experience and women's subjectivity. There was a great increase during this period in fiction about and for women, and in published writing by women. Katharine Rogers treats instrumental feminism and writing for women as part of the story of feminism, in a book which provides a very useful survey of these more broadly defined categories of pro-woman writing.[9] However, this interest in what it was like to be a woman did not necessarily lead to feminist views, although it made possible the strand in eighteenth-century feminism which emphasises women's difference from men, and their specifically feminine needs and experiences. The best-known eighteenth-century writings about women's experience convey mixed messages about women's nature and women's role in society. Many of them are less concerned with giving a naturalistic account of women's lives than with using women's experience as emblematic of being vulnerable, of having to make vital choices within narrow constraints, and of suffering bitter conflict between inner desires and external obligations.[10] The imaginative and symbolic power of these narratives of women's suffering could make it harder to imagine social change; once women's difficulties became a preferred symbol for certain general human dilemmas, they could seem inevitable and natural. There is also the simpler point that many of these texts portray women as dependent on men and focused on men: 'Alas! it was enough I knew his pleasure, to submit joyfully to him, whatever pain I foresaw it would cost me . . .' 'Oh Lord Orville! – it shall be the sole study of my happy life, to express, better than by words, the sense I have of your exalted benevolence, and greatness of mind!'[11] On the other hand, this interest in women's experience helped women to become more conscious of the constraints on them as women, even when they responded with resignation rather than with feminist protest. Patricia Meyer Spacks has described the varieties of women's self-representation at this period, and her analysis of Fanny Burney's *oeuvre* shows that Burney expresses a very subtle and complex view of the difficulties of being a woman.[12] Burney's willingness to devote great care and intelligence to discussing this subject-matter is a sign of the acceptance that the condition of women's lives is a serious subject, which was a necessary precondition of the development of feminism.

Instrumental feminism and curiosity about women's lives both made strong contributions to eighteenth-century feminism; however, they are only part of the background to it, for it was affected by the whole field of notions about women, not just by pro-woman ideas. Eighteenth-century England inherited many genres of writing about and for women; it also saw an increase in works written for a female readership, and in the number of women writing for publication.[13] Women's taste became more influential, and more important in the economics of publishing. Controversy about whether women should read seriously or write for publication died down at the end of the century, and was replaced by controversy about what they should read and write, and whether there were specifically feminine areas of intellectual life. As in earlier periods, the disciplines of theology, law, and medicine formulated ideas about women, often inconsistent with each other, which passed into educated common knowledge.[14] Women were attacked in misogynist satires and praised, more or less frivolously, in defences of women and satires against men's behaviour towards women. Their duties were discussed in sermons on marriage and on other topics. Devotional books gave more detailed advice, and so, in a different vein, did secular conduct books. Some of these ethical books have a fictional framework, such as a dying parent's advice to his or her children, and many works of fiction were strongly didactic. The rising standard of women's education led to an increase in school books written especially for girls, and an awareness of women as an important non-specialist audience. Books published by subscription often depended financially on women subscribers.[15]

Much eighteenth-century writing about women incorporates far older ideas, although the importance of women as an audience was new. However, some genres of eighteenth-century writing were favourable to the expression of new ideas about women. The greater sophistication of historical and ethnographic writing helped people to take a more relativistic view of all social institutions, including the position of women. Even within Europe, there were significant differences in the laws governing marriage and women's property rights, and there was a good deal of discussion of these differences. By the end of the century, many popular educational books addressed to women included discussion of the position of women at other times and in other places.[16] They were often reactionary in treating the position of women in contemporary English society as ideal, and the position of women in all other societies as unnatural, but they helped to create an audience for feminist ideas by ensuring that educated women and men knew that the position of women could change.

New developments in political theory suggested new ways of discussing women; theories of men's and citizens' rights made it possible to discuss the question of the rights of women. Modern discussions usually emphasise how awkwardly eighteenth-century political theories apply to feminist questions, and how there are blind spots and contradictions in feminisms which rely on such theories;[17] however, these theories made it possible to raise questions about the political status of women as a group. Political theories centred on the individual male citizen, rather than on more complex networks of hierarchy and dependence, made the exclusion of women from public life more obvious and more questionable, while theories which assumed political power was based on contract made it easier to imagine change.

Eighteenth-century feminism is often read as the beginning of the story of nineteenth- and twentieth-century feminisms, or as just another episode in the far older story of defences of women and women's complaints about their lot. Both readings are legitimate, but neither does full justice to eighteenth-century feminism's relationship to contemporary notions of woman. Feminists were affected by contemporary scientific ideas about women, by the social conventions governing women's behaviour, by moralistic and religious advice to women, and by the ways in which women were imagined in fiction. All these ways of thinking about women leave traces in feminist writing, and the development of feminist ideas at the end of the eighteenth century is involved with other shifts in ideas about women.

Part One

Eighteenth-Century Notions of Woman

CHAPTER ONE

Notions of Woman

The notions of woman current in eighteenth-century England incorporated many far older ideas, although there were significant changes in beliefs about women and in the genres of writing in which these beliefs were expressed. Middle- and upper-class women were better read than in earlier periods, and had more access to popularised versions of the ideas about women formulated in the specialised disciplines of theology, law and medicine, as well as in political, historical or ethnographic writing. Educated women and men shared access to many different and quite complex ways of talking about the social and natural conditions that made women what they were. Moral and didactic literature, designed to tell women what they should be, reflects these notions of what women were, and helps to clarify what was believed to be most crucial about women's lives, in its emphasis on women's subordination to their fathers and husbands. The genre in which women wrote and read the most, the novel, also emphasises marriage and family life, but points to their discontents in a way that the descriptive and prescriptive literatures do not. The eighteenth century developed new ways of imagining women, and heroine-centred fantasies are just as important a part of the culture's view of women as more consciously held beliefs. These women-centred imaginings, like the increase in women writers, gave women new confidence in thinking about their lives; new kinds of writing by, for and about women helped to make feminist discourse possible, even though their immediate effect was often to limit women to narrowly 'feminine' views of themselves and their lives.

Theology in eighteenth-century England provided many of the arguments in two debates about women: how far a wife's duty to be subordinate to her husband went, and whether a woman could preach or speak in church. The first question revolved round the interpretation of the story of Adam and Eve; was Eve created subordinate, or was her subordination a punishment for her part in the Fall? If the latter were the case, there was a question about the curse on her: was it a prescription for all time, or a prophecy about Adam and Eve's immediate future? These arguments translate easily into secular arguments about whether women's subordination is a matter of nature or convention. In a comment on Genesis 3.16, Locke pointed out that not all men work by the sweat of their brow, and suggested that the wife's subordination was a matter of contract, which could be varied in different social circumstances; it was as reasonable to do this as to take any measures that could be found to alleviate the pains of childbirth.[1] The second question, that of women's preaching, revolved round the interpretation of certain passages in Paul's epistles; again, the question was whether these represented valid advice for all time, or only applied to the people addressed in the epistles concerned. Practice varied between different sects; Anglicans and traditional Dissenters did not let women preach, while Methodists and Quakers did. However, by the end of the century all sides agreed that the prohibition was a matter of decorum, not of women's intellectual incapacity; women members of sects which did not allow women to preach were publishing sermons which clergymen friends had preached for them.[2]

The complexities and contradictions of English law expressed many rules which oppressed women, but many which allowed them autonomy in certain circumstances. It was a commonplace that women were better off under English law than under that of any other country, and this view was confirmed in the most influential law book of the century, Blackstone's *Commentaries*.[3] However, Edward Christian, commenting on Blackstone at the end of the century, saw much room for improvement, both in law and custom. Christian saw no legal reason why single women of property should not vote, and the history of women's votes shows how at times custom could be even more restrictive than law.[4] In 1640, Sir Simonds D'Ewes, as invigilating sheriff, had put a stop to an attempt by some widows to vote in a parliamentary election, 'conceiving it a matter very unworthy of any gentleman, and most dishonourable in such an election, to make use of their voices, although they might in law have been allowed'.[5] The judges in a 1739 case, *Olive* v. *Ingram*, found that women could hold the office of church sexton and vote for that office, and disagreed about whether there was a firm legal basis for women's exclusion from the parliamentary franchise.[6] At the end of the century in America, women voted for some years in elections in New Jersey, because the 1790 state constitution did not specify that electors had to be male. Opponents of the practice saw it as unnatural and as an unfair exploitation of a legal loophole, but not as a legal absurdity in a system based on English law.[7]

Single women and widows could own property, make wills and conduct businesses. The question of married women's property was more complex. Under common law, a wife's property, including her earnings, became her husband's, although there were restrictions on his right to dispose of land belonging to her. In equity, separate property could be settled on a married woman under the management of a trustee; rich families normally settled their daughters' money in this way at marriage, rather than allowing it to pass into their husbands' control.[8] Marriage settlements also specified what the wife's jointure, or share of her husband's estate, would be if she were widowed. In theory, if not always in practice, this meant the bride's future was provided for, whatever happened to her husband, and she would make no further claims on her own family.[9] Usually she could not dispose of the property settled on her, or borrow money against it; this was to safeguard her interests, and ensure her husband could not 'kiss or kick' her out of her property.[10] By the end of the century, legacies to married women were automatically made into trusts under the husband's trusteeship, if the testator had made no other provision.[11] Because married women's legal incapacities resulted from their married status, not from the fact that they were women, it was easy to argue that they were arbitrary, not natural. The laws of property carried an ambiguous message about women's inferiority.

Divorce was difficult and expensive, involving a private Act of Parliament. All eighteenth-century cases were initiated by husbands.[12] A necessary precondition of divorce was the husband's obtaining damages from the wife's lover in an action for criminal conversation. This transaction between two men implicitly denied that the wife was a free agent; in this it resembled the lower-class practice of husbands selling their wives to other men for a nominal sum. Many uneducated people believed that wife-selling provided a valid form of divorce and remarriage, although in fact it had no legal status.[13]

Criminal law treated the sexes equally in many respects, but also reflected beliefs about women's dependence and duplicity. A wife who was her husband's accomplice in a crime was usually deemed to have acted under coercion. A husband who murdered his wife was guilty only of murder, whereas a wife who murdered her husband was guilty of petty treason, and subject to execution by burning. There was comment on this inequality during the eighteenth century, and an increasing revulsion against this method of execution, which was also used for women coiners.[14] There were severe penalties for the abduction of an heiress followed by rape or forced marriage, but the law was concerned with the injury to the family, rather than to the woman herself.[15] The seduction of a woman without property could only be punished by means of a legal fiction in which her father or master sued for damages to compensate for the loss of her services.[16] Rape carried the death penalty, but in practice there were obstacles to getting a conviction, and a bias against the victim. Blackstone warned that accusations of rape, like those of sodomy, should be treated with the utmost scepticism, because horror at the idea of the crime could make juries overzealous in convicting, and serious writers doubted if an adult woman in full possession of her faculties could be raped by one man.[17] Sexual intercourse with girls under ten years constituted rape; with girls between ten and twelve, the crime was deemed less serious. Twelve was the legal age of marriage for girls, fourteen for boys, although fictional stereotypes usually put a girl's sexual maturity slightly later, at fifteen or sixteen. The average age of marriage was in the early twenties for women.[18] An early seventeenth-century law on infanticide received some attention because, unusually for English law, it presumed the guilt of the accused. A woman who had concealed the birth of a child which died was considered to have murdered it, unless she could prove otherwise. This law was enforced severely in the seventeenth century, but juries became much readier to acquit during the eighteenth, and the law was reformed in 1803.[19]

One factor in the increased lenience towards suspected infanticides was a well-founded scepticism about doctors' competence to decide whether an infant had been born alive. The period saw some technical developments in obstetrics, and a great deal of writing on gynaecological subjects, but doctors' ignorance could be embarrassingly obvious.[20] In 1726, Mary Toft convinced some reputable doctors that she had given birth to seventeen rabbits, while early in the next century, the 64-year-old prophetess, Joanna Southcott, persuaded a group of doctors to certify her supposed miraculous pregnancy after only a perfunctory examination.[21]

From women's point of view, the most important change in medical practice during the eighteenth century was a great increase in male interest in childbirth and the care of infants. It became normal for upper- and middle-class women to have a male doctor present when they gave birth; by the end of the century, Mary Wollstonecraft's decision to have her children with only a midwife's assistance was fairly unusual.[22] There were surgically skilled men-midwives for those who could not afford doctors. Male attendance at childbirth went against some people's ideas about propriety; many attacks on male obstetricians are prurient and obscene, and take it for granted that it should be taboo for men to attend women in such an intimate context.[23] The female midwives did not give up without a struggle, and both sides portrayed each other as ignorant butchers of the women and infants they attended. Women were not allowed to use forceps, or other instruments which had been developed to dismember an unborn child to save the mother's life; they argued that their skills made such intervention unnecessary.[24] Writers who defended male midwives argued that their knowledge and skill were greater, and pointed out that traditional female midwives did a great deal of damage without instruments.[25] Defenders of women midwives often argued that women were kinder than men, with more tenderness towards infants, and more fellow feeling for the mother's sufferings.[26] The lying-in charities which provided for many poor women by the end of the century had a two-tier system: a trained female midwife would attend all births, but was obliged to call in a doctor if there were complications.[27]

The increase in male attendance at childbirth went with a generally increased male interest in birth and early childhood, which had an ambiguous effect on attitudes to women. It meant a greater respect for women, because of the importance of their role as mothers, but also a sense that this role was too important for them to perform without help from men. William Cadogan justified his *Essay upon Nursing, and the Management of Children* with the statement: 'in my opinion, this business has been too long fatally left to the management of women, who cannot be supposed to have proper knowledge to fit them for such a task, notwithstanding they look upon it to be their own province.'[28] He argued, with some justification, that women's traditional ideas about childcare were made up of the debris of obsolete scientific views, and that a new scientific approach was needed, based on observation and experience.[29] Fathers should take more interest in their children's upbringing.[30] The importance of early childhood was to become one of the main arguments for women's education: their ethical and intellectual formation should equip them to give a child a good start in life.

This ideal of woman as rational mother, which moralists and medical writers promoted, conflicted with other medical traditions which saw femaleness as a weakness, if not actually a pathological state. Childbirth and pregnancy were sometimes equated with weakness and illness; however, many writers emphasise that women must be strong and healthy to bear healthy children. These traditions were often self-contradictory in seeing ailments like the vapours both as inherent to femaleness and as the culpable result of upper-class women's idleness.[31] It is a clear example of the fact that many eighteenth-century generalisations about the nature of women are really generalisations about non-working, upper-class women.

There is no consistent relationship between eighteenth-century feminism and other political ideas of the time, although during the periods of political uncertainty at the beginning and end of the century many people saw a strong symbolic link between female rebellion and political upheaval. Throughout the century, people made connections between women's freedom and political liberty in general:

> In Rome too liberty once reigned, in Rome
> The female virtues were allowed to bloom,
> And bloom they did . . .[32]

However, the implications of this for women's lives were as varied as the meanings of liberty.

Mary Astell, the most gifted feminist writer of the turn of the seventeenth and eighteenth centuries, links a strong feminist statement of women's rationality and moral worth to a strong Tory statement that no one has a right to rebel against authority; women and men are equal in their duty to choose obedience rationally. Her often-quoted question, 'If all men are born free, how is it that all women are born slaves?' is a *reductio ad absurdum* of Whig ideas, not a call for women's political liberation.[33] Conservative writers continued to use the question in this way, but, by the end of the century, a few democratic writers were willing to consider it seriously. Most feminist writers of the 1790s were radicals, in sympathy at least with the first stages of the French Revolution. Some writers responded by linking political conservatism with anti-feminism, but others avoided this, and combined political conservatism with a moderate feminism which recalls Astell.

Eighteenth-century political theory excluded women from public life, but made it easy to question the exclusion; it is the primary inspiration and primary opponent of many feminist theorists up to the present day.[34] Locke does not say a great deal about women, but what he says does not rule out the possibility of extending citizens' rights to women. He argues that women and men should receive similar educations, and that the extent of a wife's subordination to her husband is a matter of contract; it can be varied, or even abolished altogether, as in the case of a reigning queen married to one of her subjects.[35] He does not deny women's natural inferiority, but consistently plays it down.[36] By basing political power on contract, and arguing against the notion that it derives from a divinely instituted patriarchal power traceable back to Adam, he removes one of the principal arguments for men's power over women.

Locke's views could fit in with the side of eighteenth-century feminist thought which emphasised women's likeness to men, while Rousseau's could provide inspiration for feminists who emphasised women's separate and special needs.[37] Rousseau's anti-feminism had consequences which could be used to strengthen feminist arguments. His most important discussion of women's position occurs in the fifth book of *Émile*. Men's education should teach them to be self-reliant; women's should teach them to be dependent and submissive to their husbands. Women's duties as wives and mothers are the centre of their lives. Mary Wollstonecraft's polemic with this text in the *Vindication of the Rights of Woman* is the first of many feminist attacks on it.[38] However, parts of the book could work against the obvious anti-feminist message of the whole. Rousseau insists that women are not defective men, and that their different qualities are appropriate for them;[39] talk of superiority of one sex over the other is meaningless.[40] Parts of the book suggest genuine interdependence between the sexes, rather than dependence of women on men.[41] Rousseau agrees with feminists that women must be able to think in order to be good mothers, and that gallant and flirtatious conventions of politeness are really insulting to women.[42] His insistence on the importance of sexual difference, and on the separate and vital duties of women, could seem to offer women more dignity than the 'worldly' view to which he opposes it, the view that women should be entertaining and frivolous companions for men. He attacks the mixed-sex social life of his time, which leads to the blurring of gender distinctions, and insists each sex should be truer to its own qualities.[43] Condorcet, in his proposal to allow women political rights, found Rousseau's popularity with women readers hard to understand.[44] However, Rousseau's work encouraged women's sense of themselves as a group in society with rights and duties defined by their gender, even though it undermined faith in women's autonomy and rationality.

Rousseau's sense of the possibility of changing women's position in society is the result of a new historical and ethnographic sophistication. When writers in earlier periods talk about how men treat women, they are usually generalising about how individual men treat their wives and daughters, and the legal and social restrictions on women are seen as resulting from the sum of personal acts of control. Eighteenth-century writers have a stronger sense of an independent logic governing society as a whole, and a stronger sense of the possibility of change. Often they agree that the position of women in a society is an index of how civilised it is; the more barbarous a society, the worse off its women were.[45] At the end of the century, popular educational works directed to women often include an outline of history from this point of view.[46] A detailed and influential book directed to a female audience, William Alexander's *The History of Women*, insists that contemporary British law and custom represent the ideal for women.[47] However, arguments from history, like arguments from other cultures, were not in themselves conservative; feminist writers assume that they are at the beginning of women's historical progress, not at its culmination. Mary Hays wrote in her obituary of Mary Wollstonecraft: 'Her own sex have lost, in the premature fate of this extraordinary woman, an able champion; yet she has not laboured in vain; the spirit of reform is silently pursuing its course. Who can mark its limits?'[48]

Alexander claimed that his work 'will more gratify the curiosity of the female mind, to whatever relates to themselves, than any thing that has hitherto been published.'[49] Eighteenth-century writers and publishers were conscious of the importance of women as an audience, and published a wide range of works dealing with women, and directed primarily or exclusively at women. Some unexpected genres of writing about women could have a significant female audience. Misogynist satire could be an instrument in women's education; the moralist and educator Sarah Trimmer was inspired to virtuous behaviour in her youth by reading Young's satires against women.[50] Praises of women's virtues, and histories of exceptional women, could teach by positive rather than negative example. There is an intimate and complicated relationship between misogynist satire and a literary tradition praising women for those qualities in which they were thought to be superior to men – quick wit, social adeptness and physical beauty.[51] In the eighteenth century, as in earlier periods, this is usually less a mode of feminist argument than a vehicle for chivalrous, gallant praises of women; praise of women can be merely a way of writing about desire, just as satire against women can be about sexual disgust rather than about what women are like.[52] Statements like 'men are tyrants' are often no more than meaningless compliments to women. In *Anna St.Ives*, Thomas Holcroft puts this phrase into his villain's mouth, not into that of his feminist heroine.[53] Eighteenth-century feminists are usually even more impatient with praises of women than with misogynist satire. There is a constant tension in eighteenth-century feminist writing between the idea that misogynist satire is a libel against women, and the idea that it represents the truth about most women, which feminists must work to change. The ambiguity in Mary Wollstonecraft's chapter-title in the *Vindication of the Rights of Woman*, 'On writers who have rendered women objects of pity, bordering on contempt', is a significant one. Women have been maligned, in her view, but they have also been corrupted by bad advice.

There was a great deal of educational writing about how to form women, and numerous school books and children's books designed to provide girls with good examples.[54] Books of advice to girls usually contain some discussion of the duties of adult life, and overlap with religious or secular conduct books addressed to married women. The most successful were reprinted again and again, and were probably familiar to most middle- and upper-class women. The genre is a bibliographer's nightmare, for the most popular works were more widely available even than the number of their printings would suggest. Compendia like Steele's

Ladies' Library, or *The Whole Duty of a Woman*, are made up of lengthy extracts from earlier works and do not try to coordinate them into a consistent message.[55] School anthologies include highlights from these books, as well as more literary passages.[56]

Devotional books, which are often reprints of seventeenth-century works or incorporate seventeenth-century material, usually emphasise women's moral responsibility and play down the differences between women and men. Like some other seventeenth-century writing, but unlike most secular eighteenth-century writing, they are happy to praise women for masculine qualities, and not insist that women should always be feminine. They are often clear about the difficulties and restrictions of women's lives; one of the most influential devotional books for women, *The Ladies Calling*, by the author of *The Whole Duty of Man*, strongly emphasises the servitude of marriage in its criticism of widows who remarry, although it elsewhere describes widowhood as the most wretched stage of a woman's life.[57] The genre was one in which women wrote as well as read, apparently with no sense of inferiority; there was a school of thought which attributed the most influential Anglican devotional books, *The Whole Duty of Man* and its related works, to a woman, Lady Pakington.[58] Although these works preach resignation, the seriousness with which they take women's spiritual destiny contributed to the strand in eighteenth-century feminism which insisted on women's dignity as responsible individuals.

Books of worldly, prudential advice again assume women's subordination, but do not usually idealise men, for advice on how to deal with husbands' bad behaviour is a common theme. Most are addressed to upper- or middle-class women, though there are also books instructing women servants to make their employers' interests their own, as in the following advice to dairymaids: 'You must see that your hogs have the whey, and that it be not given away to gossiping and idle people, who live merely upon what they can get from servants.'[59] Some give a very bleak picture of a woman's life; the Countess of Carlisle's *Thoughts in the Form of Maxims* advises its readers to trust no one, expect nothing from anyone, and be as self-sufficient as possible. Men's authority is taken for granted but, until the end of the century, secular writers are less defensive than religious ones about male superiority. One of the most popular books in this genre, Halifax's *Advice to a Daughter* justifies women's subordination by their less rational nature but, as most of the book is devoted to portraying a rogues' gallery of difficult husbands, and giving advice on how to handle them, it keeps the argument light by not insisting too much on male rationality, and not indulging in pompous sermonising about the nobility of man's role, which might be vulnerable to ridicule.[60] Certainly, eighteenth-century writers were usually being ironic when they referred to men as the 'Lords of Creation', and fictional women were allowed some spirited parodies of the rhetoric of male superiority:

Men, indeed! – Men were born for no other purpose under heaven, but to amuse us; and he who succeeds best, perfectly answers the end of his creation.[61]

However, such parody addresses a heavy-handed style of insisting on male superiority, not the notion itself, and a light, friendly, chivalrous tone could convey the message just as well.

The increase in the number of didactic books addressed to women is connected with the rising standard of women's education, which created a wider audience for factual and imaginative works about women, as well as more opportunities for women writers. Men as well as women read woman centred novels, or popular factual works about women, but the implied reader in these works is usually female. Fiction, history and biography all provided women with examples; there are many references to women deriving inspiration and encouragement from women's biographies. By the end of the century, a sense of female tradition is quite common in books designed for girls' education. Elizabeth Ogilvy Benger's poem *The Female Geniad*, written when she was thirteen, lists famous women of the past and present.[62] Mary Hays' six-volume *Female Biography* seems to have been designed for educational use; it is didactic and moralistic in tone.[63]

Women wrote religious autobiographies, as they had in earlier periods; they also wrote light, entertaining, secular books of memoirs. The kind of autobiography which attracted most attention, especially at the end of the century, was the self-justifying memoir by a woman who had led a life which was immoral by conventional standards, explaining her fall and her misfortunes. Readers' response ranged from acceptance of the woman's argument, through cynicism mixed with sympathy, to disgust, outrage and disbelief.[64] These works are at best one-sided, and some of them were written to blackmail lovers into paying to be left out. Their sentimental preoccupation with the writers' fall from virtue was memorably dismissed by a courtesan of the next generation in the first paragraph of her memoirs:

I shall not say why and how I became, at the age of fifteen, the mistress of the Earl of Craven. Whether it was love, or the severity of my father, the depravity of my own heart, or the winning arts of the noble Lord, which induced me to leave my paternal roof and place myself under his protection, does not now much signify: or if it does, I am not in the humour to gratify curiosity in this matter.[65]

She also criticises the melodramatic tone of these works by adding that life with Lord Craven was 'a dead bore'. However, with all their weaknesses, the books try to discuss the injustices women suffered, and criticise conventional moral standards. Mary Wollstonecraft's posthumous novel, *The Wrongs of Woman*, is an attempt to use the genre for feminist, didactic purposes.

Women were developing a sense of their own

tradition as writers, which increased the possibilities available to them, even if it tended to restrict them to feminine genres. It was a commonplace that women were better than men at letter-writing and other kinds of spontaneous and informal writing. This idea is clearly based on traditional notions about women's quick wit and liveliness, but it may also be true that women's ignorance of Latin prevented a Latin influence from weighing down their style. The belief must have helped the market for women's writing, and many men were writing under female pseudonyms. The hack medical writer, John Hill, wrote a *Guide to Married Life* under the pseudonym The Hon. Juliana-Susannah Seymour, included cures by 'A Lady of Quality' in a book of advice to people with cancer, and was widely believed to be the author of Hannah Glasse's *Art of Cookery*.[66] However, this view of women's writing does not take it seriously, and can lead to pathetic expressions of bravado which show how little some women writers thought of their own work: 'My writings were never shackled with grammatical rules, or the fetters of deep erudition: I have suffered my sentiments to flow from my pen, totally regardless of the critic's frown, or the sneer of paltry envy.'[67] The appeal to female tradition and to women's past could be treacherous for feminists, because women's achievements appeared so few and so exceptional; Mary Wollstonecraft avoided it for this reason.[68] Yet the biographies of famous women in the past, and the corpus of writing by women, were an element in women's sense of themselves which could lead to pride and solidarity.

Women wrote novels, plays and poems all through the century, but expectations about their work changed. At the beginning of the century, women's writing was often expected to be licentious and improper:

> What has this age produced from female pens,
> But an obsceneness that outstrides the men's?[69]

The exceptions, women whose lives and works were blameless, were overpraised into invisibility. Typically, like the seventeenth-century poet Katherine Philips, 'the matchless Orinda', they were supposed not to want to publish or make money from their work. By the middle of the century, this expectation was changing; the preface to Colman and Thornton's *Poems by the most Eminent Ladies of Great Britain and Ireland* says of the works it selects: 'they are a standing proof that great abilities are not confined to the men, and that genius often glows with equal warmth, and perhaps with more delicacy, in the breast of a female'.[70] At the end of the century, many women writers were highly respected and highly moral, some of them earning a lot of money from their work. It was common for reviewers to claim women's work was judged on its own merits, and for writers attacking work by a woman to go out of their way to praise other women writers.[71] Many women expressed pride in this progress, though the century had seen no important changes for the better in women's legal, political or economic situation.[72]

The increased respectability of women's writing is related to a generally stricter demand for propriety in language and in social behaviour. 'Victorian' standards of verbal prudery had been formed in Evangelical circles by the end of the century.[73] At the beginning of the next century, Sir Walter Scott's great-aunt commented on the change, when she found it impossible to reread the novels of Aphra Behn, which she had enjoyed as a girl.[74] This shift gave women a more secure, but more restricted place in the culture. Some writers at the end of the century thought women were morally superior to men; all agreed that women were the arbiters of proper behaviour in mixed company.[75] Men needed to learn politeness in women's company for their full moral and social development. James Fordyce summed up the good effect of women's company on men:

I do not mean, that the men I speak of will become feminine; but their sentiments will contract a grace. Their principles will have nothing ferocious or forbidding; their affections will be chaste and soothing in the same instant. In their case the gentleman, the man of worth, the Christian, will all melt insensibly and sweetly into one another. How agreeable the composition![76]

This sublimates the older, worldly notion, still alive in writers like Chesterfield, that young men need to be polished by love affairs.[77] Fordyce believed the company of virtuous women was the best protection against sexual temptation.[78] If the sublimated version of this convention gave respectable women more scope for mixing with men, neither version really took women seriously. Men could speak far more freely with each other than with women. Politeness forbade them to contradict a woman, decorum restricted what they could discuss with her. Writing in the persona of a male opponent of women's education, Maria Edgeworth summed up these limitations:

> Whenever women appear, even when we seem to admit them as our equals in understanding, everything assumes a different form; our politeness, delicacy, habits towards the sex forbid us to argue, or to converse with them as we do with one another – we see things as they are, but women must always see things through a veil, or cease to be women.[79]

Any attempt to treat a woman as an equal risked looking like gross bad manners. Even women who criticised these conventions as empty flattery may have found it hard to do without them; Mary Wollstonecraft is said to have been hard on men who neglected gestures like opening doors for women or picking up their handkerchiefs, which she had written about with contempt.[80] These conventions carried as many meanings about women as formal beliefs did, but it was far harder to argue against them. They are invisible in the more erudite kinds of discussion about women, but these discussions cannot be properly understood if the conventions of politeness are forgotten. The conventions of good manners imply beliefs about women, and make it clear that these beliefs entail demands on them; chivalrous treatment is a reward for proper behaviour.

CHAPTER TWO

Advice to Women:
The stages of a woman's life

Eighteenth-century writers divided a woman's life into the three stages of maid, wife and widow, and also sometimes discussed a woman's duties as a friend and as a mother, which could continue through more than one of these stages. In every genre of writing about women, it was clear that marriage was the most important event in a woman's life; it changed her legal status and imposed a new set of duties on her. Fiction dealt with young women's entry into the world and search for a husband, while moralists, educators and preachers advised young women how to attract a husband and how to behave once married. The arts of attraction became more necessary during the century, as parents were allowing children more say in their choice of marriage partner. The Marriage Act of 1753, which forbade partners under twenty-one to marry without their parents' consent, made it easier for parents to allow children to get to know each other, as it was harder for adolescents to elope. In earlier periods, upper-class parents expected to choose their children's spouses, allowing them a limited right of veto; by the end of the eighteenth century, children expected to choose their own spouses, subject to their parents' approval.

Men chose; women waited to be chosen. Moralists warned young women against falling in love before a man had declared himself, and argued that women were more flexible than men, and loved in response to a man's love. John Gregory commented:

If attachment was not excited in your sex in this manner, there is not one in a million of you that could ever marry with any degree of love.

A man of taste and delicacy marries a woman because he loves her more than any other. A woman of equal taste and delicacy marries him because she esteems him, and because he gives her that preference.[1]

Girls were meant to be more flexible than young men at the time of marriage, but not unformed or formed only by experience. There were numerous books on girls' education, especially towards the end of the century, as well as traditional moralistic literature on the duties of daughters and of single women generally. One reason for this was that technological advances meant much less household work for upper- and middle-class women to do; foreign visitors were struck by English women's sloth.[2] This meant less work for adolescent daughters, as well as for the mistress of the household. 'Miss in her teens' had a good deal of leisure, and moralists and educators worried she would abuse it.

The vices they warn against are those of a prosperous and leisured life. Young women are warned not to eat too much, not to get drunk, not to be too preoccupied with clothes and finery, not to read romantic novels, not to masturbate, and not to go on too many outings to places of entertainment. All these vices involve sexuality, either directly, or because they are involved with qualities which make women unattractive to men.

The warnings against eating too much are partly based on general moral principles, partly on the idea that it is unattractive for women to be too strong and healthy. John Gregory commented on over-eating: 'It is a despicable selfish vice in men, but in your sex it is beyond expression indelicate and disgusting.'[3] A comic writer tells a story of a lady toying with her dinner, who is humiliated by her brother pointing out that she had a pound of beefsteak and a pint of porter brought to her room earlier in the afternoon.[4]

Novel heroines became more fragile as the century went on,[5] and educational writers argued about how much exercise was appropriate for girls. John Gregory was in favour of girls exercising and looking after their health, but he warned them to be discreet about it:

> But though good health be one of the greatest blessings of life, never make a boast of it, but enjoy it in grateful silence. We so naturally associate the idea of female softness and delicacy with a corresponding delicacy of constitution, that when a woman speaks of her great strength, her extraordinary appetite, her ability to bear excessive fatigue, we recoil at the description in a way she is little aware of.[6]

Priscilla Wakefield defended exercise for girls by arguing that the trials of pregnancy and childbirth would ensure their staying attractively weak as adults.[7] There was another strand in this distrust of exercise, the notion that girls who were physically active might not always live up to the high standards of female propriety. 'Dear creature! Did she never romp?', asks Lovelace, looking for a flaw, somewhere, in the perfect decorum of Clarissa's life.[8] Tomboyish romping is linked to early seduction in the scandalous *Life of Jenny Cameron*.[9]

However, there was more to the demands on women's bodies than a simple requirement not to be too strong or healthy. People in the period were very conscious of posture, and dance, the main form of exercise for women, did much to control this. Some manuals of conduct include illustrations showing how to hold oneself and where to put one's hands; this advice was important for both sexes, for posture was an important marker of class.[10]

People were also concerned about deformity, which was common, usually because of rickets. Its causes were not understood, and people engaged in controversy about whether it was caused or prevented by wearing stays.[11] Most discussion of the evil effects of stays occurs at the end of the century, after they had become less restrictive, although Locke had argued against putting children into them too young.[12] Stays helped an erect posture, and could disguise minor deformities. They also carried symbolic meaning about the virtues of a woman who wore them. They signified a woman's chastity and correctness; this symbolism is still alive in the word 'strait-laced'. They also carried contradictory meanings about her capacity to be a mother. The narrow waist and flat stomach produced by stays were incompatible with pregnancy, and aroused fears that unborn children could be harmed by a mother's tight-lacing, but tightness also suggested the power to carry a baby to full term. Elizabeth Montagu commented on an acquaintance's miscarriage:

> There seems to be nothing tight about that lady, I should expect her ever and anon to drop a child or a garter. There are people who have no tensities or tensions or tensitosities, which you please, and all moral and natural matters hang loose about them. . .[13]

Sarah Stone, in a book of case histories from her practice as a midwife, discusses a woman who laced tight during pregnancy; she was encouraged to do this by her neighbours, who blamed the stillbirths which had concluded her two previous pregnancies on her not lacing tight enough.[14] By the end of the century, there were stricter devices than stays to correct posture in some boarding-schools. Girls spent time suspended by their chins to straighten their necks, or strapped to backboards.[15] These devices were often attacked as potentially dangerous, or emblematic of a frivolous and excessive femininity.[16] So, for the opposite reason, that it made girls masculine, was the end-of-the-century practice of having girls drilled by a drill sergeant.[17] Yet all sides agreed that it was vital for a girl to have a straight body, even if they made fun of some of the means taken to that end.

If it was unattractive for women to eat too much, it was worse for them to drink too much; drink was an escape route women were not supposed to take.[18] In the first years of the nineteenth century, Laetitia-Matilda Hawkins was appalled at girls being allowed to take brandy back to school with them:

> We have just learnt, that a 'pretty present' for a young lady at school, is a medicine-chest elegantly fitted up, containing essences and extracts of various descriptions, and French brandy! Instances have occurred, where the young lady has been cautioned 'to say nothing on the subject, but to take just a little' of these good things whenever she finds herself low. What are liqueurs, between the courses of a dinner, compared to these comforts for youth?[19]

Girls were also warned against men who plied them with drink, presumably because drink would weaken their defences.[20] Some writers are equally severe about tea-drinking: 'Where is the difference between a lady's falling into hysterics by drinking tea to excess, and a gentleman's getting drunk with delicious liquor?[21]

However, it was important to refuse tactfully; all the advice on dealing with men emphasises keeping them at a distance without alienating them. The double bind of demanding that women be both seductive and chaste is completely articulated in the eighteenth century in a way that it is not in earlier periods. There is a similar double message in the way in which most moralists advise women not to spend too much time on clothes. They say it is immoral to pay too much attention to clothes, but they also make fun of overdressed women, and argue that simple good taste is more attractive. Sometimes they back this up by saying that simplicity and cleanliness usually go together:

> . . . to cultivate cleanliness and finery at the same time, is rather perhaps a difficult achievement. Your sex is much belied, if it be a very common one . . . But can any degree of finery compensate the want of cleanliness? A dirty woman – I turn from the shocking idea . . .[22]

However, this revulsion from finery, like revulsion from stereotypically feminine behaviour, was too clearly just the other side of intense attraction to carry much conviction; women also learnt from men to emulate the lady who was

> . . . ne'er so sure our passion to create
> As when she touched the brink of all we hate.[23]

Ned Ward shows the same ambivalence when he speculates about why homosexual men adopt feminine mannerisms to seduce each other: is their plan to arouse each other by mimicking women, or to put each other off women altogether by caricaturing them?[24]

Moralists were often disturbed by the fact that eighteenth-century English dress could blur class distinctions, and did not reliably distinguish respectable women from prostitutes.[25] Servants often dressed well, and sometimes wore their mistresses' cast-offs from the previous year.[26] Prostitutes had no special way of dressing, and by the end of the century high-class kept women were the leaders of fashion.[27] Fanny Burney's heroine Evelina is mistaken for a woman looking for a pick-up, when she strays into the wrong area at Vauxhall.[28]

Girls were not supposed to spend too much time on their clothes, but many writers saw novel-reading as a far more serious moral threat. Some writers just argue against novel-reading on the grounds that it wastes time, but others argue that it is more actively pernicious. This is not a distrust of fiction as such, but specifically a distrust of the love-novel.[29] It applied both to seventeenth-century romances and to modern naturalistic novels. There were two principal arguments against romances and novels; the first was that they gave young women a false view of life, and the second that they made them preoccupied with erotic daydreams. As a result, they were vulnerable to seduction, because they longed for love and misjudged the men who approached them. The argument that novels misled young women about life raised questions about how they were to learn about the world. Unlike young men, they could not see life by mixing with all kinds of people, and the conventions of propriety restricted what they could speak about as well as where they could go or what they could do. Everyone agreed that women's experiences had to be more restricted than men's, but there was controversy about how much they should know about the world, and the value of reading in teaching them about it.

All writers agreed that girls should do some edifying reading; the less severe allowed some reading for entertainment as well, including some fiction. Seventeenth-century romances were still widely read, and some writers argued that they were less pernicious than modern realistic novels, because their fantastic nature meant that girls could not mistake them for accurate guides to life.[30] A character in Sarah Maese's novel *The School* makes a fool of herself by volunteering information from de Scudéry's *Le grand Cyrus* during an ancient history lesson, but this is a relatively harmless confusion of fantasy and reality.[31] Those who attacked the modern novel argued that it confused them in a far more dangerous way, and promoted immoral views. Its defenders argued that only bad novels misled, and good novels could enlarge a reader's knowledge of life.[32] By the end of the century, novelists are highly self-conscious about this question, and many novels criticise novel conventions by showing a protagonist learning from experience that her view of life is novelistic and false. The masterpiece of the genre, Jane Austen's *Emma*, comes out of a long tradition.

Some of the concern about novel-reading is less to do with it creating false or misleading ideas about life than with it leading girls and women to live in an unhealthy, dreamy state of erotic fantasy. Mary Hays portrays a compulsive novel-reader in *Emma Courtney*; Emma reads from ten to fourteen circulating library novels a week.[33] The circulating library novels were formula romances, calculated to induce erotic daydreaming, and this sort of novel worried moralists the most.[34] In George Colman's words:

> 'Tis not alone the small-talk and the smart,
> 'Tis NOVEL most beguiles the female heart.
> Miss reads – she melts – she sighs –
>   Love steals upon her –
> And then – Alas, poor girl! – good night,
>   poor Honour![35]

Even if Miss in her fantasy world escaped seduction,

these self-indulgent imaginings were still morally suspect. In her first novel, Mary Wollstonecraft gives this scathing description of her heroine's mother:

> She was chaste, according to the vulgar acceptation of the word, that is, she did not make any actual *faux pas*; she feared the world, and was indolent; but then, to make amends for this seeming self-denial, she read all the sentimental novels, dwelt on the love-scenes, and, had she thought while she read, her mind would have been contaminated; as she accompanied the lovers to the lonely arbours, and would walk with them by the clear light of the moon.[36]

The satirical account of an ill-read lady's library in the *Spectator* mentions a love-novel which falls open at the warmest passage.[37]

Some of this concern about girls and women dwelling on the inflammatory passages in novels is really a way of expressing concern about masturbation. An early nineteenth-century medical writer, J.-L. Chirol, mentions in his attack on boarding-schools that easy access there to erotic fiction leads the girls to masturbate.[38] Eighteenth-century writers worried about masturbation in both sexes, believing it was dangerous as well as immoral and could even cause death.[39] They tended to view it as learned behaviour; servants were believed to teach it to children, boarding-school girls to each other. A home education under close parental supervision could probably prevent it. References to it in non-medical works, especially those directed to the young, tend to be vague to the point of inscrutability. John Essex is probably warning against it in the following passage, but the warning could easily be overlooked:

> . . . indulge not yourselves in eating or drinking immoderately, or which is worse, in having recourse to your bed for a refreshing nap after dinner; a pernicious practice that both endangers your health and your virtue; but rather fast and pray, lest you enter into temptation.[40]

Chirol argues that girls are at risk from the practice, because they do not know how dangerous it is. It is a good example of the way in which the demands of propriety made girls vulnerable, because they could not be warned against an unmentionable danger. External protection had to substitute for an internal power of decision, yet no external protection could be fully effective.

Warnings against spending too much time going out on parties of pleasure have much in common with warnings against novel-reading; simple disapproval of frivolity and wasting time is blended with dark hints of sexual danger. These warnings are an occasion for contrasting frivolous ladies of fashion with women the writer approves of, either the worthy housewives of the past or sober, well-educated women who are able to entertain themselves. Everyone allowed for some outings for pleasure; the questions were how much time should be spent on these pursuits, and what kinds of entertainment were permissible. The question of how much time one should spend on entertainments usually came down to a question of class; all but the most severe saw it as legitimate for society women to go out as much as was expected of them. The question of type of entertainment was more delicate; there was no really satisfactory solution, for respectable women and women who were not respectable both attended all places of public entertainment.

The main forms of entertainment moralists discuss are theatre, masquerades and outings to public pleasure-gardens. They assumed that women would stay away from indecent entertainments, though this was not always true; in 1740 a friend wrote to Elizabeth Montagu about a lady who went to 'Mademoiselle Chateauneuf's kicking the tambourine till she shows herself naked to the waist; she owns 'tis indecent, but she goes constantly to see her.'[41] After the middle of the century, the theatre could be defended as a respectable and edifying form of entertainment, though one writer at the end of the century warned his readers to be careful only to go to decent plays.[42] The mixed nature of a theatre audience was less troubling than that of other kinds of crowd. Masquerades, public balls to which anyone could buy a ticket, gave the greatest scope for confusion, and often represent moments of sexual danger and temptation in novels of the period;[43] yet they were popular with highly respectable people. The scholar Elizabeth Carter wrote about a masquerade in 1772:

> I think none of the characters pleased me so well as a lady in a man's domino, who talked not perhaps in the language, but upon the principles of a macaroni, with great cleverness and spirit, and with the most gallant contempt of all order, decency, good sense, and humanity, and indeed was the severest and best satirist upon these wretches I have ever heard.[44]

However, the line between travestying bad behaviour and engaging in it was not impassable. Public pleasure-gardens also disturbed moralists, because they were a haunt of prostitutes. Going out and mixing with all sorts of people involved a risk that girls would get into bad company. Dinah, the Biblical character who is seduced when she goes out visiting, was used as a warning to young women.[45]

Writers gave contradictory advice about how young women should behave in company; some said they should be silent, others said they should take part in the conversation. They also disagreed over how young women should respond when the conversation became indecent. Some advised pretending not to understand, others advised indicating disapproval. Some writers concentrated on advising how not to react: 'I blush for numbers of your sex, who not only express no displeasure at these things, but by a loud laugh, or childish titter, or foolish simper, or some other indication of a light mind, show real satisfaction, perhaps high complacence.'[46] Most writers tend to assume that sufficiently proper behaviour in young women will prevent men from making sexual advances, and so do not give advice on how to deal with them; advice concentrates on how to spot dangerous men at an earlier stage, when they say indecent things, criticise religion, or condone keeping secrets from parents. A

woman who was approached had probably already
made some mistakes:

> Let this great maxim be my virtue's guide;
> In part she is to blame that has been tried;
> He comes too near, that comes to be denied.[47]

The demands on young women's discretion were very
high. Prudery was as much to be avoided as
coquettishness, and could also arouse suspicions of
excessive interest in sex.[48] Propriety and fashion
sometimes worked against each other. Elizabeth
Montagu defended an acquaintance's morals by saying:
'she wants to have the *bon ton*, and you know the *bon ton*
of 1756, is *un peu équivoque*.'[49]

A girl entered adult society and the marriage market
in her middle to late teens; most writers assume her
education should be complete by the time she was
sixteen. Whether she was educated at home or at
boarding-school did not necessarily make much
difference to what she learnt, though there were wide
variations within both home and boarding-school
education, and women were expected to know more as
the century went on. There was constant debate about
whether women's education should concentrate on
housewifely skills, intellectual subjects, or decorative
and artistic accomplishments. No one said that
housewifely skills had no place at all in a girl's
education, but many people pointed out they need not
take much time and would have no significant place in
a rich woman's life. Plain sewing was quickly learnt;
thrifty middle-class women would spend a certain
amount of time mending household linen or making or
mending clothes, but richer women would not. Some
writers expressed concern that spending too much time
sewing could be bad for the eyes and for the posture.[50]
Cooking also took relatively little time to learn, and was
more necessary for middle-class women than upper-
class ones.

Expense and frivolity were the main objections to the

accomplishments such as embroidery, dancing, music, and painting. Lady Pennington tells a cautionary tale about embroidery in her popular advice book:

> There is not a greater extravagance, under the specious name of good housewifery, than the furnishing of houses in this manner: whole apartments have been seen thus ornamented by the supposed work of a lady, who, perhaps, never shaded two leaves in the artificial forest, but has paid four times its value to the several people employed in bringing it to perfection; the expense of these tedious pieces of work I speak of experimentally, having, many years past, undertaken one of them, which, when finished, was not worth fifteen pounds, and, by a computation since made, it did not cost less than fifty, in the hire and maintenance of the people employed in it; this indeed was at the age of seventeen, when the thoughtless inexperience of youth could alone excuse such a piece of folly.[51]

Those who defend the accomplishments never say they should be all of women's education, though some writers treat the accomplishments as just as important as literary education.[52] A few writers argue these skills can enable a woman to earn a living if she has to.[53] Writers who attack the accomplishments argue that this is rarely, if ever, true, and that they are only appropriate for very rich and aristocratic girls. Attacks on the accomplishments often identify them with aristocratic frivolity, and argue that they make middle-class girls unmarriageable because they get ideas above their station and expect a style of living which is too expensive for the men they could realistically hope to marry. If left unprovided for, they will have no way of earning an honest living, and will probably end up as kept mistresses or prostitutes.

The educational books show the standard curriculum for the middle and latter part of the century; it differed from the unspecialised education of a gentleman in not usually including Latin, or any mathematics beyond basic arithmetic.[54] A lady was expected to have a good command of English language and literature, and a good knowledge of geography and ancient and modern history; she would also know French and perhaps

Italian. By the end of the century, she would also study some botany or general natural history. Not learning Latin, some writers argue, meant girls' education was actually better than boys', as Latin was a waste of time, or even a menace to the pupils' Christian faith.[55] The aim of a girl's education was to improve her moral character, make her able to take part in a general conversation with men without making a fool of herself, and equip her to educate her own children. Most people recognised that a lady's education left her with almost no marketable skills. Girls who would need to earn a living were supposed to be apprenticed to a trade; middle-class girls would follow a more or less restricted version of a lady's education.

Intellectual subjects cause a great deal of debate, and feminist posturing sometimes introduces a very limited curriculum. All sides agree that they do not want to produce a learned lady, one of the standard butts of eighteenth-century satire. Male pedants were figures of fun too, but the taboo against displaying learning was far stronger for women. The moral purpose of a woman's education was always more important than her intellectual development.

The debate about whether girls should be educated at home or at school was primarily concerned with the effect of the different kinds of education on girls' health and morals. Defenders of home education argued that girls were safest at home; those who disagreed argued that children stimulated each other, and that they could be corrupted by servants anywhere.[56] Those who attacked boarding-school education saw it as promoting frivolity and social climbing, and argued that boarding-school girls were exposed to disease and pornography. Some writers at the end of the century gave grim descriptions of overcrowded, underheated schools, where the girls were dirty and poorly fed, and the practice of crowding several shared beds into one room facilitated the spread of infection.[57] Many writers felt this overcrowding was indecent as well as unhygienic; Mary Wollstonecraft was expressing a commonplace when she wrote in criticism of boarding-schools:

> A number of girls sleep in the same room, and wash together. And though I should be sorry to contaminate an innocent creature's mind by instilling false delicacy, or those indecent prudish notions which early cautions respecting the other sex naturally engender, I should be very anxious to prevent their acquiring nasty or immodest habits; and as many girls have learned very nasty tricks from ignorant servants, the mixing them thus indiscriminately together, is very improper.[58]

In the first years of the nineteenth century, the Society for the Suppression of Vice claimed that girls' boarding-schools were a substantial part of the market for indecent literature, and prosecuted some traders who were selling pornographic snuffboxes to girls' schools.[59] Opponents thought that boarding-school girls encouraged each other in love affairs and other kinds of mischief.[60]

The idea that relationships between boarding-school girls tended to be pernicious raises the larger question of the value of girls' and women's friendship generally. Controversy over women's capacity for friendship intersects with the home – school debate. Writers who favour a home education tend to argue that friendship is best kept within the family; sisters and brothers are the best friends for each other.[61] Hester Chapone, in one of the century's most influential educational books for girls, disapproved of friendships between adolescents, but thought a girl could learn a great deal from friendship with a woman eight or ten years older than herself.[62] A few writers go against the stereotype, and approve of boarding-school friendships.[63] Writers who are sympathetic enough to women to think it worth writing about their education do not usually take the view that women are too shallow and volatile to be capable of friendship, but this was not an uncommon belief.

Once granted that women are capable of friendship, the question of who their friends should be is still open. Jeremy Taylor, in a work dedicated to the mid-seventeenth-century poet of female friendship, Katherine Philips, gives a strong defence of women's capacity for friendship, but is primarily concerned with a woman's ability to be a friend to her husband.[64] As this view of marriage became commoner, it was harder to deny women's capacity for friendship. People accepted that men and women could have non-sexual friendships with each other, although cynics denied it and found counter-examples of hypocrisy. Some people argued that this was the best kind of friendship, challenging the classical ethical ideal of friendship between men.[65] Many people also put a high ethical value on friendship between women, and saw female friends' claims on each other as important, though a husband's claims had to come first.[66]

Descriptions of pairs of female friends could exemplify types of friendship; the eleven-year-old William Pitt was sent a didactic letter describing the friendship between Elizabeth Montagu and Elizabeth Carter as an exemplary friendship between patron and scholar.[67] Women could emulate the highest classical and Biblical examples of friendship. Richardson makes Clarissa write to her friend Anna: 'What an exalted idea does it give of the soul of Jonathan, sweetly attempered for this sacred band, if we may suppose it but equal to that of my Anna Howe for her fallen Clarissa!'[68] The most famous pair of female friends at the end of the century, Lady Eleanor Butler and Sarah Ponsonby, were described by Anna Seward as 'the celebrated votaries to that sentiment which exalted the characters of Theseus and Perithous, of David and Jonathan'.[69] Some people even argued that women's friendship was purer than men's, because it was not contaminated with self-interest; men tended to cultivate the friendships that would further their careers.[70] Describing Butler's and Ponsonby's retreat in *Llangollen Vale*, Seward says no human musician could play so movingly as their Aeolian harp, and adds:

The prouder sex as soon, with virtue calm,
Might win from this bright pair pure Friendship's spotless palm.[71]

Butler and Ponsonby insisted on the purity of their friendship, and considered suing for libel when a newspaper article hinted that they were lesbians.[72] Like some close non-sexual friendships between men and women in the period, intense friendships between women could be conducted and described in a passionate language which to a modern ear implies sexuality. An extreme example occurs in Godwin's life of Mary Wollstonecraft, when he compares her first meeting with the friend of her youth, Fanny Blood, to Werther's first meeting with Charlotte. However, this comparison may have been too much for his audience, for he deleted it from the second edition.[73]

Friendship was especially important in the life of women who remained unmarried; writers who put a high value on friendship between women also give a fairly positive view of an old maid's life. Old maids were a favourite butt of satirists, who presented them as ridiculous, pathetic, and bitter about their failure to marry,[74] but, throughout the century, some writers recognised that a woman might prefer to remain single. *The Ladies Calling* sees it as legitimate to choose celibacy for religious reasons, and other Anglican works describe exemplary single women.[75]

These exemplars always have enough money to give most of it to the poor; in reality, the economic position of single women was difficult. In the middle and upper classes, women usually had no marketable skills, and, if their families could afford to support them, they had to live with the knowledge that they were a greater drain on the family finances than they would have been if they had married. This knowledge could make the decision not to marry seem morally questionable, especially in the early part of the century. Richardson makes Clarissa financially independent, so that her offer to stay single, rather than marry in accordance with her parents' wishes, does not entail any financial demands on them.

Elizabeth Carter did not feel free to refuse a proposal of marriage until her father had given her permission.[76]

The question of whether she wanted to marry had immediate consequences for how she lived as a young woman; in 1738, when Carter was twenty, her father wrote to her: 'If you intend never to marry, as I think you plainly intimate in one of your letters, then you certainly ought to live retired, and not appear in the world with an expense which is reasonable upon the prospect of getting a husband, but not otherwise.'[77] Her nephew and editor, writing at the beginning of the following century, sees Carter's refusal to decide for herself about the proposal as an excess of filial piety. By his time, increased expectations about love between the partners in a marriage meant that many writers saw valid emotional reasons for refusing to marry. At the beginning of the century, only extreme aversion was seen as a valid reason for refusing a prospective husband, if both sets of parents approved. By the end of the century, there was sympathy for women who refused to marry because they wished to be faithful to the memory of a man they loved who had died, or because they would not marry one man when they were in love with another, or simply because they could not feel love for the men who proposed to them. Parents had the right to forbid a marriage, but not to impose one on a child.[78] Throughout the century, women wrote in praise of the single life, and though some of this writing has to be dismissed as sour grapes, or as a vehicle for satire about marriage, or as a by-product of the fact that decorum did not allow young girls to seem eager for marriage, some of it has to be taken seriously. Praise of the single life presents a religious or quasi-religious ideal of solitude, study, retirement, good works and friendship; the single, in this idea, are not less useful than the married, only more fortunate in having fewer responsibilities.

Choosing a husband was the single most important decision in a woman's life. Some writers' advice on the subject was idiosyncratic and self-serving, like the Rev. John Bennett's insistence that clergymen make the best husbands, but most of it was uncontroversial.[79] Young women were to follow their parents' advice, look for solid worth in a man, and avoid being taken in by looks and charm. Women's bad taste in men was sometimes blamed for encouraging male effeminacy; effeminate men who spend their time drinking tea with women are stock comic characters in the period.[80] Almost all writers are horrified by the maxim Richardon wrote *Clarissa* to disprove: 'that a reformed rake makes the best husband'.[81] They warn young women against the vanity and sentimentality of thinking that love for them can change a man's character. Writers later in the century emphasise love more than those at the beginning, but are still most strongly concerned with warning women not to fall in love with a man until they know he is in love with them.[82] The most crucial bit of advice is to be guided by parents, and never to consider elopement.

Elopement could have disastrous financial consequences for upper-class women, as once marriage was a *fait accompli* it was usually impossible to make a settlement which would restrict the husband's access to his wife's money. Only women of property could be protected by such settlements, and they were also the class who gained the most room to manoeuvre out of the fact that a husband was liable for his wife's debts. Writers of moral and prudential advice usually assume that a wife is provided for, and that her duty is to be thrifty and live within her husband's income. The earnings of a middle- or lower-class wife are discussed, if at all, as part of a joint income. However, there was a good deal of sympathy for women married to irresponsible men, and a sense that certain categories of a couple's property were morally if not legally the wife's rather than the husband's. The main categories were married women's earnings, property which would have been tied up in a settlement if the woman or her family had been more vigilant, and personal belongings such as jewellery which were classified as paraphernalia, the term for the belongings to which a widow had an absolute right at her husband's death. Some reformers at the end of the century criticised the fact that married women had no control over their own earnings,[83] and no one blamed Lady Cathcart for hiding her jewellery from a husband who imprisoned her.[84]

Wives were expected to obey, but husbands were not supposed to coerce them. Imprisoning a wife was an extreme step, which no one approved of, though it was not declared illegal until 1891.[85] A wife could claim legal protection against an excessively violent husband, but a husband had the legal right to beat his wife.[86] Custom probably protected wives more effectively than law, at any rate in the upper classes. Sir Francis Buller pronounced judgment in 1782 that a husband could beat his wife, provided that the stick was no thicker than his thumb, but this statement was outrageous enough to earn Buller the nickname of Judge Thumb and provoke Gillray to a caricature.[87] However, ill-treated wives were advised not to complain, on the grounds that they would lose sympathy by doing so. As *The Ladies Calling* puts it: '. . . we have naturally some regret to see a lamb under the knife, whereas the impatient roaring of a swine diverts our pity; so that patience in this case is as much the interest as duty of a wife.'[88] Wives who admitted to being ill-treated or unhappy could also be criticised for laying themselves open to approaches from would-be lovers.[89] Complaining to the husband himself was shrewish, and complaining to anyone else was betrayal. Moralists tried to suggest that submission could enable a wife to control her husband anyway, and told patient-Griselda stories in which the wife's long-suffering behaviour finally breaks her husband's will.[90] Satirists translated this into more realistic terms when they portrayed passive-aggressive, manipulative wives, and women themselves joked about managing their husbands.[91] However, emotional blackmail was a weapon that could only work as long as the husband was not prepared to insist upon his legal powers.

The legal basis of husbands' power over their wives did not change during the century, but the idea that a wife's relationship to her husband should obviously be that of a subordinate became less and less acceptable. At the beginning of the century, people were already arguing for a more equal-seeming marriage, though not always because it would benefit women:

> Now I own 'tis true that woman was made for the comfort and benefit of man: but I think it a much nobler comfort to have a companion, a person in whom a man can confide, to whom he can communicate his very soul, and open his breast and most inward thoughts, than to have a slave sitting at his footstool, and trembling at every word that comes like thunder and lightning from the mouth of the domestic Pharoah.[92]

Husbands wanted a different style of compliance, from wives who were educated enough to know what they were talking about, and who could be pleasing and ornamental companions. The relationship was a friendlier and more egalitarian one, yet still not really equal, for the husband was always the senior partner. The educationist Thomas Day took an eighteenth-century fantasy to its logical conclusion when he adopted two female orphans in order to put them through a course of education which would produce a suitable wife for him. This was eccentric, but for a woman to plan to train a husband from childhood in this way would have been unthinkable.

Works which emphasise friendship in marriage are less egalitarian than they sound, for they take it for granted that major decisions rest with the husband, and do not question his legal power. Eighteenth-century discussions of friendship between men and women often assume a great deal of deference on the women's side. Fordyce, a great praiser of friendship with women, describes a woman who contradicts a man as:

> . . . a clamorous, obstinate, contentious being, universally disgustful and odious; fit only to be chased from the haunts of humanity, those peaceful haunts which it seeks to disturb – Merciful Heaven! shelter us from its violence, in the blessed sanctuary of domestic love and joy, or in the sweet harmonious choir of friendship.[93]

The issue of authority was clearer in the debate at the beginning of the century than at the end. By the end of the eighteenth century assumptions that there would be love between married people, and that the choice of a spouse would be based on love, at any rate on the man's side, made the husband's power less visible. Ill-treatment of wives may have been less socially acceptable, but there was still little legal redress, and few writers proposed reforms.

A wife was expected to be more tolerant of her husband's idiosyncracies than he of hers. Confined to the home, she had little choice; husbands had more escape routes. Moral writers recommend emotional dishonesty; wives should not make their affection for their husbands too clear, and there were several explanations of why this was undesirable. One idea was that a husband would treat his wife better if he was always anxious to earn her love; another that too many displays of affection would bore and disgust a husband; another simply that such demonstrativeness was immodest.[94] This was one of the points on which Mary Wollstonecraft changed her mind; in her 1787 *Thoughts on the Education of Daughters* she accepts this view, while by 1792 and the *Vindication of the Rights of Woman* she found it offensive.[95] She had grown more opposed to false modesty, and more concerned to make relationships between men and women genuinely equal. Some non-radical contemporaries agreed with her second position; by the 1790s, it was more acceptable for wives to be demonstrative.[96]

One of the most obvious and most disputed inequalities between husbands and wives was the result of the double standard. A husband's infidelity was not important, a wife's was a catastrophe. Moralists advise wives with unfaithful husbands to be patient, and insist that they must not be tempted into thinking their husbands' infidelity justifies their own; the tone in which they argue against this view suggests it was quite a widespread commonsense idea.[97] The double standard can be attacked in two ways; by arguing for greater latitude for women, or for greater chastity in men. Arguments for the former position existed in comedy and satire, though it may not have been easy to transfer them into more serious contexts, and aristocratic life allowed married women considerable freedom throughout the century. The latter argument, that adultery is at least as culpable in men as in women, appears in some religious writers.[98] However, they often qualify the argument by pointing out that greater worldly inconveniences result from the wife's adultery, or blur it altogether by emphasising the wickedness of a wife who makes her husband liable for the support of children which are not his.[99] By the end of the century, writers were arguing against it on secular grounds, and implying that a husband's adultery compromised a marriage based on friendship as much as a wife's did. The stereotype of the wife who palms off the children of adultery on her husband could be countered with the stereotype of the unchaste husband who transmits venereal disease to his innocent wife and children.[100]

The friendlier, more egalitarian image of marriage was accompanied by a more indulgent attitude to children, and by both parents taking more interest in their children's welfare.[101] There was more interest in what the mother should be doing with very young children, and more insistence that she should not delegate all the childcare to the servants. Men told women what to do, but the fact of their interest in the process dignified women's work. Male interest in childbirth was also part of this interest in motherhood. In France, Jaucourt's *Encyclopédie* article on childbirth defended men's interest in the subject by arguing that compassion for women should lead men to wish to do everything possible to help women in childbirth.[102] Fiction offers examples of this male concern with birth, from Mr Shandy's fascination with technique to another character's comparison of his feelings when his lover went into labour to those of someone who had betrayed his best friend to the rack.[103] Interest in infancy and early childhood meant that women's physiology was less tabooed, a less purely female area.

Moralists had been telling women to breast-feed their own children long before the eighteenth century, but in earlier periods they tended to assume husbands would not want them to do this, because it would delay resumption of sexual relations, and affect the shape of the women's breasts.[104] By the end of the eighteenth century, breast-feeding had been glamourised, and some writers inverted earlier conventional wisdom by suggesting that the sight of a wife breast-feeding her child could win back an errant husband.[105] People began to say breast-feeding was pleasurable for the mother;[106] sometimes they also reversed earlier conventional wisdom by saying that it was healthier for her.[107] Women who bore their children in charity lying-in hospitals were often obliged to breast-feed them under the rules of the charity.[108]

People were advised to educate their children in a disciplined way; moralists criticised those who spoilt their children because they might well not live to grow up.[109] However, both parents were closer to their children than in earlier periods, and the century abounds in stories satirising spoilt upper-class children. Jane Collier, in *An Essay on the Art of Ingeniously Tormenting*, advises mothers to let the children put their bread and butter down the backs of the visitors' dresses,[110] while Charles James Fox had been notoriously spoilt as a child. In a well-known story about his childhood, the young Charles James says he must smash a watch, and his father's answer is: 'Well, if you must, I suppose you must.'[111] Because early upbringing was so crucial, the mother's role received a good deal of attention; if the mother was receiving more advice from her husband and male theorists than in the past, she could also take more pride in what she was doing. Women's sense of themselves as mothers seems to have strengthened as actual community of motherhood – advice from other women, attendance by other women at childbirth – was weakened by no longer being the only source of knowledge.

By the end of the century, moralists assumed that upper- and middle-class women were no longer vulnerable to old wives' tales about the birth and upbringing of children. Instead of telling them to follow male advice, they argued that they should cultivate a sense of female solidarity by doing charitable work with poor women, especially at the time of childbirth.[112] Usually it is poor married women who are the objects of charity. Some of the lying-in hospitals only admitted married women, and the lying-in charities providing help for poor women having children at home, which became popular at the end of the century, were also restricted to married women.[113] Lower-class unmarried mothers were treated callously, and some deaths resulted from parish officers moving on women in labour so that their children could not become a charge of the parish by being born in it.[114] Attempts to help unmarried mothers and their children risked the criticism that they would encourage vice; the Foundling Hospital was opposed for this reason.[115]

If a mother's role in bringing up her children was vital anyway, it became still more vital if her husband died. Throughout the century, moral literature addressed to widows insists on the need for them to be independent and responsible, and the risk of widowhood was probably the single strongest argument for making women independent. Throughout the century moralists advise widows with children not to remarry, but to devote themselves to their children; childless widows receive less attention.[116] A widow only had the right of custody of her sons if she had been appointed their guardian in her husband's will, but many writers assume this is normal procedure.[117] The widow must be competent to look after her husband's interests when he is gone. Some literature on marriage also emphasises the need for a wife to be competent during her husband's lifetime; this does not imply that men and women are equal, or that the wife is not the husband's subordinate, but it does mean women cannot be presented as completely helpless and dependent.[118] Widows were free to choose who they married, even if they were still under twenty-one, and most moralists assumed they would choose unwisely.[119] A widow could be a financial drain on her husband's family by taking her jointure out of the family. A widow's financial interests were likely to clash with those of her in-laws; this is one of the themes dramatised in Maria Edgeworth's *Castle Rackrent*. She might also damage her children's prospects if she or a stepfather mismanaged their affairs.[120] Concern about their children's future was a strong argument in favour of men marrying competent, independent women, once it was accepted that a mother should normally be in charge of her children's upbringing.

However, there was also some discussion of widowhood from the point of view of how it affected the widows themselves. This overlaps with the literature addressed to single women, as all adult unmarried women faced similar problems. Upper- and middle-class single women who needed to earn a living often had no saleable skills, and had to settle for the humiliating life of a governess or companion. Mary Ann Radcliffe's *Memoirs* describe how working as a governess at the end of the century did not just involve teaching duties. When Lady Traquair, her employer, felt unwell, Radcliffe and the chaplain, the Biblical scholar Alexander Geddes, had to join their hands to make a seat for her and carry her round the garden. Lady Traquair weighed between twelve and fourteen stone.[121] Clara Reeve's *School for Widows*, written at about the same period, had a heroine who argues that a poor but independent life as a village schoolmistress is preferable to a far more comfortable, dependent life as a companion.[122]

Widows and women who had never married shared many of the same problems, but the tone of moralists' advice to them differed. Women who had married were more adult in the eyes of social convention than those who had not. Even though in law they were less free, in practice married women were less restricted; there were fewer restrictions on them going out alone, and they did not have to pretend sexual ignorance. Spinsterhood could be seen as a state of perpetual dependence, in which a woman never quite grew up. Portraits of exemplary spinsters portray characters who are less involved in the world than exemplary widows are. An influential character sketch of single women makes this clear. William Law's portrait of good and bad spinsters, Miranda and Flavia, was widely read and anthologised.[123] It contrasts the devout, reclusive Miranda, who lives for prayer and helping the poor, with the frivolous, vain and sociable Flavia. Both have independent means. Law emphasises the wickedness of Flavia spending her money on keeping up her social life, and this is a common theme, whereas most writers are more tolerant of married women keeping up an appropriate level of social display. A childless widow could be expected to live like the nun-like Miranda, but a widow with responsibility for a family could not. Mary Wollstonecraft gives contrasted portraits of good and bad widows: the widow brought up to be dependent on men is unable to care for her children, cannot attract a new husband, and may well end up being seduced, while the independent widow renounces opportunities to remarry and is both father and mother to her children.[124] These portraits were not contentious, though they are used to support a polemical argument. Writers who emphasise women's natural weakness and need for direction by men tend to avoid the subject of widowhood. Advice to widows and spinsters necessarily called for them to have a certain amount of independence; only advice to the married could emphasise dependence. Once a writer emphasised a woman's duty to her children, rather than to her husband, this also required a certain level of independence, and opened the way to arguing that an independent, responsible wife was what a man should choose if he cared about his children.

This moralists' outline of what a woman's life should be like is not, of course, an accurate picture of what it was like. Other literary genres give more life to the picture, but some of the culture's crucial assumptions about women remain almost unspoken. Feminists often criticise the conventional moralistic picture in the name of greater realism, by calling attention to the needs of single women, and asking how married women should deal with inadequate husbands, but they are not free of their culture's assumptions about women. The blind spots shared by feminists and their opponents are as instructive as the points of contention; neither can avoid treating as central the classifications of married or not, respectable or not, even when they argue about how to treat women in these categories.

CHAPTER THREE

Novels and Heroines:
Clarissa and Julie

The heroine-centred novels of the eighteenth century add to the descriptive and prescriptive genres of writing about women in two important ways. Often they dramatise the social danger involved in being a respectable woman, and the constant threats to women's respectability and reputation. These woman-in-peril dramas express a real social fear, though often in a melodramatic and fantastic way. Sometimes the novels also give a vivid picture of the day-to-day minutiae of women's lives, and of what eighteenth-century social life looked like from a woman's point of view. These two kinds of writing do not always coexist comfortably; Pierre Fauchery, in an encyclopedic survey of the heroine-centred eighteenth-century novel, sees it as culminating in two writers who succeed in separating them completely. De Sade pushes woman-in-peril drama to its limits, while Jane Austen exorcises these perils, creating heroines who are not martyred or threatened with martyrdom, and who live in a world which is strongly realised naturalistically.[1]

The heroines of eighteenth-century novels are constantly at risk from events that will put them outside the categories of maid, wife and widow, and on the wrong side of the boundary between the respectable and the unrespectable. They are threatened with seduction or rape, leaving them neither maid nor wife, or faced with the prospect of marrying one man when they love another, which raises awkward questions about what being a wife really means. Many eighteenth-century novels avoid these issues by being extremely punitive, and suggesting that loss of respectability always leads to death and disaster; many others allow their heroines to come unscathed through all threats to their respectability. Moralists complained that women were corrupted by reading about

> Plot and elopement, passion, rape, and rapture,
> The total sum of every dear – dear – chapter,[2]

but eighteenth-century love novels were probably sources for compensatory daydreaming more often than for imitation in real life. However, like the autobiographies of unrespectable women, novels could implicitly undermine the barrier between the respectable and the unrespectable, by showing how easily it was crossed and how little personalities were changed by crossing it. Eighteenth-century novel-readers could identify with novel-characters more intensely than most modern readers,[3] and the actions of novel-characters could evoke passionate ethical arguments. These dramas of women's sufferings could move sophisticated readers who consciously found them pernicious or ridiculous,[4] and they are central to discussions of how women who fall from respectability should be treated. The novels by Mary Hays and Mary Wollstonecraft which try to turn the genre to feminist purposes are unsuccessful, because they are undermined by the sado-masochistic presuppositions of the genre, but their attempt was a significant one.

The naturalistic, observant side of the eighteenth-century novel provided opportunities for writers to discuss what they thought women's lives were like, or ought to be like, and to use a feminine viewpoint to make fun of boorish men or to attack exploitative ones. By the latter part of the century, many women writers were taking these opportunities, and being read with respect by both male and female readers. This kind of novel is close to satire and to didactic writing, but gives scope for a subtler account of the details of social life. Most of these women novelists were not feminists, and some explicitly criticised feminism, but the best work by women writers helped to create an audience for feminist ideas by making people aware that women could write with intelligence, perceptiveness and moral sensitivity.

Many heroine-centred eighteenth-century novels are simple dramatisations of the conventional wisdom expressed in books of advice, or self-indulgent fantasies of escape from the social constraints which made the conventional wisdom necessary. Other more complex heroine-centred novels gave readers more opportunities to disagree with the conventional wisdom, or to think about these social constraints. These novels, when read with contemporaries' comments on them, shed new light on notions about women taken from other kinds of writing, because they show how people could hold contradictory ideas about women at the same time, and how difficult they found it to resolve the dilemmas resulting from these contradictions. I have chosen to concentrate on two particularly controversial novels, Richardson's *Clarissa*, and Rousseau's *Julie, ou la nouvelle Héloïse*. Both were very popular in England, and aroused a great deal of discussion and comment; both confronted their readers with unusually difficult dilemmas. Both books address the ethical core of the sexual double standard. This is the notion that women who have once lapsed from chastity cannot redeem this lapse; sometimes this is merely described as a social fact, sometimes it is argued that women in this category really become capable of every kind of wickedness, and bad women are worse than bad men.[5] There was no male equivalent to this kind of fall; cowardice, the unforgiveable sin for men, could be redeemed by subsequent acts of courage, whereas a single lapse from chastity was supposed to mark a woman for life. This idea is obviously impossible to reconcile with respect for women as rational moral beings, but it was very difficult for people in the period to be completely unaffected by it. Feminists and moralists could be scathing about

women who behaved as if their physical chastity made
it unnecessary for them to bother with any other kind
of moral action; it was harder to consider the possibility
of a woman who had fallen from chastity becoming an
exemplary moral being who regained the respect of
society.

The fact that in real life people often compromised
and overlooked lapses does not solve the dilemma on
the level of theory. It was the physical fact of a woman's
loss of chastity, not the moral fact of choice, which
brought about the catastrophe; the idea existed on a
level which rational moral discourse could not fully
address. In the first scene of Hogarth's *Harlot's Progress*,
when the girl from the country is being hired by the
procuress, a notorious rapist of the period, Colonel
Charteris, waits in the background to introduce her to
her trade; however, by the next scene, the victim of
deception and violence has become a criminal herself.[6]
The conflict between this quasi-magical model of a
woman's life, in which she is always vulnerable to total
corruption through her sexuality in a way that men are
not, and a more rational model in which women, like
men, are always capable of moral choice, and such
choice is what gives their lives value, was hard to
articulate, because these models could coexist on
different levels of thought. A sense that unchaste
women were radically damaged could remain powerful
in people who consciously believed such women were
rational, moral beings, and should be provided with a
way of returning to respectable society. It is conflicts of
this kind, rather than more clearly articulated ones,
which fiction has a unique power to address.

The plot of *Clarissa* is a simple one, though the novel
in which it is realised is rich and complex.[7] Most of the
book is told in letters between Clarissa and her friend
Anna Howe, and Lovelace and his friend Belford; there
are very few letters from the two protagonists to each
other.

Clarissa Harlowe, a beautiful young woman of
exemplary moral character, who has inherited an estate

from her grandfather, is under great pressure from her family to marry a repulsive miser who is willing to make a marriage settlement which is extremely favourable to the Harlowe family. An aristocratic rake, Lovelace, who has already fought Clarissa's brother and flirted with her sister, tricks her into running away with him, and her father curses her. Once Clarissa has left home, there is no way back. Lovelace takes her to London, and instals her in a house with women she believes to be respectable. In fact they are prostitutes who began their careers by being seduced by Lovelace. The house is under the direction of a sinister procuress, Mrs Sinclair, who frightens Clarissa from the beginning. A long series of conversations follows, in which Lovelace's aim is to seduce Clarissa and Clarissa's is to resist him. At this stage of the novel, she is willing to marry him, in spite of her doubts about his character, and is strongly attracted to him, though her love for him never overpowers her reason. Lovelace also wavers between determination to subdue her, and willingness to marry her. Deciding that Lovelace is untrustworthy, Clarissa escapes. Lovelace tricks her into returning to Sinclair's house, where he drugs her and rapes her. She escapes again, and takes modest lodgings, where she lives in deep asceticism and penitence, obviously dying, with no friends except Belford, who has repented of his Lovelace-like life. She spends her nineteenth birthday alone, in prayer and mourning; soon after, she dies. Lovelace is desperate at her impending death, and willing to marry her, but she refuses to see him again after her escape from Sinclair's house. A cousin, Colonel Morden, returns from abroad, and is the only member of her family present at her deathbed. Clarissa's body is taken home for burial, and her will is read. After her death, her family are given the papers which make it clear that she was raped, not seduced, and Morden kills Lovelace in a duel.

The sub-plots about Anna and Belford, the protagonists' correspondents, provide some comment on this story. Belford, unlike Lovelace, listens to his conscience, repents, and abandons the rake's way of life. When the book ends, it seems likely that he will marry one of Lovelace's cousins, and get the inheritance Lovelace expected from his uncle, Lord M. Anna, who was rescued from a seducer by Clarissa's advice before the book begins, is resigned to marrying the dull but virtuous Hickman; however, she has her revenge by tormenting and teasing him, showing up his slow wit and social ineptitude.

Much of the book's richness, for both eighteenth- and twentieth-century readers, lies in the variation between the styles of the four principal letter-writers, and the conformity between their epistolary style and their characters. Belford has the most neutral style and the least differentiated character; this is in keeping with the fact that his function in the book is to portray an ordinary sinner who makes an ordinary repentance. Anna writes in a lively, witty, informal style, expressive of a character which is more wilful and impetuous than Clarissa's. Anna has more energy and spirit than Clarissa, but lacks some of her moral seriousness. Lovelace's style is a brilliant and fantastic one, in part based on that of the published letters of famous Restoration rakes.[8] It develops complex conceits, fantasies and metaphors, and has the resources to parody and pastiche the styles of other characters in the book. This style reflects a shrewdly analytic, but self-deceiving mind, and a character who develops elaborate plots and tricks to manipulate the other characters in the book. Clarissa writes in a high, dignified, sententious style, recalling that of seventeenth-century devotional books. Her character is that of 'an exemplar to her sex',[9] a living realisation of these works' commitment to self-analysis and moral struggle. A passage in which Lovelace makes fun of Jeremy Taylor's *Holy Living and Dying* underlines Clarissa's relationship to these works:

A smart book, this, my dear! This old divine affects, I see, a mighty flowery style upon a very solemn subject. But it puts me in mind of an ordinary country funeral, where the young women, in honour of a defunct companion, especially if she were a virgin, or *passed for such*, make a flower-bed of her coffin. (3.358-9)

Richardson discusses the book's central event, the rape of Clarissa, in a way which is designed to make it clear that Clarissa is innocent and Lovelace is unable to face the reality of his own actions. Writers on forensic medicine at a slightly later period doubted whether a woman could be raped by one man acting alone, unless she was drugged.[10] Clarissa is drugged, and there are strong hints that Sinclair assists Lovelace in the act. After the rape, Lovelace hopes that Clarissa is pregnant (3.243, 4.38, 4.164); this should be read as a wildly unrealistic fantasy in which he denies the rape's reality. Even at a much later date, many writers refer to the idea that rape cannot cause pregnancy as a common belief. Some eighteenth-century physiology assumes that a woman can only conceive if she has an orgasm, and it was possible to argue that the victim's pregnancy should prove her consent and ensure acquittal in rape cases.[11] When Clarissa's uncles ask her if she is pregnant, they make it brutally clear that they think she has been seduced (4.100, 104). There is another hint of Lovelace's denial of responsibility for the rape, in the language with which he reproaches Belford for delivering two of Anna's letters to Clarissa, instead of sending them on to him:

Thou hadst the two letters in thy hand. Had they been in mine, the seal would have yielded to the touch of my warm finger (perhaps without the help of the post office bullet); and the folds, as other plications have done, opened of themselves, to oblige my curiosity. (3.472-3)

Lovelace's character excited wildly opposing judgements among contemporaries. Some readers were more struck by his attractiveness and wit than by his wickedness, and wanted a happy ending for the book, with Clarissa and Lovelace reconciled and married. Richardson was disturbed by Lovelace's popularity with his readers, and added material to the third edition of the novel to make his villainy more obvious. Other readers found Lovelace unconvincing because he was too bad to be true, even judged by the first four volumes of the first edition, before the rape and without the additional material.[12]

Some contemporaries find the question of the rape less interesting than the question of Clarissa's anomalous status once she has abandoned respectable society by running away with Lovelace. However innocent she is in reality, marriage to him is her only immediate way back. It is for this reason that Anna urges Clarissa to marry him, even after the rape (3.414-18). Clarissa's refusal is based on a religious view of marriage, which prefers inward moral realities to social appearances (3.520). Some contemporaries see no excuse for her running away with Lovelace: 'any girl that runs away with a young fellow without intending to marry him should be carried to Bridewell or Bedlam the next day.'[13] Others have no patience with her refusal to marry Lovelace after the rape, attributing it to 'punctilio' and 'misplaced delicacy'.[14] Such comments see Clarissa's folly, not Lovelace's crime, as the centre of the book.

However, even writers who criticise some of Clarissa's actions usually accept that she is an exemplary and virtuous character. Dissenting voices are in a minority. Lady Mary Wortley Montagu found all Clarissa's behaviour bizarre and idiotic,[15] while Johnson was troubled by her duplicity: 'there is always something which she prefers to truth.'[16] Catharine Macaulay accuses her of conceit and folly, as well as partial responsibility for her own death: 'this catastrophe is not so much the consequence of an oppressed mind, as a rigid adherence to the discipline of fasting, whilst under the alarming symptoms of a deep decline.'[17] On the whole, Clarissa's virtue is taken for granted, though sometimes it is seen as superhuman, too forbidding to emulate, and Harriet Byron, the heroine of *Sir Charles Grandison*, is proposed as a better exemplar for young women.[18] Sarah Fielding argues that the fact that critics accuse Clarissa of contradictory faults shows the correctness of her behaviour; she also comments that all the critics' accusations are anticipated by characters in the book.[19] Some writers criticise Clarissa indirectly, by showing unwise heroines who are encouraged in their folly by identifying with her.[20] Anna's character is more controversial, because of her impatience and her rudeness to her mother and Hickman. Lady Mary Wortley Montagu thought her behaviour was unforgivable.[21] Sarah Maese, in her didactic novel *The School*, shows a headstrong and silly girl preferring her to Clarissa.[22] The *Gentleman's Magazine* thought her good qualities were 'allayed by too much fire and impatience'.[23] However, most readers seem to have enjoyed her wit, and Catherine Talbot complimented Elizabeth Carter by comparing her wit to Anna's.[24]

Just as most people accepted that Clarissa was virtuous, most people accepted that the book was edifying. Richardson himself was concerned about this, in very simple and direct ways; he appended an index of moral sentiments to some later editions of the book, and published a separate volume of moral maxims extracted from his three novels. These collections had an educational purpose; a card-game based on them was advertised at a discount for schools.[25] Some people argued that reading *Clarissa* encouraged young women to write about nothing in an affected style,[26] but Catharine Macaulay was unusual in saying it was unsuitable reading for moral reasons. In a defence of novel-reading, Mary Hays comments on *Clarissa*: 'I read it repeatedly in very early life, and ever found my mind more pure, more chastened, more elevated after the perusal of it.'[27] This emphasis on the book being uplifting in a vague and general way, rather than in its treatment of specific issues, also appears in Anna Laetitia Barbauld's account of it: 'That *Clarissa* is a highly moral work, has been always allowed; but what is the moral?'[28] She dismisses two obvious possibilities: it is not a warning against falling in love with rakes, because Clarissa is always ready to give up Lovelace, and it is not about her virtue in resisting seduction, because it would be unthinkable for a girl of her class to give in to seduction from a lover who has it in his power to marry her. She concludes that the book's aim is to make the reader love virtue by embodying it in a lovable character.

This static and limited view of the novel can easily be questioned, but the distinction between virtuous character and virtuous behaviour remains an important one. It is central to the argument of Rousseau's *Julie*, the only one of the many novels derived from *Clarissa* which can compare with it in stature.[29] Contemporaries often compared the books and argued about which heroine they preferred; both books inspired numerous imitations. *Julie* was far more controversial than *Clarissa*; Rousseau himself, in his author's preface, warns that it is not suitable for unmarried girls, and the simplest plot-summary makes it clear why.[30] This warning should not, of course, be taken too literally. As Anna Seward wrote to a friend: 'You ask me, if I expected implicit obedience when I bade you throw aside Eloisa. I cannot say I did, but I mean to hint my opinion of its very softening tendency.'[31]

Julie shares with *Clarissa* the initial situation of an exemplary heroine who faces a conflict between her own feelings and her parents' wishes about her marriage, and who is paired with a livelier confidante. Julie is in love with her tutor, Saint-Preux, who is a poor commoner, and so not a possible husband for her in her family's eyes. She sleeps with him once; the resulting pregnancy ends in a miscarriage, caused by a fall during a violent quarrel with her father, in which he beats her because she defends Saint-Preux's character. An English lord, Bomston, tries unsuccessfully to persuade Julie's father to consent to the marriage, and then offers the lovers refuge on his estate in Yorkshire. Julie refuses, from loyalty to her parents; her cousin and confidante, Claire, has ensured the refusal, by insisting that she will come too, if Julie and Saint-Preux elope, in spite of her own impending marriage. Julie's mother dies, and Julie decides to marry the man her parents proposed, Wolmar, who is one of her father's oldest friends. Bomston arranges for the despairing Saint-Preux to join Anson's voyage round the world.

Several years pass; Julie is living happily with Wolmar, the now widowed Claire, and her and Claire's children. Saint-Preux returns; Wolmar, who knows about Julie's affair with him, invites him to join the family and act as tutor to the children. There is much discussion of Wolmar's virtue and his exemplary management of his estate at Clarens; the only flaw, for the devout Julie, is that he is an atheist. Wolmar tests the lovers' virtue by going away on a journey and leaving them alone together; they pass the test, but realise they are still in love with each other. Saint-Preux goes to Italy to prevent Bomston from making an unsuitable marriage to a mistress. While he is away, Julie becomes ill after diving into the lake to rescue one of her children, and dies. Her death, like her life, is far more controversial than Clarissa's. Clarissa dies with traditional Christian devotion, but Julie argues that deathbeds are not the time for prayer. God will judge her on her life as a whole, and she will spend the time left to her with her family and friends, confident in God's mercy. Her dying wish is for Claire and Saint-Preux to marry; Claire refuses, but admits she was in love with Saint-Preux, and tells Saint-Preux and Bomston to come and join the family at Clarens in their cult of Julie's memory.

The novel is told in letters, but Rousseau does not have Richardson's brilliance at differentiating character by style. However, he shares Richardson's concern with psychological analysis and the process of self-deception; the novel is a brilliant meditation on the difficulties of sincerity.[32] With its many digressions, it also provides a summary of Rousseau's moral and social ideas. Some eighteenth-century readers picked out favourite passages, such as the letter where Saint-Preux describes his and Julie's realisation that they are still in love, for their emotional intensity.[33] Some of this power derives from Rousseau's use of landscape; the book created a thriving tourist industry in the area round Lake Geneva where it is set.[34]

The book was immediately successful in England, and was recognised at once as a derivative and rival of *Clarissa*.[35] Its morality disturbed some readers from the beginning, but it aroused the harshest criticism after the French Revolution, when people looked at it more in the light of Rousseau's politics. The first point which aroused controversy was the virtuous Julie's agreeing to sleep with Saint-Preux. Elizabeth Carter was shocked to find that all the young women she met 'defend and applaud' Julie.[36] Carter blamed the book's influence for a famous scandal of the year after its publication, Kitty Hunter's elopement with the married Earl of Pembroke.[37] However, an influential article in the *Critical Review* argues that *Julie* is a more edifying book than *Clarissa*, because Clarissa is too forbiddingly virtuous for readers to imitate, while Julie's frailties make it possible to live up to her. This reviewer adds:

> If we may speak our own sentiments, Rousseau hath furnished the more useful instruction, as he hath taught us the means of retrieving the esteem of mankind, after a capital slip in conduct; than which he could not have read a more instructive lesson to the female world, who generally resign over to vice and wretchedness those of their own sex, who have once deviated from the paths of virtue, though earnest to redeem their errors, and more valuable members of society than those boasters of their single quality – their *honour* and unsolicited chastity.[38]

This issue aroused feminist interest at the end of the century, but here is argued from the basis of a traditional chivalrous set of ideas; there is misogyny in the reviewer's dig at 'good' women, as there is in his summary of *Clarissa*, which does not mention the rape, and attributes Clarissa's refusal to marry Lovelace to 'punctilio' and 'false delicacy'. Many writers who are unhappy about Julie's affair with Saint-Preux follow Rousseau's own argument in his preface, that the first part of the book needs to be redeemed by the second.

Novels can imply this by showing foolishly romantic heroines who only read the first part of the novel.[39]

The affair between Julie and Saint-Preux also raises the question of whether Saint-Preux should be forgiven for exploiting his position as Julie's teacher, and abusing the trust placed in him by her family. Burke saw *Julie*'s portrayal of this situation as part of a systematic scheme by Rousseau to destroy all social and family relationships, thus enabling the French revolutionaries to take power.[40] The revolutionary government can use the substance of the book to encourage servants to betray their masters, and its style to make aristocratic gallantry unfashionable with upper-class girls:

> Through him they teach men to love after the fashion of philosophers; that is, they teach to men, to Frenchmen, a love without gallantry; a love without anything of that fine flower of youthfulness and gentility, which places it, if not among the virtues, among the ornaments of life. Instead of this passion, naturally allied to grace and manners, they infuse into their youth an unfashioned, indelicate, sour, gloomy, ferocious medley of pedantry and lewdness; of metaphysical speculations, blended with the coarsest sensuality.[41]

As a result, the upper classes are less civilised, and class barriers are weakened; lower-class men can seduce in this style, though not in the traditional aristocratic one.

On the whole, though, readers were more interested in the sexual aspects of the plot than in the class ones. Some readers were troubled by Julie's decision to marry Wolmar. At the end of the century, Clara Reeve thought the first section of the book should be altered to make it as morally acceptable as the second:

> I thought it might be possible to give a different turn to the story, and to make the two lovers stop short of the act that made it criminal in either party to marry another, for were they not *actually wedded* in the sight of heaven? and could Eloise with any pretensions to virtue, or to delicacy, give herself to another man?
>
> If this insuperable objection was removed; then might the lovers renew their friendship with honour and dignity on both sides, then might the husband in full confidence in his wife's

principles, invite her friend, and even leave them together without appearing so justly ridiculous in his conduct as he now does to impartial judges.[42]

Even with this alteration, the book would still have been troubling; by the end of the century, the question of whether a woman in love with one man should marry another was very controversial. John Bennett, a far from radical writer, describes this as the worst pain he can imagine for a woman, and calls marriage for money legal prostitution.[43] However, Hannah More makes a woman in this situation forget her love and become the exemplary heroine of a patient-Griselda story.[44]

The way in which Julie and Wolmar conduct their marriage also troubled critics. Wolmar's welcoming of Saint-Preux was easy to make fun of, and novelists of the conservative reaction to the French Revolution wrote about sleazy *ménages à trois* which parody the triangle at Clarens.[45] However, the questions which the situation at Clarens pushes to the limit, those of the competing claims of friendship and marriage, and of trust in marriage, were important ones. Wolmar insists on the importance of friendship; his respect for Julie's friendship with Saint-Preux is consistent with his respect for her friendship with Claire. Once Claire is widowed, he thinks it would be scandalous if Julie and Claire did not live together (4.1), and he refuses to read Julie's letters to Claire (4.7). This sort of explicit statement is not very common, but many people agreed with this view of the importance of friendship; fictional husbands who disapprove of female friendship are often unsympathetic characters.[46]

The religious aspect of the book also aroused controversy, especially when read in conjunction with the *Profession de foi du vicaire savoyard* in *Émile*, Rousseau's statement of a deistic faith which could be expressed in the worship of any denomination. Some people were offended by the portrayal of Wolmar as a virtuous atheist, because they did not believe such a person could exist.[47] Julie's religion could be read as deist rather than Christian, and her deathbed scene is unorthodox and provocative. A comparison of her deathbed scene with Clarissa's gives some sense of how shocking it could seem to Anglican readers. Clarissa dies with the name of Jesus on her lips, after long repentance and long meditations on death; she has had her coffin brought in to her room days before she dies, and separated herself from earthly wishes, though she is scrupulous about her duties to the very end. Eighteenth-century readers were still familiar with this style of devotion, and could see Clarissa's death as an example of how to die that might be helpful when their own time came.[48] Julie dies without praying at all, confident that God will judge her in accordance with her devout and virtuous life. To severer Christian readers, this would be appalling presumption, and the idea of not praying on one's deathbed could seem utterly perverse. Her wrong religion and wrong behaviour could be seen as all of a piece. On the other hand, many people found the second part of the book deeply moving and edifying, and were in no doubt that it redeemed the first part. More liberal Christians were not troubled by the deathbed, and Mary Wollstonecraft found it an acceptable model of how to die; she too died without praying and without religious fear.[49]

Julie was the most popular of Rousseau's works in eighteenth-century England, and disseminated many of the notions about sexual difference which he developed in more detail in *Émile*.[50] It was possible to look at both books as love stories: Mary Hays' heroine Emma Courtney says of the man she falls in love with: 'He was the St. Preux, the Emilius, of my sleeping and waking reveries.'[51] Just as Julie is an inspirer to virtue, rather than a virtuous agent, Émile's bride Sophie is educated for him, rather than for herself. Rousseau insists that women are utterly different from men, find the meaning of their lives in relation to men, and are female in every aspect of their lives, whereas men are only male in certain contexts. Many women were offended by this, but many were not. Rousseau's views had a corollary which could appeal to women, the idea that women are not inferior men, but something quite different and perfect in its own way. Also, his belief in a good deal of social separation between the sexes made him interested in intense relationships between women, and willing to portray them as important. Sophie spends the day after her wedding lying in her mother's arms, while Claire shares Julie's bed when she is dying, and plans to be buried with her.[52]

Julie, or Julia, became a stereotypical name for a novel heroine who is seduced; it could also signify a heroine who is tempted but remains virtuous.[53] Henry Mackenzie's Julia de Roubigné, in the novel of that name, agrees to marry Montauban, a man she does not love, after he pays her father's debts and says that he will renounce all hope of marrying her.[54] She has heard that the man she loves, Savillon, is to marry, and her mother on her deathbed has urged her to marry Montauban to restore her father's fortune. Savillon had been the de Roubignés' ward, and grown up with Julia. He returns from abroad, unmarried after all, and arranges an innocent meeting with Julia; Montauban assumes that she is guilty, and poisons her. When she is dying, he realises she is innocent, goes mad, and commits suicide. Earlier in the novel, Julia expresses doubts about whether it is right to marry a man she does not love, and only does so because of extraordinary pressures. Mackenzie's triangle is like Rousseau's, but his views on love in marriage are the opposite; Mackenzie thinks love and marriage should go together, while Rousseau doubts whether they are compatible.

Helen Maria Williams, in her novel *Julia*, exploits a different triangle, also derived from *Julie*.[55] Williams' Julia falls in love with Frederick, the fiancé of her cousin Charlotte; he returns her feelings, but is in honour bound to go ahead with the marriage. Julia behaves nobly; Frederick, a weaker character, lets the situation prey on his mind until he falls ill and dies, while Charlotte is giving birth to their child. Julia takes care of him on his deathbed, and spends the rest of her life bringing up the child with Charlotte. Julia and Charlotte are poorly characterised, but the conflict between their love for each other and their love for the same man is the emotional centre of the book. Williams' novel is less competent than Mackenzie's, but both, as simple problem-novels developing ideas from Rousseau's more complex novel, suggest what aspects of *Julie* contemporaries found ethically interesting.

Both these novels disregard the class difference between Julie and Saint-Preux; however, this question is at the centre of Thomas Holcroft's *Anna St Ives*.[56] Holcroft was a radical, in sympathy with French revolutionary ideas, who was to stand trial for treason in 1794. His novel draws consciously on both *Julie* and *Clarissa* to preach a moralistic and radical message: human worth is independent of class, so love and marriage should be too; women are as rational as men; rape, like other kinds of violence, cannot subdue the mind of a virtuous person. However, elements in his plot undermine his message, paradoxically making his book less subversive than the novels he draws on. At the beginning of the book, Anna St Ives, his exemplary and rational heroine, believes that reforming men is an appropriate task for women. Her father, Sir Arthur St Ives, wants her to marry the book's Lovelace-like character, Coke Clifton, who is the brother of her best friend, Louisa. Sir Arthur is being swindled by his steward, Abimelech Henley, whose son, Frank, is the book's other exemplary character. Anna and Frank fall in love; the declaration scene comes about when Anna finds Frank weeping over a copy of *Julie* (p.241). Meanwhile, Clifton is trying to seduce Anna by arguing that belief in marriage is a mere prejudice; this provides the opportunity for Holcroft to state that marriage is necessary in society as it is, though it would not be in an ideal society (p.281). Anna decides that Clifton, like other rakes, cannot be reformed by marriage: 'Let us never cease our endeavours to reform the licentious and depraved, but let us not marry them' (p.332). Clifton kidnaps Frank and Anna, planning to kill Frank and rape Anna, but fails to do either. Holcroft seems to assume that Clifton could not rape Anna if she were conscious, and she protects herself from drugs by not eating the food brought to her in captivity till the day after her maid has sampled it. Frank and Anna escape, and Sir Arthur consents to their marriage. Clifton contemplates suicide, but Frank talks him out of it, and converts him to his and Anna's moral views.

Two points about this plot undermine Holcroft's conscious message. The first is the fact that Frank is the son of a dishonest steward. In spite of Frank's own virtue, this associates his love for Anna with disloyalty, and shows that Holcroft perceived the betrayal in *Julie* that troubled Burke. The second problem is Holcroft's treatment of rape; points in the text where he criticises *Clarissa* by arguing that rape victims should not feel grief and shame are undermined by the fact that he seems not really to believe in the possibility of rape. Anna's behaviour during her imprisonment is designed as a critique of Clarissa's; for example, the fact that she forces herself to eat a good breakfast the morning after Clifton has tried to break in to her room (p.418) is a comment on Clarissa's frequent, and ultimately fatal, inability to eat. Her speech of defiance to Clifton also criticises Clarissa's suffering after her rape:

> While I have life I fear you not! – And think you that brutality can taint the dead? Nay, think you that, were you endowed with the superior force which the vain name of man supposes, and could accomplish the basest purpose of your heart, I would falsely take guilt to myself; or imagine I had received the smallest blemish, from impurity which never reached my mind? That I would lament, or shun the world, or walk in open day oppressed by shame I did not merit? No! – For you perhaps I might weep, but for myself I would not shed a tear! Not a tear! (p.423)

She does not believe Clifton can rape her while she is conscious, and because of her foresight in suspecting drugs, she escapes untouched. Anna's heroism is not tested, and Holcroft only raises the issue of rape to deny it.

Holcroft's choice of the name Anna for his heroine may be a hint that he prefers Anna Howe's spirit and defiance to Clarissa's devoutness and submission to her fate. Another Jacobin novelist, Robert Bage, criticises this side of Clarissa's character in his novel *Hermsprong*; the heroine almost loses the love of the exemplary hero when she insists on obeying her father, even though his demands on her are unjust. An account of *Clarissa* and *Julie* which concentrates on their plots is bound to neglect the importance of Claire and Anna, and of the double-heroine formula the books have in common. The formula became very popular, because of the scope it provided for portraying different female types, and for developing female characters outside the formula of a love story. If one heroine carries the love plot, the other has more scope to develop other characteristics which might not suit a love story heroine. Anna's fire and liveliness, like Claire's cunning and her worship of Julie, would have been troubling in the primary heroine of a love story, but readers could easily feel closer to Anna and Claire than to the books' primary heroines. An Anna-like liveliness and disregard of strict good manners may have became more acceptable as the century went on. In *Julie*, Rousseau reserves most of this sort of liveliness for his secondary heroine, but Sophie, in *Émile*, is allowed some of it. She is educated to exist for her husband, but she is also educated to be natural and to be impatient with gallant conventions of politeness to women. When confronted with this kind of good manners and mild flirtation, she reacts rudely.[57]

However, Clarissa and Julie themselves represent vitally important feminine ideals, and their misfortunes crucial beliefs about women. The novels give a deeper sense than the moralistic literature of what eighteenth-century feminists were addressing. Neither novel can be called feminist; they portray women's goodness and misfortune, but without taking the further step of saying that change is possible. However, both have a great deal to do with the side of eighteenth-century feminism which is concerned with improving women themselves, rather than their situation. Clarissa realises a seventeenth-century devotional ideal of woman; she is always rational, and bases her obedience to authority on a reasoned acceptance of the need for hierarchy, not on the idea that those in authority are intrinsically superior. She is at least as intelligent as Lovelace, and he finds her consciousness of this hard to forgive (2.14). Anna Laetitia Barbauld compared the dialogues of seduction and entrapment between Clarissa and Lovelace to a chess game which he can only win by cheating.[58] Julie represents a different ideal; she is also rational and devout, but her intelligence is not as strongly emphasised as Clarissa's. Her heart, her capacity to inspire others, and her self-sacrificing devotion as a mother are all crucial to the ideal she represents. Julie's life and death as the beloved mistress of Clarens exemplify an ideal involved with social usefulness, while the ideal exemplified by Clarissa's lonely death is more purely religious. The idea that women's place in society matters because of their moral influence on men and the importance of their role as mothers was exploited by both feminist and anti-feminist writers at the end of the century, and emphasises the importance of sexual difference in a way that the earlier ideal does not.

Both heroines represent ideals, and struggle to be virtuous; neither lives an exemplary life. They cannot be placed accurately in the categories of good woman/bad woman, or maid/wife/widow, but they take the categories seriously. Their stories call these categories into question, but also suggest that the compromises available to women who fall outside them are morally dubious. Both heroines are exemplary moral subjects; neither can survive for very long as a woman in an anomalous category. Their paradoxical status, as good human beings who are also 'bad' women, cannot be maintained for long. Clarissa will not compromise by taking any of the steps which could gloss over the scandalous anomaly of her position; she will not marry

Lovelace or anyone else, she will not prosecute for the rape, she will not go abroad and wait for the scandal to blow over. Julie's decisions implicitly criticise Clarissa's; her marriage to Wolmar is not made less valuable by her past affair with Saint-Preux. However, the younger Julie remains present in the older one, and in the end it is as impossible for her to resolve her dilemma in life as it is for Clarissa. Both heroines die because their creators have no other way of resolving the clash between the demand on them as women to save appearances and not break conventional categories, and the demand on them as moral beings to live in accordance with the truth.

On a simple level, the novels discuss the question of whether a woman who has lapsed from conventionally correct behaviour should return to being accepted in society, and seem to give opposite answers. Clarissa refuses to return; Julie consents. However, the depth with which both heroines are portrayed, and the terrible price of their decisions, make easy answers impossible. There is contemporary polemic about this problem, but it rarely achieves the respect for women's moral autonomy which is present in these novels, and tends to reduce the women in question to stereotypical victims or whores, who must be completely innocent or completely guilty. Clarissa and Julie are neither, and they are more than mere vehicles for their creators' conscious beliefs about women. Clarissa's refusal to compromise and return to society is not intended as a literal exemplar for fallen women, for Richardson was interested in their rehabilitation, and supported the foundation of the Magdalen Hospital, whose aim was to reform prostitutes and return them to society.[59] Julie expresses her feelings for Saint-Preux, and takes the initiative in arranging an assignation with him (1.53). However, elsewhere Rousseau argues that women should not express their feelings for men, and says that men would die of exhaustion if women were allowed to take the initiative sexually.[60] It is the quality of these woman-centred novels, and the depth of their characterisation, not any explicit message, which makes them an important part of the background to the feminist thought at the end of the century. Both novels enriched the language in which the minutiae of women's lives could be discussed, and gave a deep sense of the importance of women's moral choices.

Part Two

Feminist Responses

CHAPTER FOUR

The Beginnings of
Eighteenth-Century Feminism

The feminist writing of the end of the seventeenth
century has affinities with earlier discussions of
women's education, and of women's responsibility for
their own religious duties, but it was original in
transferring religious arguments about women's
equality into a secular context. It argues clearly for
women's rationality, and for their duty to educate
themselves, and to base their decisions, including the
decision to obey a husband, on a rational understanding
of life, not mindless submission to custom.
Contemporaries often misread this writing,
disintegrating it into its less controversial sources. Parts
could be read as religious exhortation, with no
implications for women's social position, parts could be
dismissed as satire about relationships between the
sexes. It is still a long way from the later, unified,
discussion of women's rights and responsibilities, but it
represents a move towards it.

Changes in the intellectual life of the period made it
easier to argue seriously for women's rationality. Earlier,
light-hearted defences of women's intelligence, which
oppose women's wit to the male pedantry of the
schools, could take on a different meaning once the
value of the ancient languages and ancient learning was
under serious attack. After Descartes, the defence of
untutored reason was no longer an exercise in mystical
paradox. The increased use of the vernacular meant that
being trained to think no longer depended on a long

apprenticeship in Latin which was usually given to boys only. Cartesian emphasis on the mind's independence of the body weakened arguments from physiology against women's rationality. Poulain de la Barre's work, which argues that only custom and prejudice, not Nature, exclude women from the professions and public life, was translated into English in 1677. Poulain does not call for change, but points out that the male monopoly of power is arbitrary; he argues that someone must have the monopoly, just as only one family can be the royal family.[1]

This feminist writing was made possible by the uncertainties and changes which affected people's notions of women in the period. Ideas about women were intimately involved with ideas about the moral tone of society, and about social and political hierarchy; both were anxious and controversial areas. Many people thought the period from the Restoration onwards was far looser sexually than earlier periods, and some people were troubled by this. This period saw the first publication of pornographic literature in England, and the formation of the Societies for the Reformation of Manners to hound the immoral.[2] People worried about male homosexuality, 'which though felony by the laws was never so much talken on, and I doubt, not without cause, as of late years'.[3]

Women were publicly conspicuous in some new ways. The Quakers, who gained toleration during this period, maintained women's right to preach and pray in public. They also formed local women's meetings, which were responsible for administering relief to poor Quaker women, and had a role in approving forthcoming marriages.[4] In a rather different milieu, that of the theatre, women also had a position which they had not held before in England. After the Restoration, women's roles were played by actresses; many actresses had doubtful sexual reputations, but a few were ostentatiously respectable. The same is true of the numerous women playwrights. Aphra Behn and her less famous colleagues represent a new, more professional type of woman writer, less restrained in their subject-matter and more willing to promote themselves than earlier women writers. Katherine Philips, the exemplary woman poet of the mid-seventeenth century, had not been responsible for the publication of her poems or her translation of Corneille's *Pompée*; writers at the end of the century could vilify contemporary women writers, while treating Philips as a model women should emulate in private study.[5] Robert Gould, the author of some violent misogynist satires, also wrote a poem urging a lady to study Philips's work:

> But O! when you have read this matchless book
> And from its excellence a judgment took,
> What the fair sex was then, how will you mourn,
> To see how justly now they're branded with our
> scorn?
> Farces and songs obscene, remote from wit,
> (Such as our *Sappho* to *Lisander* writ)
> Employs their time – so far th'abuse prevails,
> Their verses are as vicious as their tails:
> Both are exposed alike to public view,
> And both of them have their admirers too:
> Though which is least was ne'er distinguished yet,
> The writer's virtue, or the reader's wit.[6]

Gould's poem shows clearly how misogynist satire was compatible with an ideal which honoured women's virtue and intelligence, so long as they behaved with propriety. This primarily religious ideal was not easy to transform into more secular arguments in favour of women. It was serious in its defence of women, but extremely limited, and made severe moral demands on women. Some kinds of humorous secular writing in defence of women, which address misogynist satire directly, seem to be much stronger, but this strength is deceptive, because the misogynists and the defenders do not disagree substantially about women's nature. Both agree that women's seductive power over men is the central fact about them; the difference is whether they react with rage or with pleasure. Often what is being defended is the idea that women can be pleasant and civilised companions for men, not the idea of their intrinsic human worth. The difference is subtle, but crucial. The serious defences of women as civilised companions for men imply some assertion of their human worth, but this assertion is weak and unstable, and these defences slide very easily into frivolous, chivalrous defences of women as beautiful and lovable. Frivolous defences of women often praise women for much the same qualities for which misogynists condemn them; vivacity, wit and physical beauty. This type of defence of woman could also absorb the religious ideal of the educated woman for its own purposes, and bring it down to its own level; Philips appears in its pantheon of examples beside Aphra Behn, while more religious works do not mention Behn at all, or do so with regret.[7] The shifting, half-serious tone of these defences, and the ease with which they could incorporate more serious material, made it hard to articulate serious secular defences of women, as there was no unambiguous way of marking that they should not be read frivolously. Contemporaries misread serious feminist arguments as satirical defences of women, and often external evidence is the only way to be sure of a writer's feminist intentions.

Satires against women evoked some satires against men, as well as defences of women.[8] However, anti-male satire did not attack male dominance as strongly as misogynist satire affirmed it. Misogynist satire attacked women as women, even when its writers claimed an educational, reforming value for it; anti-male satire attacked particular types of male fool – philanderers, men who behaved badly in women's company, jealous husbands – and gave the attack piquancy by putting it in the mouth of a woman. Satires against women often attack marriage, and there is a corresponding genre which attacks marriage by giving the point of view of the unhappy wife. However, both genres usually agree that wives will be unfaithful if they get a chance; the difference is whether they view the wife's adultery with horror or with sympathy, and whether the butt is an insatiably lustful wife, or a husband who is 'jealous by day, and impotent by night'.[9]

Comedy also portrayed provoked wives, but comic sympathy for them was hard to translate into a serious questioning of husbands' power, because moralists often argued that ill-treated wives were always partly to blame. They argued that women were more adaptable than men, and so had a greater obligation to make an effort to please in marriage, and that wives are responsible for much of their husbands' bad behaviour.[10] A wife who would consider committing adultery, whatever the provocation, could never deserve sympathy.[11] In other comedies, the adulterous triangle is softened into a courtship triangle, in which the young lover wins the woman from the man her parents want her to marry. Here the real focus of interest is on the problem of youth and authority, rather than women's situation specifically. The triangle could be resolved by marrying the lovers, but the question of the power relationships between them once they are husband and wife is left untouched. The unloved husband, or the unwanted suitor, is a particular comic type who does not call the whole institution of marriage into question. This genre of satire and comedy may have encouraged a cynical approach to marriage as some contemporaries feared, but it is not concerned with women's rights.

Cynicism about marriage bothered moralistic writers, who were concerned to encourage people to marry. The wish to promote marriage could lead to an instrumental feminism, which aimed to educate women so as to make them more interesting companions, and to an increased willingness to give children some say in their choice of marriage partner. Available figures suggest that the proportion of the population who never married was unusually high at this period; because there were many clandestine marriages, the figures are not wholly reliable, but this seems to be true of the children of peers, who are better documented than most of the population.[12] Upper-class families had to spend more money on dowries for their daughters than in earlier periods, and marriage settlements fixed jointures at a smaller proportion of the dowry than earlier; husbands were becoming more expensive.[13]

Styles of authority within the family were changing, and people had varying expectations about how the subordinate partners, wives and children, should behave. Real changes in behaviour could arouse fears about other kinds of social upheaval; rebellious women, wives who wore the trousers, were an old emblem of anarchy and misrule.[14] This uncertainty about authority within the family was compounded by the uncertainty about political authority during this period. The revolution of 1688 raised difficult problems in political theory, and its supporters took a long time to arrive at a coherent justification of it.[15] The difficulty was to analyse the deposition of James II and the accession of William and Mary in a way that did not make other depositions seem too easy, and make Parliament too powerful. The usual solution was to argue that James had effectively abdicated before anyone took action to bring William and Mary to power. Sometimes this was argued in terms of a contract theory of government; tyrannical abuse of power by the ruler broke the contract, and released subjects from the duty of obedience which was their side of the bargain.

People who did not support the revolution argued that subjects' duties were unconditional. Subjects had no right of resistance against an immoral ruler, and if confronted with a command which they could not in conscience obey, they were still bound to the duty of passive obedience, or accepting whatever punishment was imposed for non-compliance. Not accepting the revolution raised problems about the nature of subjects' duties to the effective government of William and Mary, once James had definitely lost power. The usual solution rested on the distinction between the ruler *de jure* and the ruler *de facto*; even if James were King by law, William and Mary had a claim on their subjects' obedience once they were thoroughly settled in power. If Providence willed wicked or usurping rulers to take power, they still had to be obeyed. Biblical models for this situation showed *de facto* rulers in a very bad light; the Jews owed obedience to the Babylonians and Romans, although they, not their pagan rulers, were the chosen people, and the legal basis of these rulers' authority was often doubtful.[16]

Both sides in the argument were usually reluctant to draw all the logical conclusions from their positions, or state them in their strongest form; some people tried to give illogical, hybrid accounts of the nature of authority. The outlines of the argument could easily be transferred to arguments about the basis of the husband's authority in marriage, though few people did this in a consistent way. The question of whether kingship was a matter of contract or divine right resembled the question of whether the husband's authority in marriage was a matter of contract or of innate male superiority. The literature of the period is full of jokes about husbands who expect passive obedience and non-resistance from their wives, although this is not the way they behave towards their own superiors.[17] The links between the theory of the divine right of kings and the theory of natural male dominance, which a few writers tried to formalise in a theory tracing the origins of kingship to the paternal authority of Adam, were obvious on this sort of joking, informal level.[18]

At the end of the century, many writers either questioned the natural basis of male dominance, or asserted it so violently that they obviously felt it was threatened. Locke thought that there might be some basis in Nature for the husband's dominance, but argued that marriage was a contract the terms of which could vary widely. He also considered the anomalous case of a reigning queen married to one of her subjects; clearly she could not owe him obedience, so male dominance was not an absolute rule.[19] In his educational writings, Locke allows there may be some difference between the sexes and some natural male superiority, but in a tone which makes it clear that he thinks that such difference and superiority are neither interesting nor important.[20] His attitude contrasts with the violent tone of some preachers on the subject, who insist that men's natural physical and mental superiority is shown by the fact that women depend on men for money and protection.[21] These preachers also insist that there must be a clear superiority, within the family, and the issue is not whether equality is possible, but who should rule:

> Though there be many women superior to many men, in strength of body, and abilities of mind, in fineness of parts, greatness of capacity, soundness of judgment, and strength and faithfulness of memory, yet the number of such, neither is, nor ever was, nor ever will be, great enough to show that Nature intended to give that sex the superiority over the men . . ..[22]

Sophisticated readers probably treated the stronger and more naive assertions of male dominance as a kind of misogynist satire; they could laugh at them as absurd and extreme, without having to formulate a position that disagreed with them in substance. It was harder to oppose this position seriously than to make fun of its style, or undermine it by a weakened acceptance, in the manner of Locke. There is a good example of this in the response to John Sprint's sermon *The Bride-Woman's Counsellor.*[23] This work expresses a very strong view of male dominance, and was probably read as a joke as much as for serious edification. A collection of wedding sermons printed in the 1730s, which includes a reprint of *The Bride-Woman's Counsellor,* was clearly aimed at the market for mildly *risqué* light reading, not the market for spiritual edification.[24] Sprint argues that the principal end for which women were created, after the glory of God, is to be serviceable to men; wives should obey their husbands, and defer to them externally and internally, not even thinking ill of them. The sermon provoked two replies, one ridiculing it mercilessly, and expounding an instrumentally feminist position which differs from Sprint's position in style more than in substance; the other treating it more seriously and trying to articulate a feminist position in response to it.

The Female Advocate, by a writer who uses the pseudonym Eugenia, makes fun of Sprint, and gives an idealised picture of marriage, where the harmony between the partners means there is no need for 'an unsociable majesty on the one hand, or a vile submission on the other'.[25] Internal evidence suggests Eugenia is a man; he is well-travelled, has a good command of Greek and Latin, as well as 'the more solid parts of learning', and writes about Sprint with an air of confident superiority.[26] He is in favour of educating women, and argues that it is not only bad wives who disagree with Sprint.[27] Women were made 'for the comfort and benefit of man', but it is 'a much nobler comfort' to have a companion than a slave.[28] Sprint's argument that women should not even think ill of their husbands is dismissed by an appeal to experience:

> Let it be granted that 'tis the part of a woman, being the weaker vessel, to submit and learn as well as she can the hard lesson of *Passive Obedience*; yet I defy the meekest woman in the world, if she meets with an unreasonable, imperious, domineering, insolent creature, I defy such a lady with all her virtue and patience to forbear wishing at least it were otherwise. . ..[29]

However, this expression of sympathy for ill-treated wives does not really address the question of how they should behave, or what can be done about their situation. Much of Eugenia's criticism of Sprint consists of ridiculing points of detail. He makes fun of a passage where Sprint writes: 'the Persian Ladies have the resemblance of a foot worn on the top of their coronets, in token that the height of their glory, top-knot and all, does not stoop to their husbands' feet'; for Eugenia, this is a far-fetched and silly conceit.[30] He also makes fun of Sprint's disapproval of women who call their husbands by their Christian names,

> as if they esteemed them at no higher a rate than their very servants that attend them . . . Those women who will not condescend to give their husbands the title of *Lord* and *Master*, it is to be feared will not scruple in little time to usurp that authority

which that title doth imply, and the husband may quickly experience what it is to be under the discipline of the Apron.[31]

Eugenia gives a friendlier, more egalitarian picture of marriage than Sprint does, but takes the inequality of power between husband and wife for granted. *The Female Advocate*'s picture of a friendly marriage denies the problem of conflict between husband and wife, rather than looking for a different solution.

Mary, Lady Chudleigh's reply to Sprint, *The Ladies Defence*, which seems milder and more hesitant than Eugenia's, is more authentically feminist in its assertion of women's rationality.[32] Chudleigh does not complain in general terms about Sprint condoning ill-treatment, but specifically that he asks women to resign their reason and will to their husbands. Her epistle dedicatory urges unhappily married women to obey their husbands, but recognises how difficult this can be, and respects the moral achievement of women who have bad husbands and behave well. She urges women to read and educate themselves, and ground their behaviour in a Christian Stoicism. They should read Seneca and Epictetus, and realise that external evils such as poverty are not real evils.[33] Her preface appeals for men to treat their wives better; in choosing wives, they should 'prefer virtue and good sense, before either riches, beauty, or quality'.[34] She criticises parents who force children to marry against their inclinations. In tone the preface is quite conventionally moralistic, and emphasises that she is not using polemic with Sprint as a pretext for attacking religion. The main text is a verse dialogue; the participants are a Parson, who expounds Sprint's views on male dominance in marriage, Sir John Brute, borrowed from *The Provok'd Wife*, complaining of the tedium of marriage and speaking up for free love, and Sir William Loveall, who is willing to marry, thinks wives should be kindly treated, and admires women's beauty; however, he thinks that if women were educated they would become vain and 'none but the men of sense would dare to love'.[35] Finally there is

Melissa, who expounds Chudleigh's own point of view, which rejects both Sprint's justification of male dominance, and Vanbrugh's sympathy for Lady Brute's rebellion in *The Provok'd Wife*. Husbands have duties as well as wives, the Parson's ridiculous exposition of male dominance amounts to a satire against men, women should educate themselves and act morally, men can retain the power in the world as long as women are free to think and act virtuously:

> The tyrant Man may still possess the throne,
> 'Tis in our minds that we would rule alone:
> Those unseen empires give us leave to sway,
> And to our Reason private homage pay.[36]

It is a modest demand, but in its insistence on women's right to intellectual and moral autonomy, even when married, it is stronger than Eugenia's glossing over of the problem. Even if women must obey, they must freely choose to do so, as rational and autonomous beings. Sermons on natural male dominance, and comic sympathy for rebellious wives, seem to carry contrary messages, but in fact both articulate the idea that, for women, independence and rebellion are the same. Chudleigh's reply, that women can choose obedience freely, had been stated before in religious contexts; however, because her writing also addresses comic material, and the obedient wife is intended as a contrast to a character as vividly realised as Lady Brute, her demand for mental freedom gains concreteness, and cannot be dismissed as a sermon ideal.

Chudleigh complained that the work was misread as an attack on marriage, because of its pessimism about a wife's position.[37] She had satirised marriage elsewhere, urging women to live single, because

> Wife and servant are the same,
> And only differ in the name . . .[38]

However, the freedom to choose to live unmarried without financial worries was not available to most women. Works which satirise marriage, or give an idealised picture of a single woman's life, avoid this problem. Attacks on marriage carry the message that it is men who are better off single, even when they are written from a woman's point of view. *The Ladies Defence* can be read as a stronger and more serious assertion of women's autonomy and rationality than this kind of anti-marriage writing, because of its greater realism about women's limited choices.

A work with a similar argument to *The Ladies Defence*, Mary Astell's *Some Reflections upon Marriage*, was misread in the same way.[39] Astell shares Chudleigh's view that women's rationality should make them see that an ill-treated wife has a duty to obey, but she articulates this view in terms which have clear political implications, and ridicules men more sharply than Chudleigh does. Her pamphlet is not a response to Sprint, but to a text by St-Évremond defending the conduct of the Duchess Mazarine, who had just died.[40] The Duchess, a niece of Cardinal Mazarin, had brought her husband a huge fortune on their marriage. The Duke turned out to be overbearing and insane; his madness took the form of religious mania and excessive sexual prudery. The Duchess left him, as a result forfeiting much of her property, and after various adventures, came to England. A period as Charles II's mistress earned her a pension.[41] However, St-Évremond, like Astell, speaks of her only as indiscreet; neither writer discusses her adultery explicitly. St-Évremond argues that the Duke's behaviour was so intolerable that it automatically created a legal separation, and the Duchess had a right to leave him and expect financial provision:

> Our first engagements are to reason, justice and humanity, and the quality of a husband can't dispense with so natural an obligation. When a husband turns extravagant, unjust, or inhumane, he turns tyrant, he breaks the society, which he contracted for with his wife. The right of separation is already made; the judges make it not, they only publish its validity by a solemn declaration.[42]

As Lady Brute asked on stage in 1697: 'The argument's good between king and people, why not between husband and wife?'[43]

Astell disagrees strongly with this contractual account of the nature of authority. For her, the duty to obey a husband's authority, like the duty to obey political authority, is unconditional. In politics she takes this doctrine to its limits, and says that Locke's argument that the right of self-preservation can override the duty to obey is shockingly unChristian, conflicting with the duty to accept martyrdom and love one's enemies.[44] However, she insists that husbands' authority, like political authority, is ordained arbitrarily by Providence; it is not based on any natural male superiority. She is critical of husbands who behave tyrannically, and has some sharp satire against men who think they are superior to women, or who think they are doing women a favour by proposing to them: 'Scarce a man who can keep himself clean, or make a bow, but thinks he is good enough to pretend to any women, no matter for the difference in birth and fortune. . .'[45] Only an heroic Christianity, reinforced by a rational education, can enable an unhappy wife to do her duty; Cato's suicide, when he had been defeated by Caesar, shows that Stoic philosophy is not enough to sustain people in desperate situations.[46] Woman should be educated, because otherwise their natural good sense will make them see that they are unfairly treated, and they will mistakenly conclude that they have a right to rebel.

In her preface to the third edition of the work, Astell insists that the work is a serious appeal for obedience, not the satire against marriage or authoritarian political views which it had been mistaken for, and develops her argument against natural male superiority. She also makes it clear that she is writing as a woman; there would have been no way of telling this from the first edition, and she says that a male author had claimed the work. She argues that the belief in natural male superiority undermines other kinds of social hierarchy, and comes close to sedition against the reigning monarch, Anne. The fact that female subordination is a universal custom does not mean it is natural or right, and Biblical texts which refer to women's subjection are descriptive, not prescriptive. Adam and Eve may have been more nearly equal before the Fall.[47]

> However this be, 'tis certainly no arrogance in a woman to conclude that she was made for the service of God, and that this is her end. Because God made all things for himself, and a rational mind is too noble a being to be made for the sake and service of any creature. The service she at any time becomes obliged to pay to a man, is only a business by the bye. Just as it may be any man's business and duty to keep hogs; he was not made for this, but if he hires himself out to such an employment, he ought conscientiously to perform it.[48]

The Duchess's story was a suitable example for Astell's argument, for the fact that her husband was mad and that she had brought a great deal of property to the marriage made it clear that the usual arguments for natural male dominance could not apply in this case. These are the arguments that men are stronger and more able than women, both mentally and physically, and that women need men to protect them and provide for them financially.[49] Astell disposes of these arguments by pointing out that physical strength and mental ability do not necessarily go together, and by giving a sad portrait of an heiress whose husband marries her for her money, 'and now he has got that into his possession, she must make court to him for a little sorry alimony out of her own estate.'[50]

Astell was able to make such a clear distinction between the duty to obey authority, and belief in the worth of the person in authority, because of her strongly Tory political views. She detested William III, but accepted the duty to obey his government.[51] Although she herself believed it was legitimate for those who had sworn loyalty to James II to take the Oath of Loyalty to William and Mary, she was close to some of the most eminent of the non-jurors, the ecclesiastics who felt conscientiously unable to do this. Sancroft, the non-juring Archbishop of Canterbury, helped her when she first came to London from Newcastle upon Tyne; she presented him with a manuscript volume of her poems in 1689, before she had published anything.[52] Henry Dodwell, one of the non-jurors' principal theorists, corresponded with her.[53] She wrote several authoritarian political pamphlets opposing the relaxation of the penalties imposed on the Dissenters; these show that she was a strong churchwoman, and accepted the Tory political doctrines of passive obedience and non-resistance.[54]

Astell came from a family of merchants, but much of her work expresses an aristocratic point of view. She speaks with devotion of her patron, Lady Catherine Jones, a daughter of the Earl of Ranelagh and a great-niece of Robert Boyle, and she lived with Lady Catherine for part of her life.[55] She was also close to other pious and philanthropic aristocratic women, Lady Elizabeth Hastings and Anne, Lady Coventry.[56] *Some Reflections upon Marriage* is critical of women who marry beneath them; in her first and best-known work, *A Serious Proposal to the Ladies*, she also criticises aristocratic men who marry for money, and praises German aristocrats for being more concerned with purity of blood than the English.[57] The strength of her belief in imposed, providential order and hierarchy is the other side of her disbelief in natural hierarchy among human beings.

A Serious Proposal to the Ladies has two principal suggestions. The first is a general argument that women should be educated for their own moral and religious good. The curriculum Astell proposes emphasises general intellectual training, rather than particular subjects:

> . . . it is not intended she should spend her time in learning *words*, but *things*, and therefore no more languages than are necessary to acquaint her with useful authors. Nor need she trouble herself in turning over a huge number of books, but take care to understand and digest a few well-chosen and good ones. Let her but obtain right ideas and be truly acquainted with the

nature of those objects that present themselves to her mind, and then no matter whether or no she be able to tell what fanciful people have said about them: And thoroughly to understand Christianity as professed by the Church of England, will be sufficient to confirm her in the truth, though she have not a catalogue of those particular errors which oppose it.[58]

As ladies usually know French, they should read Descartes and Malebranche, instead of wasting this skill on novel-reading.[59] Astell's second suggestion is a plan for a kind of convent without vows, where single women could spend their time studying, doing charitable work, and educating girls. She had serious, and apparently realistic, hopes of raising money to endow an institution of this kind; there is a tradition that Queen Anne was willing to endow it, but was dissuaded by Bishop Burnet, who felt that it would be too reminiscent of a Catholic convent.[60] Astell dedicated the sequel to *A Serious Proposal* to Anne, and she made an appeal to her to consider founding such an institution in a work published ten years later.[61] The fund-raising purpose of the book means that Astell spells out how such an institution would be a cheap and efficient way for upper-class families to provide for their unmarried daughters; the endowment each lady would bring with her could be much less than what would be needed to keep her in suitable style as a single woman. It would also prevent women from contracting unsuitable marriages out of fear of becoming old maids:

> . . . she flies to some dishonourable match as her last, though much mistaken refuge, to the disgrace of her family, and her own irreparable ruin. And now let any person of honour tell me, if it were not richly worth some thousand pounds, to prevent all this mischief, and the having an idle fellow, and perhaps a race of beggarly children to hang on him, and to provide for?[62]

An aunt of Lady Catherine Jones's had eloped with a footman; Astell's heat in this passage may reflect the family's outrage.[63]

The book was well received, but no one took any steps towards founding the proposed college. Astell was not the first person to make such a proposal; the convents which had been closed at the Reformation had not been replaced by other institutions providing refuge for single women or adequate education for girls, and some people recognised that there was a need for them. Some non-Catholic parents educated their daughters at convents abroad, because of the frivolous reputation of English girls' boarding-schools.[64] In the mid-seventeenth century, Letice, Lady Falkland had hoped to found institutions for girls' education and widows' retirement, but the Civil War had made this impossible.[65] Slightly later, the author of *The Ladies Calling* openly regretted that convents had been closed; however, this was controversial, for works plagiarising material from *The Ladies Calling* often omit this passage.[66] Edward Chamberlayne, who was English tutor to Queen Anne's husband, Prince George of Denmark, proposed colleges for single women and widows, suggesting similar institutions in Germany and the Netherlands as a model. His 1671 pamphlet on the subject is a serious fund-raising proposal, which suggests that he knew women who were eager to live in such an institution.[67] Writers who approved of Astell's project and wrote proposals of their own for such an institution included Sir George Wheeler, and, in a semi-serious vein, Defoe.[68] Wheeler pointed out that some institutions where women lived communally already existed, such as almshouses or homes for clergy widows, so that opponents' fear of monasticism was exaggerated and unjustified.[69]

Three years later, when it had become clear that the proposed women's college was not likely to be founded for some time, Astell published a second part to the work, which goes into more detail about what women should study.[70] It is a serious, if limited, curriculum; Astell argues that it is more important for women to develop their reasoning capacities than for them to master particular bodies of knowledge. This is a moral project, not a purely intellectual one; for Astell, intellectual training is worthless if it is not accompanied by religious discipline. One of the books Astell recommends is the *Port-Royal Logic*, and she shares much of its view of human life.[71] It argues that moral and intellectual education are intimately linked; its translators describe it as 'no less useful for the conduct of human life, than to instruct and guide us wandering in labyrinths of unsettled reason'.[72] Astell agrees with the *Port-Royal Logic* both that intellectual error is the cause of many wrong actions, and that many intellectual errors result from laziness, or from prejudices which are really a wilful moral blindness:

> Indeed if we search to the bottom I believe we shall find, that the corruption of the heart contributes more to the cloudiness of the head, than the clearness of our light does to the regularity of our affections; and 'tis oftener seen that our vicious inclinations keep us ignorant, than that our knowledge makes us good.[73]

However, this does not mean intellectual effort is unnecessary; women should train themselves to think logically, and speak and write clearly. Astell's advice that women should do this by reading the *Port-Royal Logic* and parts of Locke's *Essay concerning Human Understanding* expects more of women than some other educational proposals which suggest wider reading and more learning of languages.[74]

Astell's commitment to women's education was supported by some churchmen; she was particularly close to John Norris, who publicised the Christian Cartesianism of Malebranche in England.[75] In 1695 she published a religious correspondence with Norris, which sparked off a theological controversy about the love of God.[76] Another woman correspondent of Norris's, Damaris, Lady Masham, also wrote anonymously in the controversy, disagreeing with Norris.[77] Lady Masham, who is best known as a friend of Locke, was a well-read and intelligent woman, who taught herself Latin in order to teach it to her son.[78] The fact that she had not learnt it as a girl, although her father was an extremely erudite theologian, the

Cambridge Platonist Ralph Cudworth, is an index of how little women's education could be taken for granted. Norris also knew Mary, Lady Chudleigh, and his views on women's education are close to Chudleigh's and Astell's. In a letter answering a woman's request for advice on reading, he insists that learning to think is more important than memorising information, and recommends beginning with the Port-Royal Logic.[79]

Astell and Norris agree that this kind of basic logical training is what is essential for women, but their argument does not imply that all women should be restricted to this. Astell quotes a passage from William Wotton's Reflections upon Ancient and Modern Learning, discussing Tudor ladies' classical erudition, which makes it clear that learning does not injure a woman's moral character.[80] The non-juring cleric and Anglo-Saxon scholar, George Hickes, translated Fénelon's De l'éducation des filles, which recommends a serious, but narrow and moralistic curriculum; he also encouraged Elizabeth Elstob in her scholarly work in Anglo-Saxon.[81] Elstob herself mentions Hickes' praise of Fénelon as a proof of his commitment to the cause of women's learning.[82] At this period, even promoting a very simple curriculum for women could have feminist implications, because it was providing women with the tools to educate themselves further, which could not be taken for granted. Elstob wanted to encourage other women to take up Anglo-Saxon, and found at least one pupil.[83] She argued that Anglo-Saxon was worth studying, because all parts of learning were valuable.[84] In the preface to her Anglo-Saxon grammar, she insists that her work must stand on its own merits. She says her subject-matter demands a rough style, and adds, 'If I am mistaken herein, I beg pardon: I might allege that which perhaps might be admitted for an excuse, but that I will not involve the whole sex, by pleading woman's frailty.'[85] Like Astell, she complains about women who are hostile to women who are better educated than they are; both Elstob and Astell insist on the duty to be generous about other people's achievements.[86] Elstob knew Astell, and Lady Catherine Jones was one of the subscribers to Elstob's *English-Saxon Homily.*

These writers put forward views about women's rationality and their duty to educate themselves which are very like the views in some earlier religious writers, but the changed context in which they wrote gives their views a newly feminist content. They are not writing in a private context, or a purely religious one, but publicly responding to kinds of writing which earlier works for women's spiritual edification had not addressed. As a result, their assertions about women's spiritual and moral equality gain weight and carry more implications for everyday life. The pessimistic rational feminism of Chudleigh and Astell is largely made up of ideas from earlier religious writers, but it represents a change in the field of secular writing about women. The response to Astell's *Serious Proposal* is a curious mixture of respect and ridicule. Extracts from it appear in the *Ladies' Library,* and no one objected to the ideal of women's self-improvement.[87] However, the proposed college was ridiculed in the *Tatler,* as was Elstob's study of Anglo-Saxon.[88]

The *Tatler* piece shows the college breaking up as soon as the women are courted by men; light secular writing preferred to deal with women in the context of love. It could dismiss assertions of woman's moral and intellectual autonomy as empty moralism, by suggesting that in real life women would always be more interested in men than in self-improvement.

When Astell and Chudleigh asserted this autonomy in their writings on marriage, they were misunderstood in a more extreme way; contemporaries could think they were making a violent satirical attack on the institution of marriage. However, these works were still available later in the century; *Some Reflections upon Marriage* was reprinted in 1730, and *The Ladies Defence* appears in Colman and Thornton's 1755 collection, *Poems by Eminent Ladies.* What Astell and Chudleigh were saying appeared comic and nihilistic in a secular context; the pious assertion that an ill-treated wife has a duty to obey her husband seemed subversive once marital tyranny was linked seriously to political tyranny, and once the picture of a rational and virtuous wife victimised by an irrational and vicious husband was made concrete. Their argument that a happy marriage should be based on a virtuous friendship was not contentious, but the clarity with which they exposed power relationships within marriage was.

The exemplary educated woman, and the exemplary patient wife, are old religious ideals which change their meaning when read in the context of new comic portrayals of witty and autonomous women. The old religious statement of women's spiritual autonomy was too other-worldly to carry strong feminist implications. The satirical and comic portrayal of independent, self-willed women, with legitimate grievances against men, was not easy to translate into more serious assertions of women's right to autonomy; strict moralists could always point to these heroines' failure to live up to the duty of patience. A woman who combined a religious sense of her own worth with the secular self-assertiveness of a comic or satirical heroine represented a more serious challenge to male dominance.

CHAPTER FIVE

Women's Education and Women's Rationality

The questions of women's rationality and women's education were central in eighteenth-century feminist discussions. Astell's demand for an education which would give women intellectual and moral maturity was treated with respect at the beginning of the century, but views like hers were still controversial at the end. Beliefs about education necessarily implied views about what sort of intellectual and moral being a woman should turn out to be, and, as the century went on, some writers not only argued that education should make women intellectually and morally mature, but criticised features of society which kept women immature. Education became an instrument of social reform, and educational writing did not only discuss how to form the ideal woman, but also discussed what her place in society should be.

At the beginning of the century, people usually discussed the question in terms of how much women should be educated; later, the question was more often posed in terms of how male and female education should differ. Locke's casual dismissal of the question of difference evoked a violent contradiction from Rousseau in *Émile*; Émile's education in self-reliance contrasts dramatically with Sophie's education to please him and depend on him.[1] Sophie's education is neither a traditional masculine intellectual education, nor a traditional feminine ornamental education; it is a specifically feminine moral education. It seems to offer a way out of an earlier dilemma about women's moral education; either women are inferior, and must be educated to take their morality on trust, or they must be educated to make rational moral choices in the same way as men, but accept that their field of action is much more limited. Rousseau insists that men and women are radically different, and women's different field of moral action should be seen as just as important as men's, but demanding different kinds of moral action and training. Wollstonecraft, like many other writers, saw this as no more than a restatement of the idea of women's inferiority, but others saw it as compatible with a more affirmative notion of women's separate sphere and necessarily different education.[2]

There were genuine changes in women's education during the eighteenth century; upper- and middle-class women were much more literate and well-informed at the end of the century than at the beginning. There was also a greater interest in the education of the poor, including poor women, although it was as much concerned with preventing rebellion as with the welfare of the poor themselves.[3] Most writers on women's education are primarily concerned with middle-class women. Everyone agreed that the daughters of aristocrats or people with substantial inherited wealth, who would never need to earn a living, could study subjects which might be a waste of time for other girls, such as foreign languages or music, although there was debate about how much serious reading they should do. There was more controversy about the education of daughters of the class below – professionals, and wealthy tradesmen – and some criticism of them for imitating upper-class education. Anti-feminists thought that their education should make them pleasing to their husbands, and tolerated an intellectually undemanding curriculum, which often included many ladylike accomplishments such as music or embroidery. Moralists and feminists wanted an education with more practical and intellectual content, and were more concerned about women's ability to educate their children, help their husbands in their business, and earn their own living if necessary. A woman from this class would have had to be rather unlucky to need to earn a living; writers who discuss such cases are usually sympathetic, and aware of the difficulties of moving socially downwards with grace. Most writers are much harsher towards girls from the next class down – small tradespeople and skilled workers – who emulate ladylike accomplishments. Moralists argue that their expensive tastes and lack of useful skills make them unattractive as wives to men of their own class, while their vanity and pretension make them easy prey for upper-class seducers. Most writers emphasise the need for them to be hard-working and useful wives, rather than the possible need for them to earn a living independently. On the other hand, when really poor girls' education is discussed, making them able to earn a living is the primary aim.

The principal debate over the education of women was whether it should be ornamental, making them pleasing companions for men, or useful, making them good mothers and heads of households, and perhaps capable of earning a living. Feminists usually argue for a useful education, but add a stronger emphasis on the need for women to develop their rationality and moral sense, and not to rely on the judgements of others. The range of the curriculum, and the extent of its demands, could vary considerably in both categories. Ornamental education could include time-consuming and serious study of art and music, as well as fairly wide reading, and useful education could include quite intellectually demanding subjects.

Neither kind of education was necessarily feminist, for neither necessarily respected women's minds or taught them to think. Increases in the range of women's education are not in themselves advances in respect for women's rationality. An expanded curriculum did not imply greater respect for women's minds, if it only covered more subjects without making greater intellectual demands. Apparently new subjects, such as natural science, could be treated in an old-fashioned, decorative way, as just another accomplishment:

> In her closet she has a large collection of insects, which her microscope clothes with most exquisite beauty, and a museum, filled with shells, corals, and petrefactions, the sparkling of which is exceeded by nothing, but the vivacity of her eyes, or the stronger and more permanent lustre of her virtues.[4]

The collection of this exemplary woman is not to lead to serious study; John Bennett, the author of this passage, thinks Linnaeus is too technical for women. A more reliable index of respect for women's minds is advice to read demanding texts, such as Locke's *Essay*. Norris and Astell were recommending Locke to women at the beginning of the century, and Catherine Trotter Cockburn had published a vindication of Locke in 1702.[5] However, advice to read Locke was still controversial a hundred years later. John Bennett took it for granted that Locke was unsuitable reading for women, while Hannah More expected that her advice that young women should read Locke would startle her audience.[6]

The improvements in women's literacy and general knowledge were substantial and genuine, even if their education still lacked intellectual rigour. Early in the century, many women could not spell correctly or write coherently, and knew nothing about subjects which were commonplace later. Charlotte Charke, describing her education in the 1720s, thought it was unusual that she had learnt geography.[7] Even in the middle of the century, educational writing pays a good deal of attention to quite simple skills. Women should be able to tell a story coherently, without interjecting phrases like 'And so, – in short, – however, – well to be sure, – do you see, – do you mind me, – without any more ado', and they should be able to purge their speech of slang and exaggerated language: 'We must not talk of an *immense* tea-cup, not a *prodigious* fly; we are not allowed to *detest* a daffodil, *doat* on a rose, or *adore* a honeysuckle'.[8] By the end of the century, upper- and middle-class women were expected to be able to spell correctly, write coherent and readable letters, and have a good grasp of geography and history. At the beginning of the nineteenth century, Anna Laetitia Barbauld commented on the change that had taken place in expectations about women's knowledge in the fifty years since the publication of *Sir Charles Grandison*:

> The prejudice against any appearance of extraordinary cultivation in a woman, was, at this period, very strong. It will scarcely be believed, by this generation, that Mrs. Delany, the accomplished Mrs. Delany, objects to the words *intellect* and *ethics*, in one of the conversation pieces, in Grandison, as too scholastic to proceed from the mouth of a female. What would some of these critics have said, could they have heard young ladies talking of gases, and nitrous oxide, and stimuli, and excitability, and all the terms of modern science.[9]

Barbauld had mixed feelings about this change; she continues:

> The restraint of former times was painful and humiliating; what can be more humiliating than the necessity of affecting ignorance? and yet, perhaps, it is not undesirable that female genius should have something to overcome; so much, as to render it probable, before a woman steps out of the common walks of life, that her acquirements are solid, and her love for literature decided and irresistible. These obstacles did not prevent the Epictetus of Mrs. Carter, not the volumes of Mrs. Chapone, from being written and given to the world.

Barbauld's ambivalence reflects another genuine change, the great increase in the number of women writers. Some contemporaries agreed with Barbauld that more meant worse. Hannah More commented: 'Capacity and cultivation are so little taken into the account, that writing a book seems to be now considered as the only sure resource which the idle and illiterate have always in their power.'[10] Others had no doubt that this represented progress.

Many women expressed a particular interest in the work of women writers, and pride in other women's achievements. Elizabeth Elstob collected information about other women scholars; Elizabeth Carter was delighted when she found out that plays she had admired on their anonymous publication were by a woman, Joanna Baillie.[11] Some women writers appeal to this sense of female solidarity in their audience; Catherine Trotter Cockburn, in an appeal for the Queen's patronage, argues that royal patronage of her work will help to promote women's learning, regardless of its merits:

> If not the work, give the attempt applause,
> And patronise in her the sex's cause.[12]

Interest in women writers often implied feminist views. Mary Scott's poem *The Female Advocate* pleads for improvements in women's education, and includes a tribute to Chudleigh's feminism:

> 'Twas thine O CHUDLEIGH (name for ever dear
> Whilst wit and virtue claim the lay sincere!)
> Boldly t'assert great Nature's equal laws,
> And plead thy hapless injured sex's cause:
> For that, thy fame shall undecaying bloom,
> And flowers unfading grow around thy tomb.[13]

Here a sense of female tradition includes a sense of feminist tradition; Scott recognises that women's education has improved, but argues it needs to be improved much more.[14] She does not criticise women's social position:

But zealous as I really am in the cause of my sex, yet I would not be understood to insinuate that every woman is formed for literature: the greatest part of both sexes, are necessarily confined to the business of life. All I contend for is, that it is a duty absolutely incumbent on every woman whom nature hath blest with talents, of what kind soever they may be, to improve them; and that that is much oftener the case than it is usually supposed to be. As to those ladies whose situation in life will not admit of their engaging very deep in literary researches, it surely is commendable in them, to employ part at least of their leisure hours in the advantages of useful knowledge; the advantages of an understanding in any degree cultivated, are too obvious to need pointing out.[15]

Scott's moderate feminism in this passage needs only a subtle shift of tone to become a much more limited plea for women's education. Many writers say much the same things – that exceptional women deserve respect, and that all women should do some serious reading – but emphasise how few the exceptional women are, and how little most women need know. They damn women's achievements with faint praise, or insist on their specifically feminine qualities, thus removing them from competition with men's. Sometimes discussion of women's achievements becomes a rather condescending educational device, justified by the argument that girls must be engaged emotionally in order to learn: 'Their understandings are principally accessible through their affections; they delight in minute delineation of character, nor must the truths which impress them be either cold or unadorned.'[16] Anti-feminist writers at the end of the century exploit complacency about the progress in women's education, as well as traditional mockery of learned ladies, and praise some women writers in order to attack others more effectively.

Some feminists used the achievements of exceptional women to plead for greater respect for the talents of women in general; however, there were several possible anti-feminist replies to this argument. Some writers simply asserted that exceptional women were too few and anomalous for their achievements to have any general implications, or that their work had been grossly overrated, and could not stand comparison with men's.[17] Both these approaches could be combined with making fun of exceptional women, treating them as freakish, or vain and self-deluding. It was also possible to argue that the achievements of exceptional women proved that women had all the opportunities they needed; women who complained about male oppression and men's monopoly of learning were just trying to avoid the blame for an ignorance that was due to their own laziness.[18] Mary Wollstonecraft avoided arguing from exceptional women, pointing out that heroes and heroines are both exceptions, and that education must consider the average woman: 'I wish to see women neither heroines nor brutes; but reasonable creatures.'[19]

Distinctively feminist arguments in favour of improving women's education are often hard to disentangle from instrumental ones. The idea that improving women's education will have desirable results for society in general implies more respect for women than the view that they should not be educated, and feminists agreed that it was true. However, writers who argue for improving women's education on these grounds cannot always be called feminists; sometimes they are insensitive to women's own intellectual capacities and needs, and differ from anti-feminist writers in the details of what they recommend, not in their tone and attitude. To grant that men's and children's needs should determine what women were taught left the way open for arguments in favour of a restricted or frivolous education. Mary Wollstonecraft stated this with uncompromising religious fervour:

> . . . considering woman as a whole . . . the inquiry is whether she have reason or not. If she have, which, for a moment, I will take for granted, she was not created merely to be the solace of man, and the sexual should not destroy the human character.
> Into this error men have, probably, been led by viewing education in a false light; not considering it as the first step to form a being advancing gradually towards perfection; but only as a preparation for life. On this sensual error, for I must call it so, has the false system of female manners been reared, which robs the whole sex of its dignity, and classes the brown and fair with the smiling flowers that only adorn the land.[20]

An immortal being, advancing towards perfection in heaven, should not be taught to please men, but should learn 'the power of generalizing ideas, of drawing comprehensive conclusions from individual observations'.

Wollstonecraft is insisting here that women are capable of abstract thought, which was the type of intelligence anti-feminists were most reluctant to allow them. Praise of women's quick wit, taste, and so on, often carries the implication that women are perceptive at the level of individual objects precisely because they cannot go higher or deeper. Praise of women's light touch is very close to contempt for women's superficiality. The knowledge anti-feminist writers expected from women was a second-hand knowledge, based on easy guides, anthologies, and selections, not the sort of knowledge that comes from extensive or serious reading. Women educated in this way had to take opinions on trust, or be called pretentious when they formed opinions of their own. Contempt for the childishness of this elegant feminine education comes out clearly in a mid-century satire against homosexual men:

> The gravity of dull knowledge is at last happily exploded: masculine sense and wit are rejected as obsolete and unfashionable talents; and better supplied by the more engaging charms of the contrary qualities. Nothing is now heard, but sweet chit-chat, and tender prittle-prattle, shreds of sentiments, and *cuttings* of sentences – all soft and charming, elegant and polite.[21]

Among Wollstonecraft's contemporaries, the principal debate was between those who thought women's lack of capacity for abstract thought meant their education should be oriented towards developing taste and feeling, and those who thought that, though women might be incapable of the highest flights of abstract thought, they could still benefit from a more intellectually demanding education than they were getting. However, as long as the arguments for better education were primarily instrumental there was an inevitable pull towards mediocrity, as in this passage from Hannah More's *Coelebs*, where the hero is reflecting on what he should look for in a wife:

'In such a companion,' said I, as I drove along in my post-chaise, 'I do not want a Helen, a Saint Cecilia, or a Madame Dacier; yet she must be elegant, or I should not love her; sensible, or I should not respect her; prudent, or I could not confide in her; well informed, or she could not educate my children; well-bred, or she could not entertain my friends; *consistent*, or I should offend the shade of my mother; pious, or I should not be happy with her, because the prime comfort in a companion for life is the delightful hope that she will be a companion for eternity.'[22]

This ideal of a rational woman includes much that some anti-feminists would ridicule – the ideal wife receives her husband's respect and confidence – but the instrumental tone of this passage undermines the feminist, rational element in it.

What people thought about women's rationality determined much of what they thought about women's education. The apparently simple question of whether women were as rational as men, and, if so, whether they were rational in the same way, yielded confusing and ambiguous answers, with unpredictable consequences for feminism. The first possibility, that women are as rational as men and in the same way as men, could form the basis of a feminist argument; it could also undermine it by presenting women as slightly weaker, inferior men, with no distinguishing characteristics of their own. It could suggest that women's education should give as much scope for individual intellectual development as men's; it could also suggest that education should cure women of their intellectual pretensions, and lead them to a rational recognition of their inevitable inferiority to men.

The idea that women were less rational than men, or expressed their rationality in ways that had more to do with taste and intuition, and less with logic and abstract thought, could lead to a wide range of views about education. Some writers thought women's weaker rationality meant that they needed stronger moral indoctrination than men; the common eighteenth-century view that disbelief in Christianity is far more disturbing and repugnant in a woman than in a man is obviously related to this idea.[23] Even if upper-class educated men could be trusted to be good without religion, women probably could not. Other writers thought women's superior taste and sensibility meant their education should concentrate on the arts. These attitudes could be accompanied with overt contempt for women's weakness and frivolity, or with admiration for women's sensitivity, which often disguises contempt. However, this anti-feminist view attracted some women writers, because it put a positive value on women's difference from men. A specifically feminine ideal could seem less daunting than a generalised human ideal which a woman could never realise as well as a man. By the end of the century, some people shifted to seeing virtuous behaviour as the result of right feeling rather than rational choice, and this could lead to the view that women, more ruled by feeling than men, were morally superior. The view that women had a finer aesthetic and moral sense than men, even if their role in life was a subordinate one, could give women a self-consciousness and a sense of group identity which could sometimes lead to a strong commitment to women's education and philanthropic work directed towards women. It could also, more surprisingly, be used to argue that women should be more involved in male professions and be educated more like men because they would be a good influence on men.[24]

There was a stronger basis for feminism in a variation on the belief in women's equal rationality. This is the view that women are as rational as men, and exercise their reason in much the same way; virtue depends on rational choice. However, the unique importance of their role as mothers, which they must fulfil rationally, means they must be well educated; it also means they must be psychologically and economically independent, in case they have to bring up their children alone. The rational mother deserves the same consideration as any other citizen performing a valuable task; her duties as a mother are more important than her obligations to men. This view can lead to a more genuine respect for women than do generalised assertions of women's finer aesthetic and moral sense, or statements of their equal rationality which do not connect it to any specially valuable task in life.

A final, illogical compromise position forms the basis of most frivolous defences of women, and is present in the background of some more serious feminist discussions. This is the view that women are as rational as men, but that in addition they are more sensitive and have finer aesthetic and moral perceptions. Eighteenth-century psychology normally assumes that excessive sensitivity compromises rationality, so this view breaks down if it is seriously challenged; however, it could be superficially attractive as a basis for women's self-assertion. The confidante of a novel-heroine exclaims:

> They think a woman their property, and imagine they have a right to treat her as they please. – Insensible wretches! Has not nature endowed us with the same reason? – Are not our feelings more exquisite, and our passions stronger than theirs? – In what does their superiority consist?[25]

Belief in women's equal rationality and belief in women's finer sensitivity probably coexisted in many people. The two beliefs could undermine and compromise each other, but they could also work together as motives for claiming better education for women.

Most educational texts do not make an issue of their view of women's rationality, and it has to be deduced from casual comments. A simple moral interpretation of women's education remained available throughout the century, though the content of women's education changed greatly. The popular moralistic texts which were central to most women's education had very long careers. The *Spectator* was read all through the century, and Mary Wollstonecraft ridicules a fifty-year-old text,

Wetenhall Wilkes's *Letter to a Young Lady*, without
commenting on its age.[26] Texts from the 1760s and
1770s – Fordyce's *Sermons*, Chapone's *Letters*, Gregory's
Father's Legacy, Lady Pennington's *Mother's Advice* –
were all read into the nineteenth century. What women
were told about the purpose of their education did not
change as much as its content. However, the recognition
that women's education had improved became an
important element in discussions about it; arguments
about whether women should be educated acquired an
historical dimension. Had progress gone far enough?
Had it gone too far and become decadence? Had its
price been the loss of something that had been of value
in the past?

Usually progress in women's education was linked to
social progress in general. By the end of the century, all
writers agree that women have a vital influence on the
well-being of society. Their views about women are
affected by the fact that they had available to them far
more complex ways of thinking about the nature of
society than were available at the beginning of the
century. Earlier moralistic notions did not disappear,
but social ideas were added to them. The early
instrumental feminism which argued that men would
gain from improvements in women's education was
enlarged into the view that these improvements would
benefit society as a whole. Alexander Jardine's summing
up of the message of his *Letters from Barbary* shows this
new confidence in the malleability of society and the
power of education:

> . . . the most remarkable conclusions to be drawn from these
> *Letters* seem to be, that the improvement of the world depends
> most on education, and principally on that of princes, of women,
> and of the lower classes; and then on legislation, the form and
> formation of which seem to be of the utmost importance.[27]

Belief that society could be changed through
education was closely linked to ideas about the power
of society and education to form personality. Debates

about the roles of nature and education in human development generated new ways of discussing what women were like. Seventeenth-century discussions suggested either that women's physical difference from men compromised their rationality, or that this difference was no more important than other differences between individual human beings, and that women and men shared a common rationality and standard of ethical behaviour. Eighteenth-century writers were more likely to discuss sexual difference in terms of whether nature or education made men's and women's minds different, and, if education was the major factor, whether it should aim at perpetuating this difference, or at making men and women more alike. Even writers who emphasise nature insist on the importance of education; the argument is between those who see education as something like training and pruning a growing tree, and those who see it as more like moulding a substance like wax. Writers who, like Rousseau, believe in a different feminine nature, are often deeply interested in programmes for a specifically feminine education. Writers who recommend an education closer to men's are more inclined to emphasise that women have been damaged by their upbringing, and that most of what contemporaries thought of as a feminine character was a socially caused warping of the personality. Catharine Macaulay argues that an empiricist psychology, which denies innate ideas and innate affections, and considers that character is formed by experience, removes any basis for believing in special qualities in the female mind.[28] This denial of an innate feminine character is one of the cornerstones of Mary Wollstonecraft's arguments; it is also important in her friend, Mary Hays. This denial could lead to sorrow and anger about what had been made of women. In her personal writings, Hays shows a deeply pessimistic feminist self-consciousness, seeing herself as a damaged being. She wrote in a letter to Godwin:

I sometimes blush after you have left me from the recollection of the many follies and weaknesses I have betrayed; among which, feminine foibles make no inconsiderable share: I mean, by feminine foibles, those errors which result from the present absurd systems of female education. There is a tenacity in some parts of my character, a proneness to habit, which makes reformation of my mistakes at a great distance from their direction: this perhaps, proceeds from the small number of my impressions, their consequent force and distinctness.[29]

Hays identifies her weaknesses with her femininity; however, this femininity is not a fact of nature, but an injury done her by society in exposing her to ill-chosen and restricted experiences. Women's weaknesses are not inevitable, nor are they a simple matter for moral reform; Hays argues that the effects of education must be understood scientifically.

The real changes in women's education meant that everyone admitted that choices had to be made. Most people recognised that these choices were largely governed by what men wanted women to be like, and some criticisms of frivolity in women's education are connected to criticism of men's frivolous tastes. Alexander Jardine argued that men's liking for women's frailty and frivolity was either hypocritical or corrupt:

Many of those female weaknesses which we term delicacy, etc. and pretend to admire, we secretly laugh at; – or when our taste is so far vitiated as really to like them, it is chiefly from their being symptoms of inferiority and subordination, that soothes and feeds our pride and domineering spirit.[30]

Other writers criticised men's taste for frailty and frivolity in women on practical grounds; a frivolous education might make a woman more attractive as a mistress, and perhaps more vulnerable to seduction, but it would not make her a good or useful wife.[31] However, in many upper- and middle-class households there was very little for a wife to do, and men could indulge a taste for attractively childish women. Many people argued that, as long as they did, women would continue to behave childishly. Chesterfield's provocative statement 'Women . . . are only children of a larger growth' aroused angry replies from moralists and feminists.[32] These writers argued that if women were childish, it was because they had been taught to behave in this way. Mary Hays expected that women who had learnt how to think would be angry about the harm bad education had done to them, and the way society treated them: 'Thus awakened to a sense of their injuries, they would behold with astonishment and indignation, the arts which had been employed to keep them in a state of PERPETUAL BABYISM!'[33]

Women who had not been made childish by their education often complained about being treated like children. Some writers satirise boorish husbands who refuse to talk to their intelligent wives; others criticise men who refuse to discuss anything serious in mixed company, or listen to what women have to say. A few women complain about having to leave the men to their port after dinner, assuming that they would turn to more interesting conversation after the women were gone.[34] The mildness of some appeals for reform suggests how severe these restrictions could be, as in this text from the 1760s, praising older women who talk about learned subjects in mixed company:

> Those who do so are of service to their sex, as they will in time emancipate us from the fetters laid on our conversation; and by rendering such subjects more common in mixed company, will make discourse more rational, and prevent the charge of pedantry from being so liberally applied to any young woman, who ventures to stray from the trifling topics generally assigned to us; but, my young friends, I would have you wait till this change is effected, before you indulge yourselves in the most moderate display of your reading; for more than *moderate*, even custom could not sanctify.[35]

Lady Carlisle, writing some twenty years later, urges women to be very sure of their facts before venturing an opinion about geography or history, as people expect women to get names and dates wrong, and are highly critical of them when they do.[36]

These criticisms do not give a complete picture of how educated women were treated in society, but the impression they give helps to put the well-known exceptions in context. There were famous women, and there were friendships between men and women where there was real respect on both sides; there was also overpraising of famous women, which played into the hands of those who wanted to deny their achievements, and dishonest and patronising politeness to women. Mixed company could be identified with fun and frivolity, all-male groups with serious activities. "'Let us divert the Wenches, " "Let us amuse the Ladies," has been the cry now for these fifty years, I think – as though the Ladies, like Leviathan, came only into the world to take pastime,' remarks a broadside of 1803, urging women to behave responsibly if the French invade.[37] Elizabeth Montagu's Bluestocking parties, at which a mixed company spent their time on serious conversation rather than cards, represent a conscious departure from the usual practice.

These gatherings were exceptional, but the fact that they were possible at all is a sign of change. The common complaint that men underestimated women's intelligence and education is itself a sign of how much women's education had improved. By the end of the century, women's right to better education was generally accepted, although people had different views about what this better education might be, and women themselves could express a wide range of opinions about it. Several writers argue that the case for a serious education for women does not depend on their rationality being equal to men's, and dissociate themselves from strong feminist arguments. The improvements in women's education could make it seem that the strong feminist assertion of women's rationality was no longer necessary; they also meant that this assertion could carry much more weight. Writers at the end of the century take it to imply more demands for change in men's treatment of women than at the beginning. Mary Hays was puzzled by Chudleigh's couplet

The tyrant Man may still possess the throne,
'Tis in our minds that we would rule alone,

and thought this demand was absurdly modest; if women's knowledge that they were enslaved was not to lead to any change, they might be better off ignorant.[38]

Educated women could articulate a wide range of views about their own education and rationality, and a wide range of attitudes to exceptional women. Formal and informal writing by women gives life to the different genres of writing which deal with women's education – theoretical treatises, sermons, conduct books, didactic fiction, prospectuses for boarding-schools. Discussions within families and between friends show how women thought about these questions from childhood on. Two sisters, Sarah Scott and Elizabeth Montagu, provide a good example of the different opinions and possibilities open to upper-class educated women. Their own education was marked by seventeenth-century proposals for reform, and correspondence between them and their friends covers much of the eighteenth century. Born in 1720 and 1723, they were largely educated at home, in a lively family, freely competing and arguing with their brothers.[39] Their mother controlled the children's arguments; she herself had been educated at Bathsua Makin's school at Tottenham. Makin had taught Charles I's daughter Elizabeth, and Anna Maria van Schurman wrote to her in Greek. She wrote a plea for the improvement of women's education, which concludes with a prospectus for her school; the school offered Greek and Hebrew, as well as the usual arts and crafts.[40] Montagu, the older child, received a good deal of attention from her mother's stepfather, the Cambridge theologian Conyers Middleton. She was temperamentally like her father, who encouraged her in her liveliness and wit. Some early letters between Montagu and Scott show them disagreeing about Young's satires against women; Scott is angered by them, and finds them misogynist, while Montagu accepts that they have a benign, reforming intention, and likes Young when she meets him.[41]

The difference between the sisters here is congruent with the differences between their later lives. As the wife of a rich, much older husband, and later, as a rich widow, Montagu enjoyed close friends of both sexes, fame as a hostess, and admiration for her letters and for her few published writings. Her assertions of women's rights are humorous and moderate, and her respect and affection for Elizabeth Carter did not prevent her from occasionally making fun of other learned women.[42] Scott lived a more retired life, and her closest friendship was with another woman; Lady Bab Montagu lived with her before, during and after her short and unhappy marriage.[43] Scott's writings show a stronger feeling for injustice to women than Montagu's, and her best-known novel, *Millennium Hall*, describes a community of women living in the country and doing philanthropic work, who have found happiness in this way of life after being ill-treated by men. The sisters remained friendly with each other, both critical of men who despised women, both interested in improvements in women's education, neither arguing for major changes in the way law and institutions affected women's lives. In 1794, Scott wrote disapprovingly to Montagu about a doctor's daughter who spoke at a Jacobin meeting in Norwich.[44] It is likely that this radical woman was Amelia Alderson, who was soon to move to London, make friends with Godwin, Wollstonecraft and other radicals, and marry a divorced man, the painter John Opie. One of her novels, *Adeline Mowbray*, was recognised by contemporaries as a bitter attack on the morality of the institution of marriage. Her world is utterly different from Montagu's and Scott's; yet her career would have been impossible without what they represent, the diffusion of women's education and the deepening of respect for women's capacities. It may have been as difficult to make a strong assertion of women's and men's intellectual equality at the end of the century as it was at the beginning, but the area of intellectual territory that was exclusively male was smaller, and people were more conscious that this equality might have social implications.

CHAPTER SIX

Women in Society

Eighteenth-century writers on women's education often argue that it matters because of women's influence on society, and that it should fit them to play a more useful role in society. They argue that women should be reformed for the benefit of society as a whole; sometimes they also emphasise that women themselves are harmed by a bad education. Some of them see a need for changes in the way society treats women, as well as changes in women themselves.

General discussions about what position women should hold in society, or what sort of work they should do, are often hard to interpret. Sweeping statements about male tyranny, or suggestions that women's access to learning and the professions should change dramatically, are often part of satirical praises of women which make fun of the status quo without seriously proposing change. Context makes it clear that a remark like 'women in general are as fit for the offices of state, as those who most commonly hold them,' is a joke about politicians, not a feminist demand.[1] These satirical works contain powerful arguments about injustices to women, but neutralise them by their satirical tone. As a result, it could be difficult to propose these arguments seriously, because it was natural to read them as satire. The way in which Poulain de la Barre's works were used by eighteenth-century writers shows how potentially serious feminist arguments could be transformed by tone. Poulain's trilogy,

De l'égalité des deux sexes, De l'excellence des hommes, and *Dissertation ou discours pour servir de troisième partie au livre de l'égalité des deux sexes*, makes serious points about prejudice against women, and argues that the restrictions on women are the result of custom and prejudice, not Nature.[2] The middle work, *De l'excellence des hommes*, is a parody of male prejudice, put into the mouth of an uncouth Aristotelian academic. An English trilogy, by a writer using the pseudonym Sophia, uses Poulain's structure and some of his material, but negates its seriousness by lightening the tone, concentrating on character sketches of male and female fools, and concluding with a traditional praise of women's superiority because of their beauty and wit.[3] It expresses an instrumentally feminist position, arguing that well-educated, sensible women are good companions for men, and attacking male effeminacy, prejudice and boorishness, but it is not a serious claim for the equality of the sexes. On the other hand, by reproducing some of Poulain's material, and asking why women should not be in the professions or the army,[4] it disseminated arguments which could be turned back to seriousness, or ritually denied as a proof of moderation by writers who were making milder feminist demands.

Discussion of women in society addressed the values of the society which were symbolised by women, as well as particular injustices in law and custom. There were some shifts in what women symbolised during the eighteenth century, which generated some changes in traditional misogynist writings and traditional praises of women, and were challenged by feminist writers. The first of these was a strengthening of the association between women, and the frivolous or ornamental aspects of life. This could lead to attacks on women's idleness, or praise of their refining, civilising influence. It could also be used to argue for their restriction to less serious intellectual pursuits:

Whilst men, with solid judgment and a superior vigour are to combine ideas, to discriminate, and examine a subject to the bottom, you are to give it all its brilliancy and all its charms. They provide the furniture; you dispose it with propriety. They build the house; you are to fancy, and to ornament the ceiling.[5]

Women here are associated with interior decoration and social graces, with things that add pleasure to life, but are not really important.

This association had not been so strong in the seventeenth century; seventeenth-century moralists could attack male frivolity without insisting on its unmanliness, as in this attack from *The Gentlemans Calling* on men who waste their education:

They can discern exactly the most minute error in their garment, hold their artificer most rigidly to the laws of the mode, are most exquisite judges in all that relates to vanity or pleasure, and can they ever think fit to trouble their heads (whose least lock must not be disturbed) with abstruser speculations, who have found out so much a more easy exercise of their faculties?[6]

By the eighteenth century, this sort of attack was usually directed against women and homosexual men. Satires against women's frivolity and homosexual men's effeminacy fed off each other, promoting an idea of an artificial, immoral femininity, which, for misogynist or homophobic writers, constituted the nature of women or homosexual men. Defenders of women sometimes try to dissociate femininity and effeminacy; they argue that qualities can be good in women and bad in men, or they argue that effeminate homosexual men are not really like women at all, and their taste for women's company is no reflection on women:

So if Lord Thimble prefers our company to the men's, let them blame themselves for it, but not fall out with us. It is neither likeness nor sympathy makes him take refuge among us. He has no more of the women in him than he has of the man: but a kind of species himself of no one sex, he has just sense enough to distinguish which of the two sexes have the most temper and mastery over their passions to bear with him. And would it not be quite barbarous, as well as unpolite, not to bear with a poor good-natured inoffensive thing, and a lord too?[7]

Other changes in what women symbolised gave them a more positive value. The idea that women were more religious than men became a commonplace in this period, and this associated women with one of the highest values of the culture. However, the idea is not an assertion of women's superiority, for several reasons. It can imply that women are less rational than men, more emotional, more superstitious, or more willing to obey authority. Sometimes writing on this theme becomes voyeuristic, and authors indulge in rhapsodic descriptions of beautiful young women at prayer, comparing them to angels and saying this is when they are at their most beautiful.[8] Mary Wollstonecraft commented that men who compared women to angels always had young and beautiful women in mind.[9] Implicitly, this undermines the value of religion, rather than increasing respect for women.

Sometimes women were thought to be morally superior to men, as well as more religious; however, this also is not the statement of female superiority it might seem to be at first. If women behave better than men, it is because they lead more restricted lives than men, and are not exposed to so many of the world's temptations. If they have less scope for doing harm than men, they also have less scope for doing good. By the end of the century, restrictions on what men could talk about in women's presence, and what women could mention, had become much more severe. In 1782, Hester Thrale wrote:

> How great a change has been wrought in female manners within these few years in England! I was reading the letter in the third volume of the Spectator, 217, where the man complains of his indelicate mistress; I read it aloud to my little daughters of eleven and twelve years old, and even the maid who was dressing my hair burst out laughing at the idea of a lady saying her stomach ached, or that something stuck between her teeth. Sure if our morals are mended as much as our manners, we are grown a most virtuous nation![10]

Mary Wollstonecraft, who opposed excessive delicacy in language, was appalled that French women would mention having indigestion.[11] Helen Maria Williams was also distressed by French women's willingness to discuss their bodies in mixed company:

> . . . the manners of an English female are in danger of becoming contaminated, while she is only endeavouring to suffer without pain the customs of those she has been taught to consider as models of politeness . . . so little are these people susceptible of delicacy, propriety, and decency, that they do not even use the words in the sense we do, nor have they any others expressive of the same meaning.[12]

In the conventions of propriety, women's virtue was tied up with their refinement; the stereotype of women as moral and religious turns out to be close to the stereotype of women as frivolous arbiters of taste and good manners. Women were associated with a sheltered world of domestic virtue, which could be idealised, or despised as unreal.

Propriety could infantilise upper- and middle-class women, confining them to a domestic universe of decorative and pseudo-thrifty activities. However, it could also give women a more positive and powerful sense of their separate sphere. Evangelical reformers took women's moral influence very seriously, and the tightening of the demands of propriety made people more dubious about whether men should be in charge of philanthropic work with poor women. This negative argument could be reinforced by the positive argument that women understood each other. Hannah More praised the Quaker women's meetings for their work with the poor, and the Society for Bettering the Condition of the Poor set up a separate women's committee in 1804.[13] This sense of female separateness and solidarity could lead to arguments that upper-class women should be more sensitive to the needs of poor women; a midwifery book from the 1790s attacks upper-class women who allow poor pregnant women to do heavy physical work.[14]

Philanthropic work with poor women usually included a desire to make them conform to upper-class standards of femininity; earning money at home spinning was preferable to going out to work, and poor women who made their houses and gardens attractive would encourage their husbands to spend their leisure time at home gardening, instead of drinking in the pub.[15] The position of poor women may have got worse during the century, and women were concentrated in badly paid occupations.[16]

Eighteenth-century writers are often concerned about female unemployment because they see it as a cause of prostitution, and argue that some prostitutes have no other way of earning a living. They show more imaginative sympathy for these women than their opponents do, but often are concerned with protecting the moral tone of society as a whole, rather than with the women's own welfare. Other writers deny the problem, and argue that these women are unable to make a living because they have been educated above their station, and that they end up as prostitutes because they have aspirations to gentility without the money to support them, rather than because there is no work available. The stereotype of the recruit to prostitution was a girl from the lower professional or upper working classes, without the money to support her pretensions to gentility; a clergyman's daughter or milliner's apprentice.[17] Apprenticeships to milliners were sometimes a way to entrap girls into prostitution.[18] The magistrate Saunders Welch insisted that prostitutes were not recruited from the labouring poor;[19] others said that they were, and argued that the poor should recognise their duty to work hard. 'What are most of these tawdry and gigantic women who stalk through the streets, like grenadiers in disguise, and exhibit so much wanton and ferocious effrontery, but servants out of place?[20]

One possible reason for the idea that prostitutes did not come from the labouring poor is that women who were used to hard physical work may have had more chance of earning a living, though a poor one, than women from slightly more prosperous classes. Writers do not say much about female unemployment in the poorest classes until the end of the century. Again, it is only then that writers begin to show much concern about the effect on poor women of hard physical work. Most eighteenth-century statements about feminine weakness have to be read as applying to upper- and middle-class women only. Accounts of women who lived in male disguise and served in the army or navy do not make much of their unusual physical strength, though they sometimes discuss their height, or their tomboyish childhoods.[21] In the eighteenth century, the authorities sometimes acknowledged the value of their service by granting them pensions – Christian Davies, a female veteran of Marlborough's wars, spent her old age as a Chelsea pensioner – whereas in the nineteenth century they refused applications for medals from women who had served, arguing that if they granted any it would open the way to a flood of applications.[22] Eighteenth-century transvestite women could not stay in the army or navy once they were discovered, but accounts of women who lived in male disguise were often quite sympathetic. In 1766, a jury convicted a blackmailer who had revealed a transvestite woman's true gender.[23]

Discussions of the position of women in society usually paid little attention to these anomalous cases, or to working-class women in general. General discussions of women's position, and particular questions of injustice to women, were both popular subjects in the eighteenth century. Most writers who find women worth discussing say that they think women should be better treated; however, by the end of the century, this is sometimes an anti-feminist ploy which introduces reactionary ideas in the guise of what is best for women. The fact that anti-feminists sometimes use pro-woman rhetoric, rather than the language of traditional moralism, is a sign of how commonplace the idea of improving women's position had become. The idea that women should be better treated was more widespread than the developed feminism which also thought they were as rational as men, and criticised the double standard.

Some arguments for treating women better, like arguments for educating them better, are primarily instrumental; improving the position of women will be good for society as a whole. Others are more concerned with women's welfare, but discuss women in a chivalrous, patronising tone, and emphasise that women need to be protected; they plead for charity rather than justice. Even writers who insist on women's equal rationality and moral worth, and express strong feelings of female pride and female solidarity, often use instrumental or chivalrous arguments as well. Some writers call for better treatment for women, but are vague about what this implies in concrete terms. This pro-woman literature has affinities with the anti-slavery literature, as some late eighteenth-century writers recognised. Abolitionist writers compared misogynist prejudices to belief in the innate inferiority of blacks;[24] writers who opposed the anti-slavery movement complained that charity should begin at home, and middle-class women's sufferings deserved more compassion than those of slaves. 'What are the untutored, wild imaginations of a slave, when put in the balance with the distressing sensations of a British female, who has received a refined, if not a classical, education, and is capable of the finest feelings the human heart is susceptible of?'[25]

Eighteenth-century pro-woman writing is often hard to interpret for the same reasons as writings on slavery during the period. Much fiction about the sufferings of slaves was produced and enjoyed by people who had no commitment to abolishing the slave trade, or actively opposed abolition.[26] Mary Robinson, who wrote poems about the cruelty of the slave trade, also wrote the parliamentary speeches of her lover, Banastre Tarleton; his principal duty, as MP for Liverpool, was to defend the slave trade.[27] However, the hypocrisy or inconsistency of individual authors did not remove all political content from this literature, and abolitionists used it in their propaganda, as well as producing similar work of their own. Sentimental and self-serving writings about slaves acquire meaning from an abolitionist context, as well as helping to make abolitionism conceivable. In the same way, feminist writings and writers who sentimentalise about women's position without seriously wishing to change it can sound very similar. On the other hand, even very patronising and sentimental accounts of women's sufferings acquire new meanings when people are discussing possible concrete changes, and may have contributed to making people willing to think about these changes.

There was no single issue comparable to slavery in eighteenth-century discussions of women; instead, there were vague and general assertions of the need for women to be better treated, and discussion of possible minor legal reforms. Politicians and lawyers usually proposed these reforms without much general discussion of principle; it is their tone which indicates whether they are motivated by a sense of the need for women to be treated justly, or a chivalrous sense of the need for women to be protected. People were interested in the details of women's legal situation; several books on the laws affecting women were published during the century. These are aimed at a general audience, and often are concerned to entertain as much as to inform. 'Buggery with man or beast is felony in women as well as men. The case of a lady of quality, who committed this crime with a baboon, and conceived by him, may be read in 3. Co. Inst. 59.'[28] Laws about women were seen as a mass of curious information, rather than as a system in need of rationalisation and reform. There are surprisingly few proposals for legal reform in general works on women; some of the social issues these writers discuss are not the sort of thing that could be dealt with by legislation. However, eighteenth-century feminism is not a purely literary phenomenon; it exists in a context where real, if minor changes in the laws affecting women were possible.

The question of married women's property, and of the legal incapacities of married women, received a good deal of attention during the century. The law governing the wife's separate property underwent some minor adjustments during the century, all tending to limit the husband's control. These shifts resulted from judges' decisions, not from legislation. Eighteenth-century judges insisted that a wife's property had to be viewed as in trust for her use, not simply as part of her husband's property; decisions from 1725 onwards reinforced this principle.[29] In 1785, Lord Mansfield stated clearly that judges had a duty to interpret the law in a way that answered new problems arising from changes in social behaviour; he was referring to a decision which laid down that a wife regained her power to make financial contracts even when a couple had separated voluntarily, a decision which was overturned in 1800.[30] Mansfield and Thurlow, as well as other judges, saw this duty as involving a duty to interpret the law in a way favourable to women's independence.

There were arguments in favour of changing the law, as well as reinterpreting it. A text of 1735, *The Hardships of the English Laws in Relation to Wives*, parts of which were printed in the *Gentleman's Magazine*, goes into details about how hard English law was on married women, and compares it with points where Roman law treated them better.[31] Most of it deals with disabilities relating to property, although it criticises the fact that men could imprison and beat their wives. It argues strongly that English law is unjust: 'A good husband would not desire the power of horse-whipping, confining, half-starving his wife, or squandering her estate; a bad husband should not be allowed it.'[32] It does not argue for full equality for women, although it accepts that women are not naturally inferior to men; instead, it argues that English law's oppression of women goes beyond the necessary subordination which was imposed on women by the curse on Eve.[33] It criticises the law in detail, but without drawing up

specific proposals for reform; when it discusses the
difficulties of married women traders, who must trade
under a friend's name because of their legal incapacity
to make contracts, it does not bring up the obvious
model for reform, the Custom of London, which
allowed married women traders in the City of London
to be treated legally as if they were single for the
purposes of their business.[34]

Most discussion of married women's property deals
with their inherited wealth, in spite of interest in the
Custom of London as a curiosity, and occasional
references to wage-earning women. Safeguarding this
money was in the interests of the wife's family, as well
as of her own; it ensured that a married daughter was
off her family's hands for life. In earlier periods, rich
families had normally settled land on their daughters,
rather than money, and husbands' power over freehold
land belonging to married women was limited by
common law. The new legal devices protecting money
belonging to married women probably resulted from a
wish to make it as safe to provide for them by giving
money as by giving land, as much as from a new
concern for women.[35] However, to see these legal
developments purely as safeguards for the wife's family
is as simplistic as to see them purely as advances for
feminism. The wife, with her property in the hands of
trustees, had little more power to decide what should be
done with it than if it was in the hands of her husband,
but the protection of the wife's estate as her own was
symbolically important, and the arguments in favour of
it take it for granted that women's needs matter. The fact
that the wife's separate estate was seen as a response to
women's needs is itself significant. People became more
sensitive to the need to provide for women as the
century went on, and discussed it in a way which makes
it easy to exaggerate the importance of the legal changes.

By the end of the century, writers also discuss parents'
obligation to provide for daughters who remain
single.[36] Some people argue that daughters should be
given more money than sons, if there is not enough to

go round, as sons should be able to provide for themselves.[37] Writers throughout the century revived Astell's idea of an institution for single women, and small groups of women lived voluntarily together. However, these groups often quarrelled and disintegrated; conventional wisdom expected them to do so, and they were sometimes gossiped about as communities of lesbians.[38] Writers who propose setting up communities accept that they need rules and authority. In 1737, William Cunninghame wrote to Archdeacon Thomas Sharp, asking for help with setting up a 'Protestant convent' in the diocese of Durham, and Sharp replied with a detailed account of his objections to such an institution.[39] Cunninghame's decision to approach Sharp may have been influenced by the fact that Sharp was the son-in-law of Sir George Wheeler, who had proposed such an institution in *The Protestant Monastery*. Cunninghame argues that the 'convent' is necessary because single women are treated with scorn once they are alone in the world; Sharp denies this, and says that setting it up would make single women think the world despises them, when this is not true. Sharp respects voluntary celibacy, and argues that single women can lead religious and useful lives in the world. The idea was widely circulated in the middle of the century, when Richardson mentioned a need for Protestant nunneries in *Sir Charles Grandison*.[40] At the end of the century, there were proposals for such institutions by Mary Ann Radcliffe, Clara Reeve and Helena Wells Whitford: these emphasise single women's economic needs more than earlier proposals. Whitford and Reeve proposed institutions which would be schools for poor girls, as well as communities of adult women.[41] Radcliffe proposed a community where women with no money could live and work, which would distinguish 'between the well-bred female, who is reduced by the unseen hand of fate, and the very poor and abject, whose birth has deprived them of the knowledge of refinement or delicacy'.[42]

Radcliffe argued that impoverished women needed

such a refuge to save them from being seduced and sinking into prostitution. Seduced women were a popular theme in sentimental literature of the second half of the century, and were usually portrayed as innocent victims.[43] Most discussion of them belongs to general discussion of the double standard; however, there were some arguments that the law should provide for them better. Some writers argued that parents should be able to recover damages from their daughters' seducers.[44] Martin Madan, in an eccentric work which aroused a storm of controversy, used Biblical precedent to argue that a man who took a woman's virginity should be financially and legally responsible for her, and that women would be better protected by polygamy.[45] He argued that the system in which an unmarried mother swore to her child's paternity, and could claim its maintenance from the father, was inadequate to protect the mother, and was simply a device to ensure the parish was not liable for maintaining the child; this analysis was probably correct.[46] A writer in 1800 suggested making seduction a criminal offence.[47] Some speakers in a 1772 parliamentary debate over an unsuccessful attempt to repeal the infanticide law which required the mother to prove her innocence, showed sympathy for the single mother's position, arguing that it was unjust to impose standards of modesty which forced her to conceal her pregnancy, and then to punish her for that concealment.[48] Much of the literature on seduced women is implicitly anti-feminist in its treatment of women as helpless victims, but an interest in providing for these women and rehabilitating them is part of feminists' agenda at the end of the century; it was not necessary to view women as helpless in order to argue they should not have to suffer all their lives for one mistake.

The rights of mothers, both married and unmarried, received some attention, because increased respect for mothers made it troubling that they had no guaranteed right to custody of their children. Separated wives did not automatically have a right of access to their children, and widows could have custody willed away from them, although they had guardianship of daughters under sixteen, if no other provision had been made.[49] This law did not change till the following century, but there was criticism of it as early as 1735.[50] In 1773 and 1802 there were unsuccessful attempts to pass Bills protecting the rights of pauper mothers by reforming the system of parish nursing; the 1773 Bill proposed that a child should not be taken from a mother without her consent, and that if she decided to give it up, she should approve who it was boarded with.[51] This Bill may reflect a wish to reduce infant mortality, rather than concern for mothers' feelings; children did not usually survive with parish nurses. However, the implied trust in mothers' concern for their children itself indicates respect for them.

Arguments that women should have more power in the public sphere were more controversial than suggestions that they should be better treated in the private sphere, and were made rarely and hesitantly. Opponents often simply answered them by jokes and appeals to prejudice: '. . . it would be highly ridiculous should the most important national affairs be interrupted, while her excellency the Prime Ministress should lie under the care of an accoucheur.'[52] Others pointed out that a few upper-class women already wielded considerable power through their influence at court and on politicians, and argued that women already had too much covert power.[53] Feminists sometimes accepted this, and answered that the solution was to give women some publicly recognised power, and encourage them to exercise it responsibly. However, the nature of this power is usually left very vague; Catharine Macaulay, though radical in her proposal that boys and girls should study the same curriculum, and in her disbelief in an innate femininity, says only:

. . . when the sex have been taught wisdom by education, they will be glad to give up indirect influence for rational privileges, and the precarious sovereignty of an hour enjoyed with the meanest and most infamous of the species, for those established rights which, independent of accidental circumstances, may afford protection to the whole sex.[54]

The question of women voting received little attention, apart from jokes such as an obscene ballad, *The Lady's Choice of a New Standing Member*, and arguments by opponents of reforming the electoral system, who say that the fact that women are excluded from the suffrage shows that voting is not a natural right.[55] However, by the end of the century, people who favoured electoral reform were prepared to think about extending the vote to women, at least as a theoretical possibility. An article on this subject in the *Gentleman's Magazine* for 1788 mixes traditional praise of women's innate good sense, gentleness, and civilising influence with apparently serious arguments linking women's oppression to other political issues of the day: women's exclusion from the vote is an abuse, like the exclusion of residents of Manchester, Sheffield and Birmingham, and arguments for men's power over women are as specious as arguments in favour of enslaving blacks.[56]

By the end of the century, writers often explicitly identify men's lives with the public sphere and women's with the private.[57] This notion, which made women's participation in politics seem obviously absurd and impossible, also excluded them from the professions; the subject was difficult to raise seriously, for the image of a woman preaching, pleading at the bar, or engaging in other professional activity, could easily seem self-evidently ridiculous. Alexander Jardine was unusually bold in suggesting that 'women might be of great use in all the learned and sedentary professions', and that they might be university professors, as they already were in Italy.[58] Mary Wollstonecraft only suggested that women should conduct businesses, and be physicians and midwives; women were already represented in all these fields, although women physicians were not fully trained or eligible for membership of professional bodies.[59] Both Wollstonecraft and Mary Hays suggest that decorum means women should receive medical attention from other women, although Hays admits to feeling prejudice: 'I would do anything but die, rather than have a woman physician. I never knew but one, and the very sight of her acted upon me like an emetic; and she had nearly the same effect upon most of her female acquaintance.'[60] The moderation of Wollstonecraft's and Hays' suggestions indicates how difficult it was to think seriously about women engaging in the professions.

When lower-class women were under discussion, the problem was not whether women should be allowed to practise male professions, but whether men should be prevented from taking over women's jobs. By the end of the century, some writers were also concerned about women doing heavy physical work: 'Nor do I see less cruelty in depriving women of those employments which are essential to their maintenance, than in putting them to labour beyond their strength.'[61] Mary Robinson saw injustice in the fact that some women had to do hard physical work, while some men were in easy service occupations:

If woman be the weaker creature, why is she employed in laborious avocations? why compelled to endure the fatigue of household drudgery; to scrub, to scour, to labour, both late and early, while the powdered lackey only waits at the chair, or behind the carriage of his employer? Why are women, in many parts of the kingdom, permitted to follow the plough; to perform the laborious business of the dairy, to work in our manufactories; to wash, to brew, and to bake, while men are employed in measuring lace and ribbons; folding gauzes; composing artificial bouquets; fancying feathers, and mixing cosmetics for the preservation of beauty? I have seen, and every inhabitant of the metropolis may, during the summer season, behold strong Welsh girls carrying on their heads strawberries, and other fruits from the vicinity of London to Covent-Garden market, in heavy loads which they repeat three, four, and five times a day, for a very small pittance; while the male domestics of our nobility are revelling in luxury, to which even their lords are strangers. Are women thus compelled to labour, because they are of the WEAKER SEX?[62]

However, most discussion of protecting women's occupations concentrates on two devices of persuasion. The first is to ridicule men who perform feminine tasks, such as serving in shops catering to women; Rousseau makes fun of male shop assistants in *Émile*, and this kind of ridicule became very popular.[63] The other is an argument from propriety; by the end of the century, writers argue that it is indecent for men to attend women as hairdressers, dressmakers and staymakers.[64] Priscilla Wakefield added the suggestion that undertakers should hire women to attend to female corpses.[65] They also suggest that upper-class women should make a conscious effort to do something about female unemployment by boycotting shops with male assistants and refusing to hire men as hairdressers, and so on.[66]

This suggestion reflects a new self-consciousness among some women, a sense that they had certain social obligations and certain powers, simply because they were women. It had been possible all through the century to use networks of aristocratic women to help philanthropic projects, but reformers were more conscious of women's power by the 1790s.[67] Evangelicals made a conscious effort to reform the upper classes, including upper-class women, in order to reform society in general.[68] Philanthropists argued that it was more decorous for poor women to be helped by women's charitable organisations.[69] The stricter standards of decorum in women's speech and behaviour placed women under restraint, but gave women's role as arbiters of taste and manners a stronger moral content, which some women were happy to exploit.[70]

This female self-consciousness did not necessarily imply feminist demands. In the 1790s, many women who express it, and argue that women should be more respected, are careful not to claim equality with men, and to dissociate themselves from demands for change. Even the writers who were seen as the most strongly feminist, and express the most anger with the status quo, are more concerned with general pleas for respect and better treatment from men, than with particular institutional changes. It was more often their opponents who discussed women in Parliament, the professions, and so on. Eighteenth-century changes in women's legal position were minor, but many people felt women's position had improved greatly, because they were better educated and more respected. People who proposed legal reforms argued that the law should reflect the fact the women's social position had improved, not that legal reform should promote social change. A general assertion of women's equal intellectual and moral worth was the core of eighteenth-century feminist arguments about women in society; feminists insisted on this principle, rather than on particular proposals for reform which might be deduced from it.

CHAPTER SEVEN

The Double Standard

Arguments that women were intellectually and morally equal to men, or that they should be given a wider field of action in society, were hard to reconcile with the double standard.[1] In its strong form, the double standard does not only argue that sexual lapses are more serious in women than in men, but that chastity is the most important virtue in women. Once this is granted, the need for women to lead sexually sheltered lives overrides the possible value of them exploring the world and acting in society without special restrictions; it is simply too dangerous for them to learn and act in the way men do. Rousseau saw that the double standard made nonsense of talk of women's equality,[2] and feminist writers were beginning to criticise it at the end of the century, though hesitantly and with difficulty.

One consequence of the double standard is that women are divided into 'good' and 'bad' on the basis of their sexual history, regardless of their other moral qualities. Most eighteenth-century women writers did not question this division; if anything, they reinforced it, by insisting that there are 'good' women who deserve consideration, and denying the misogynist view which reduces women to purely sexual beings, and argues that they are all 'bad', in thought if not in deed. They insist that 'good' women can be genuinely good in being chaste by choice, and that they may have other qualities which deserve respect; sexuality is not the only area of moral choice for a woman. However, they usually accept that unblemished chastity is a necessary condition of real virtue in a woman, even when they deny that it is a sufficient one. Some writers complain that 'good' women are too hard on 'bad' women, and blame women for the strictness of the division; this complaint shows a failure to understand how precarious the position of a 'good' woman was.[3] To be classified as 'bad' could make it impossible to earn a living in any of the few ways open to middle-class women, and discredit the ideas of women with intellectual ambitions.[4] Archibald Hamilton Rowan describes his reaction to meeting Mary Wollstonecraft with her maid and her baby in Paris:

> I started: 'What!' said I within myself, 'this is Miss Mary Wollstonecraft, parading about with a child at her heels, with as little ceremony as if it were a watch she had just bought at the jewellers. So much for the rights of women,' thought I.[5]

The severity of these penalties made it understandable that many women saw it as vital to maintain a category of 'good' women who were respected, and not to risk breaking the categories and exposing all women to the treatment 'bad' women suffered.

In theory the division between 'good' and 'bad' women was absolute, and the traffic between them was all one-way; the 'good' could become 'bad', but the 'bad' could never be fully rehabilitated. However, there was a vast gap between theory and practice, and there were great differences between the behaviour of different classes. Middle-class behaviour came closest to theory; many working-class people tolerated pre-marital sex, or never bothered to marry, or left their spouses and formed new unions. Aristocratic women had considerable freedom once they were married; at the end of the century, moralists criticised the fact that adultery in women was tolerated more in practice than pre-marital sex, when religious and ethical principle would suggest it should be treated more severely.[6] As the century went on, people began to argue more seriously that the division reflected real differences in character between 'good' and 'bad' women, and was not simply a penalty for their actions. Writers in the latter part of the century often wish the distinction were more clearly marked and lecture young women on the importance of making their status clear by modest dress and behaviour. The division is one of the principal themes of Fordyce's influential and popular *Sermons to Young Women*. His treatment of the subject shows the problems that arise from the wish to see the distinction as marking women's inherent qualities. Fordyce insists on the need for women to cultivate modesty, and avoid the possibility of being confused with the immodest, while simultaneously claiming that modesty is an infallible indicator of innocence and cannot be disguised or simulated.[7] Other writers complain about the lack of visible distinctions between different classes, and between employers and servants. Sarah Trimmer explicitly connects modesty in female dress with dress appropriate to one's class. The rich should set a good example,

> then would the outward appearance of every woman secure the respect due to circumstances and character; and we should no longer see the modest virgin, with dishevelled hair, inviting the insults of libertines, and lessening herself in the esteem of the worthy and good.[8]

Helena Wells Whitford mentions being shocked by both these areas of confusion when she came to England from America as a loyalist refugee, because she was used to these distinctions being marked by race. She had never seen a white woman who was not respectable, and she was horrified by English people's familiarity with their servants, attributing her own superior reserve to the fact that she was used to being waited on by blacks.[9]

The wish to see the division between 'good' and 'bad' as reflecting real differences between the women concerned indicates a wish for a single set of ideas on sexual morality to be true in all contexts, and for the gap between the ideals held up to the young and the maxims which people implicitly followed in their behaviour to be narrowed or closed. Earlier in the century, and in aristocratic circles, people accepted that there was a gap, and were more interested in keeping the categories clear and saving appearances than in judging individuals. Elizabeth Montagu wrote to Elizabeth Carter about a man who had married his mistress, 'The age is wicked when men make w----s, but it is shameless when they marry them; from infamy to virtue there is no return.'[10] However, both women showed kindness and discretion in helping a married woman who had had an affair to keep her secret and return to respectable society.[11]

Translating this sort of practical sympathy and tolerance into general criticism of the double standard was not easy. In the same way, it was hard to bring the maxims which governed people's behaviour once they had departed from what was strictly correct into discussion of the abstract standards to be upheld and appearances to be maintained. There is evidence for this sort of informal ethical belief, and some discussion of what to do once these rules have been broken makes its way into moral philosophy and law, but it does not undermine the theoretical strictness of these rules. The theologian William Paley discusses a man's duty to provide for his illegitimate children, while defending a faithful monogamy as the ideal.[12] The courts upheld gifts and legacies to mistresses, without suggesting that their status was comparable to wives.[13] Other ideas are expressed informally, in correspondence and memoirs: Lady Mary Wortley Montagu discusses the ethics of the child of an adulterous relationship inheriting money from both the legal and the natural father, while a woman who had lived as a kept mistress, Elizabeth Gooch, defends her conduct by saying she only got involved with single men and did not undermine any marriages.[14] However, to translate informal ideas about obligations to mistresses and illegitimate children into proposals to make formal institutions of polygamy or concubinage was highly controversial, even though the institutions were familiar from the Old Testament. Locke considered the possibility of legal concubinage in a diary entry, but not in his published work.[15] Paley's *Moral Philosophy* articulated clearly both the duty to recognise these informal obligations, and the refusal to countenance formalising them.

The interplay between formal severity and informal elasticity can be seen vividly in discussions of the Magdalen Hospital, which was founded in 1758 as an institution for the rehabilitation of prostitutes.[16] Most of the inmates probably were not experienced street prostitutes, as they had to be free of venereal disease on entry. Eighteenth-century writing about prostitutes does not distinguish clearly between professional prostitutes in the modern sense and women cohabiting with men; the fact that the absurdly high figure of 50,000 prostitutes in London, which had a population of about one million, was widely accepted at the end of the century, is one index of this.[17] Some moralists opposed the founding of the charity, because it would encourage immorality; women would be less afraid of the consequences of illicit sexual activity, and men who subscribed could use their right as subscribers to nominate beneficiaries as a cheap way of providing for cast-off mistresses. The subscription lists include some notorious characters who might have done this.[18] Other upper-class supporters may have used the institution to threaten their female relations. Horace Walpole describes a visit there soon after it was founded; some of the inmates seemed to be no more than twelve years old, and one, the niece of an acquaintance, Sir Clement Cotterel, fainted when she recognised Walpole.[19] Even if 'niece' here is a euphemism for illegitimate daughter, the incident makes it clear that the inmates could come from quite upper-class backgrounds.

The services at the chapel of the Magdalen Hospital were open to the public, and extremely popular; the Magdalens were shown to young women as a warning of the consequences of error. A story in a conduct book for girls emphasises the punitive side of the institution. The beautiful, rich and upper-class Miss G—is seduced and abandoned, and becomes a prostitute.

> At last, wearied and worn out with a life of lewdness and debauchery, she fled to the Magdalen-house, where, I am told, she is now endeavouring to wash out the guilt of her former crimes, by her tears and repentance, and preparing to enter the world afresh, in the humble character of servant: for I am well assured, that her friends are firmly resolved never to see her more, nor to afford her any relief or assistance.[20]

A novel published soon after the institution was opened, [The Histories of some of the Penitents in the Magdalen-House] in which the inmates tell each other their stories, also emphasises the disastrous consequences of error. This warning to the young was only one aspect of the Magdalens' image; some writing on the hospital treats them with sympathy, seeing them as victims rather than sinners, and claims that some inmates married into high society when they left.[21] Here the theme is not that of sexual misconduct leading to social catastrophe and humiliation; it is closer to the Pamela myth, the story of rising socially by marrying a man who is socially superior. The story of a girl who is seduced and abandoned by an upper-class lover, and the story of a girl who traps a social superior into marrying her, are fundamentally the same story; Magdalens who marry well suggest that there is a second chance for the seduced. This account of the Magdalen Hospital emphasises its power to rehabilitate, rather than to punish, and plays on the attractive, essentially virtuous nature of the inmates; it plays down the severity of the double standard, while the use of the inmates as a warning reinforces it.

The Magdalen Hospital was founded very soon after the passing of the Marriage Act of 1753. There is no direct connection between the two events, but one effect of the Marriage Act was to make it harder for seduced women or their families to push men into marriage.

Before 1753, it was very easy to contract a legally binding marriage; exchange of vows before witnesses sufficed, or any marriage ceremony performed by a clergyman, even if the circumstances were not those which the church canons required. After 1753, all marriages had to be held in church, at the place of residence of the one of the couple, after the banns had been read for three consecutive weeks; if either of the partners was under twenty-one, the parents' consent was needed. The need for time, and for parental consent, made it impossible for a woman or her family to force a marriage against the will of the man or his family.

Theoretical sympathy for seduced women increased as the century progressed, though censoriousness, and doubts about whether women who had fallen from virtue should be restored to society, also increased. Both movements are part of the shift from a morality based on appearances to one that is more inward-looking. The older morality was ruthless when certain boundaries had been crossed, but willing to overlook anything not absolutely forced on its attention; the newer, which paid more attention to motives and to individual cases, was more flexible, but more inquisitorial. Adherents of the two views of morality could disagree explicitly about whether it was a duty to appear as well as to be correct, in order not to scandalise others, or whether it was enough to behave in the way one believed to be right, regardless of what other people thought.[22] The disagreement represents serious differences about whether duty to self or society comes first; either side could see the other as hypocritical and irresponsible.

The increase in theoretical sympathy for seduced women is tied to a greater willingness to see them as virtuous, because increased faith in female modesty made people reluctant to think women could fall as a result of desire; it was their loving and trusting natures which led them astray. Earlier in the century, this was not so. The double standard was interpreted as meaning that the rules were different for men and women, not that there was a natural difference between men and women in their attitude to sex. A female character in a late seventeenth-century satire wishes she were a man, because

> Like that wild creature, I would madly rove,
> Through all the fields of gallantry and love.[23]

In mid-century Lady Mary Wortley Montagu could still complain about girls 'that declare if they had been born of the male kind they should have been great rakes, which is owning they have strong inclination to wh—ing and drinking, and want only the opportunity and impunity to exert them vigorously.'[24] This view of the double standard as the result of external constraints, not internal differences between men and women, made it easy to complain about its unfairness in a comic mode, but hard to criticise it seriously. There was always available a circular argument in defence of the double standard, that women who committed sexual sins were more culpable than men precisely because the penalties for them and their families were greater.[25] This view could make virtuous behaviour seem less admirable in women than in men, because it was determined by external constraints, and leave women open to the misogynist charge that 'every woman is at heart a rake'.[26] The recognition that women had the same desires as men could lead to practical kindness and sympathy towards women who had broken the rules; it was less likely to lead to a criticism of the double standard which was connected to ideas about women's equal rationality and rights to more respect in society. Logically, it could make it seem that women's chastity had to be protected by social restrictions and naive religious faith.

On this view of the double standard, the crucial point was what women did, or, more realistically, what they were caught doing; their thoughts and desires were unimportant. Religious writers and early feminists could criticise this by arguing that conforming to the minimum standard of virtue was not enough, and that there were other dimensions to women's moral lives. They might also insist on the sinfulness of male unchastity, but they do not question the unequal social penalties. In *Reflections upon Marriage*, Mary Astell's severe prescriptions for how an ill-treated wife should behave are also an assertion of women's moral capacity and moral dignity. Feminists early in the century are not concerned to argue for leniency towards 'bad' women, but to argue that 'good' women are as rational and deserving of respect as good men. Complaints that the double standard was unfair in restricting women are usually comic and superficial, because they have no answer to the standard defence of it – the need to preserve legitimate patrilineal inheritance. Arguments that 'bad' women should be better treated can be a way of devaluing 'good' women, just as saying the sexes are equal can be a pretext for satirising male folly and irrationality, not an argument for treating women with more respect.

However, there is some force in comic dismissals of male censoriousness and hypocrisy, as well as in complaints such as Laetitia Pilkington's: 'Of all things in nature I most wonder why men should be severe in their censures on our sex, for a failure in point of chastity: is it not monstrous, that our seducers should be our accusers?'[27] Like comic assertions of women's equality, they represented potentially powerful arguments which could be given weight in the right context. By the end of the century, a more individualistic morality, increasingly concerned with motives, could give these arguments legitimacy. A morality concerned with appearances and clear categories was not troubled by the fact that its penalties were sometimes arbitrary. In a morality concerned with what a person was like rather than what they had done, it was less easy to explain why one sexual lapse should transform the value of a woman's character. Rousseau's Julie, the virtuous woman who had broken the rules without ceasing to be fundamentally good, provided a powerful fictional denial of this idea.

This emphasis on inner virtue, rather than on virtuous actions, gained force from the more intense concern with female modesty at the end of the century. It became more plausible to represent seduced women as innocent dupes, and adulterous wives as victims of loveless marriages, who had found love too late, once desire without love was seen as a property of men, or of women who had been masculinised by unchaste living. Fiction expressed greater sympathy with women's emotions, and a willingness to pay more attention to the claims of feeling. The most exalted emotion could be involved in seduction; a poem from the 1790s by Ann Batten Cristall, an acquaintance of Mary Wollstonecraft's, draws a general moral from the story of a young woman who is seduced in a moment of visionary religious ecstasy, rather than in more mundane circumstances.[28] Sexual boldness in either sex was seen as masculine. This view of femininity embodied a confusion about whether it represented women's nature, or whether it represented an ideal of refinement which was almost impossible to reach. A warning from the 1780s against friends who are not perfectly innocent suggests the difficulty of attaining femininity: 'Their minds may be coarse, however delicate their form; and their manners unfeminine, even without being masculine.'[29] Both femininity as nature and femininity as ideal could play a part in arguments against the double standard. The idea that women were naturally modest and chaste suggested that all but the most depraved could be rehabilitated, and that a fundamentally chaste nature could survive a good deal of experience. If women became corrupt, it was probably not so much the fault of their initial lapses, as of the cruelty with which they were treated afterwards. Women, like men, should be allowed a few mistakes. Feminists at the end of the century were still claiming rights for 'good' women, but expanded the category by arguing that many apparently 'bad' women were victims of male exploitation; they were not able to deny these categories altogether. The other view, of a modest femininity as an ideal, was often a powerful reinforcement of the double standard, but could provide more than one starting-point for criticism of it. One possibility was to take the view that chastity was a virtue in both sexes, and draw the conclusion that unchaste men should also suffer social penalties. Catharine Macaulay suggests that men are penalised too little and women too much,[30] and, though she urges women to change their treatment of men and women accordingly, her account of what she would teach girls about the origin of the double standard makes it clear that she sees it as a product of male oppression.

> I shall intimate, that the great difference now beheld in the external consequences which follow the deviations from chastity in the two sexes, did in all probability arise from the women having been considered as the mere property of the men; and, on this account had no right to dispose of their own persons: that policy adopted this difference, when the plea of property had been given up; and it was still preserved in society from the unruly licentiousness of the men, who, finding no obstacles in the delicacy of the other sex, continue to set at defiance both divine and moral law, and by mutual support and general opinion to use their natural freedom with impunity.[31]

The view that chastity was an ideal both sexes should respect could lead to another criticism of the double standard, the argument that it corrupted both sexes by making men too coarse and women too refined. As a result, men and women could not really care for each other, and marriages were unlikely to succeed. The old argument that prudish women were disguising an excessive interest in sex changed into the argument that excessively refined women were partly to blame for male immorality, by being too unapproachable, or even too physically feeble to satisfy their husbands' sexual needs.[32] Some women also complained that men were only attracted to 'bad' women, in a tone whose self-righteousness often fails to disguise unhappiness and insecurity. The problem of how to retain a man's interest without sleeping with him was not a new topic; an early eighteenth-century poem by Catherine Trotter Cockburn, *The Platonic*, portrays a woman telling a man that her love for him is much greater than that of another woman 'warmed with grosser fires' who might be willing to sleep with him.[33] However, this straightfoward approach became harder once the division between 'good' and 'bad' women became more absolute.

Some of the more strident comments about male grossness and female virtue must be read in the context of women's insecurity. A letter from Mary Hays to William Godwin provides a full criticism of the way in which men and women were taught different attitudes to sex, and makes it clear that she sees her own painful experience of unrequited love as the result of this division:

> It is from chastity having been rendered a sexual virtue, that all these calamities have flowed – Men are by these means rendered sordid and dissolute in their pleasures; their affections blunted and their feelings petrified; they are incapable of satisfying the heart of a woman of sensibility and virtue – *supposing such a woman has the power (which I believe is not often the case) of fixing, in any degree, their attentions!* – Half the sex, then, are the infamous, wretched victims of brutal instinct – the other half – if they sink not in mere frivolity and insipidity – are sublimated into a sort of – what shall I call them? – refined, romantic, unfortunate, factitious beings, who cannot bear to act, for the sake of the present moment, in a manner that should expose them to complicated, inevitable evils – evils that will, almost infallibly overwhelm them with misery and regret! – And beside which these refinements, however factitious, are, in time, incorporated into, and become a part of, the real character. Woe be, more especially, to those who, possessing the dangerous gifts of fancy and feeling, find it as difficult to discover a substitute for the object as for the sentiment![34]

When Hays published a rewritten version of this letter in her novel, *Emma Courtney*, she left out the words italicised above, substituting a weaker and vaguer phrase: 'the simplicity of modest tenderness loses its charms'.[35] The pain of rejection has to be disguised as righteous indignation.

Hays' complaints about the way in which both men and women have been corrupted are related to her two main subjects in *Emma Courtney*, the taboo against women taking the initiative in expressing their feelings for men, and the possible conflicts between love and marriage. In a letter to Godwin, Hays is perceptive about the way in which falling in love could assume a distorted and exaggerated position in a woman's life, because finding a man was the way to acquire a position in the world, but in the novel she insists on the importance of love.[36]

The plot revolves around Emma's unrequited love for Augustus, who has made a secret marriage; it is not clear if this, or simple indifference, accounts for his coldness towards Emma. It is a weak novel, but it acquired some notoriety; Charles Lloyd's *Edmund Oliver* and Elizabeth Hamilton's *Memoirs of Modern Philosophers* both contain criticisms of it.[37] Both avoid the question of what a woman should do if she falls in love before a man has declared himself, by making their heroines wilful and silly, motivated by theories about women's right to love, rather than true feeling. *Emma Courtney* touched on a real problem, because contemporaries had more expectation that wives ought to be in love with their husbands, and more acceptance of them showing it. This implied acceptance of the power and value of women's feelings, and made it harder simply to dismiss emotions women felt in unsuitable contexts.

At the end of the century, many writers suggest that the partners' emotions, and not the legal bond, constitute the reality of marriage; this could be seen as implying that, when they clash, feeling, not law, should take precedence.[38] Mary Wollstonecraft thought a marriage should last only as long as the partners' feelings for each other; Godwin criticised marriage as a monopoly in early editions of *Political Justice*.[39] However, these defences of feelings do not think through the practical economic consequences, and conservatives like Paley who argued that marriage was needed to protect women's interests could make a convincing case. James Lawrence's utopia, *The Empire of the Nairs*, first published in English in 1811 but written some years earlier, represents a rare consistent attempt to imagine a society without marriage: inheritance among the Nairs is matrilineal, so female chastity is not needed to preserve legitimate inheritance, and the book includes strong criticism of the double standard's cruelty to women. It uses two different idealised models of what such a society would be like; some Nairs live in idyllic monogamous relationships, the result of their free choice as adolescents, while others have a series of easy, amicable affairs, in a world which resembles an idealised picture of aristocratic life. Lawrence deals with the *Emma Courtney* problem, and makes it clear why contemporaries found it threatening; one of the un-European features of Nair life is that it is acceptable for a man to reject a woman's advances.[40] Lawrence's book is subtitled *The Rights of Women*, and he refers to Wollstonecraft, but his feminine utopia does not represent the feminism of her *Rights of Woman*.[41] Its fantasy takes the instrumental feminism of the century to a logical conclusion – the Nair women are charming and intelligent lovers and mothers – but does not deal with the question of how women can become more self-sufficient. The public Treasury provides for their children, but Lawrence disapproves of the idea that they should play a larger part in public life, although he favours a better education for them.[42]

Sympathy for women's feelings, and a tendency to favour the claims of love over those of marriage, did not always go with the belief that women were as intelligent and rational as men, or that they should be given more legal rights or economic power. However, people who held these views often attacked the double standard, usually by denouncing male hypocrisy and corruption, and pleading for some way back for women who had fallen, rather than by arguing that women should be free to follow their feelings. They argue that virtue is the same in both sexes, but emphasise chastity for men, not greater freedom for women.[43] Opponents of a feminism promoting women's education and wider social freedom for women sometimes argue that it will lead to sexual anarchy, and so its defenders are concerned to argue that free, educated women can choose to be good.[44] They argue that chastity is not the sole virtue in a woman's life, and that some mistakes can be redeemed; they do not claim it is unimportant, but argue that it is important for men too. Questioning the value of female chastity could play into the hands of those who argued that women's lives should be restricted; those who seriously criticised conventional standards usually did so in the name of a truer chastity and modesty. All through the century, male licence and exploitativeness, and not the restrictions on women, were the principal objects of feminist attack. A novel by Mary Robinson, published at the end of the century, shows a villain who immediately recognises that criticism of male immorality and deception of women has wider feminist implications. When reproached by the heroine for arguing that a man can be honourable and exploit women, he replies:

> I make no doubt but you will shortly become a *he* – *she* philosopher; that you will pretend to inculcate new doctrines on the potency of feminine understanding, and the absurdity of sexual subordination. You will preach on the sublimity of intellectual gratification, and oppose the majesty of mind against the supremacy of the senses. You will become an advocate for universal toleration: you will hope to equalise the authority of the sexes, and to prove that woman was formed to think, and to become the rational companion of man; though we all know that she was merely created for our amusement.[45]

Robinson implies here that criticism of the double standard has feminist consequences, but some of her language in this passage is quite uncontroversial. Because feminists agreed with conventional moralists in disapproving of men's exploitation of women, they often found it hard to criticise the high value conventionally placed on female chastity; those who defended the rights of women were often primarily concerned with the rights of 'good' women.

CHAPTER EIGHT

The 1790s

In one of the rhetorical high points of *Reflections on the Revolution in France*, Burke lamented that the age of chivalry was dead, and implied a connection between denial of the mystery of kingship and denial of the mystery of gender:

> On this scheme of things, a king is but a man; a queen is but a woman; a woman is but an animal; and an animal not of the highest order. All homage paid to the sex in general as such, and without distinct views, is to be regarded as romance and folly.[1]

Throughout the decade, ideas about how women should act and how they should be treated were closely connected to fears and hopes about the French Revolution and the war with France. French women were believed to be more powerful in their society than English women, and French society and the French character more feminine. Many writers compare Frenchness and femininity, and anti-French writing draws on misogynist stereotypes: the French may be quick-witted and attractive, but they are volatile and unreliable, and easily rush into extreme actions. Mary Wollstonecraft herself uses the femininity of the French character as an excuse for the failures and excesses of the Revolution.[2] This symbolic opposition between worthy British masculinity and pernicious French femininity colours much discussion of women during this period. Interest in women was often connected with the idea that moral reform would prevent revolution and defeat in war. There was an increase in anti-lesbian feeling, as well as general moral severity, and increased awareness of lesbianism, because of rumours about Marie Antoinette and her circle.[3] The revolutionary activities of lower-class French women made people more concerned about poor English women, and the changes in French law dealing with marriage, divorce and parents' power over their children, stimulated discussion of these issues.[4]

There was no simple correlation between attitudes to the Revolution and ideas about women, though discussions about women always involve hopes and fears about social change in general. Radicals usually spoke in terms of freeing women, conservatives in terms of restoring them to their proper place; however, this does not mean that all radicals were coherent feminists, or that all conservatives were anti-feminist. Either side could view women primarily as rational beings, or primarily as objects of men's love. Radicals who emphasised women's rationality argued that women should be better educated, have more opportunities to work, and generally be treated with more respect. Some conservative writers argued much the same thing; both sides agreed on the central importance of women's role as rational mothers, and often both agreed on the importance of moral reform and chastity for men. However, radicals were more likely to sympathise with couples in love who were unable to marry, or women who had been seduced and wanted to return to respectable society, and they criticised the hypocrisy of conventional sexual morality, while conservatives were stricter; even those who wrote most fulsomely about married love did not condone marriages against parents' wishes, let alone anything extra-marital. Some radicals defend the claims of feeling over those of law, but often are more concerned with women and love as a symbol of emotional life than with realistic ideas about women's needs. The glorifying of women's emotions was not always accompanied with respect for their rationality.

Similarly, conservatives sometimes combined expectations that a couple would be in love when they married with a strong emphasis on the wife's intellectual inferiority and dependence on her husband. However, many conservative writers insist on women's rationality, and differ from radicals in their ideas about how women should behave, rather than in their estimation of women's capacities.

The most famous example of radical rationalist feminism is Mary Wollstonecraft's *Vindication of the Rights of Woman*; parodists answered it with *The Rights of Boys and Girls* and *A Vindication of the Rights of Brutes*.[5] The title suggests political radicalism, recalling Paine, and Wollstonecraft's own *Vindication of the Rights of Men*, a reply to Burke's *Reflections*.[6] The date and circumstances of the book's publication gave a new political weight to a title which had precedents in a satire, *Female Rights Vindicated*, or a mild defence of women, Thomas Seward's *The Female Right to Literature*.[7] The book was provocative in its sympathy with the Revolution, and its attacks on British institutions and the British ruling class, as much as in the details of its ideas on women. In her dedication to Talleyrand, Wollstonecraft pleads for civil and political rights for women, and makes it clear that she thinks the Revolution has not gone far enough in this respect.[8] She criticises the fact that 'hard-working mechanics' as well as women are excluded from the vote, and attacks the immorality of the upper classes: '. . . it is in the most polished society that noisome reptiles and venomous serpents lurk under the rank herbage.'[9] She describes the Fellows of Oxford and Cambridge colleges as 'indolent slugs, who guard, by sliming it over, the snug place, which they consider in the light of an hereditary estate.'[10] The book expresses deep, but heterodox, religious belief; it contains no unequivocal reference to the divinity of Christ, it denies the existence of eternal punishment, and it treats the Bible as a poetic allegory rather than an irrefutable authority.[11]

Much of what Wollstonecraft says about women's

education and women's place in society was relatively uncontroversial; many of the most violent attacks on the book came from people who had very little idea of its contents.[12] Elizabeth Hamilton, an intelligent and moderate conservative writer, respected it, and regretted that minor details of the book prevented many people from taking it seriously.[13] Arguments that women should be better educated, physically healthy, able to bring up their children rationally, capable of earning a living if necessary, and free to express their affection to their husbands in an honest and direct way, appear in reforming writers of the period who are not politically radical. However, other aspects of the book were more controversial. Contemporaries were shocked by her belief in co-educational day schools, and her advice that children should be spoken to honestly about sexual matters.[14] Wollstonecraft is unusually forthright, for a female writer, in arguing that seduced women should not be treated like prostitutes, and their lovers should be responsible for them and their children. This advice is not substantially different from Paley's, and the courts could order fathers to maintain their illegitimate children, so that Wollstonecraft's position does not depart radically from existing practice; however, she is provocative in referring to such an arrangement as a 'left-handed marriage'.[15] Her insistence that women should be better educated is not controversial, but her refusal to limit the kinds of intellectual inquiry women should engage in is; most writers assume that women should avoid subjects which demand very concentrated thought. She speculates more freely than most writers about the possibility of women voting or taking a more active part in political life.[16] Most other writers emphasise the improvements in women's education which took place during the eighteenth century; Wollstonecraft is unusually pessimistic about the contemporary position of women. She is also unusually direct about the idea that marriage should be based on friendship and respect, not love.[17] This is commonplace in earlier moralists, but many of

Wollstonecraft's contemporaries assume that friendship and love should be blended in marriage, and dismiss kinds of love which conflict with this ideal as infatuation. Hannah More summarised the new ideal some years later:

> Love itself appears in these pages, not as an ungovernable impulse, but as a sentiment arising out of qualities calculated to inspire attachment in persons under the dominion of reason and religion, brought together by the ordinary course of occurrences, in a private family party.[18]

In this suspicion of love, as in her argument that a rational understanding of their duty will make women more obedient, Wollstonecraft is close to the tradition of rational moralistic works addressed to women which had absorbed much from early feminist works such as Astell's *Serious Proposal*, and which was also a source for more conservative contemporary writers. If Wollstonecraft disapproves of two of the most popular writers for young women, Gregory and Fordyce, she has deep respect for the equally popular, but more rationalist, Hester Chapone.[19]

Wollstonecraft agrees with other rationalist moralists that much stereotypically feminine behaviour is silly and reprehensible, and insists that it represents bad habits which have been learned, not a spontaneous expression of women's nature. Like other feminists of the period, she uses the transvestite former French Ambassador to London, the Chevalier D'Eon, as an example of what a masculine education can do for a woman.[20] At this stage in his career, D'Eon was believed to be a woman who had been brought up as a boy and lived as a man. Wollstonecraft also plays with the satirical convention of a combined attack on women and effeminate men. Her comparison of women's frivolity to that of soldiers provoked some of her readers, even though frivolous and effeminate soldiers appear as comic characters in other writers of the period.[21] Mary Robinson refers to an officer who

changed regiments three times in search of a more
becoming uniform; Elizabeth Hamilton portrays a
cavalry colonel who answers a question about his
duties: 'Me ride, Ma'am? How could you petrify me by
the mention of anything so horrid?'[22] However, the
point of this sort of satire is usually that soldiers ought
not to behave like this, just as the point of misogynist
satire is to blame women themselves for their
shortcomings. Wollstonecraft's point is that soldiers and
women are inevitably corrupted by their enviroment,
although she also believes in the power of the will, and
does not absolve either soldiers or women from blame.
Women's weaknesses are the result of bad education
and unjust treatment in society, but they are not
irremediable, and Wollstonecraft implies that women
can do a good deal to help themselves, and bear some
of the responsibility for their own folly.

There is an instructive and extreme contrast with the
Rights of Woman in a book published a year later, Laetitia-
Matilda Hawkins' *Letters on the Female Mind*. The book is
a polemic with Helen Maria Williams, a radical who was
living in France and publishing sympathetic accounts of
the progress of the Revolution.[23] Hawkins opposes the
Revolution, and expresses reactionary views about
women: 'Our Maker never designed us for anything but
what he created us, a *subordinate* class of beings; a sort
of noun adjective of the human species, tending greatly
to the perfection of that to which it is joined, but
incapable of sole-subsistence.'[24] She is concerned about
the effect on women of easier divorce in France, and
afraid that rebellious behaviour by English women will
provoke English men into refusing them education.[25]
Women's education, which had a good effect in making
women pleasanter companions for men, may have gone
too far, and made women arrogant and rebellious. The
defenders of women's education are wrong to say that
it makes women morally better; in fact, by strengthening the passions, it makes women more liable to
err.[26] This idea of women's moral life is the direct opposite of Wollstonecraft's view that the experience of

struggling with strong passions is necessary for full moral development in both men and women.[27] Hawkins thinks that women should have nothing to do with politics, justifying her own political remarks by saying she is only repeating the statements of 'the best historians'.[28] Repetition is an appropriate intellectual activity for a woman:

> We are not formed for those deep investigations that tend to the bringing into light reluctant truth; but when once she has appeared, when *vera incessu patuit Dea*, then it is within the female province to give her spirit and decoration, which the less flexible and less volatile male mind would fail in attempting.
>
> That we were not designed for the exertion of intense thought, may be fairly inferred from the effect it produces on the countenance and features. The contracted brow, the prolated visage, the motionless eyeball, and the fixed attitude, though they may give force and dignity to the strong lines of the male countenance, can give nothing to soft features that is not unpleasant . . .[29]

Hawkins provides a vivid illustration of the fears and prejudices Wollstonecraft addresses. Her views on women's education, and her praise of women as ornamental, subordinate companions, recall writers such as Fordyce or John Bennett, though she is less fulsome about love in marriage. This kind of praise of women was still fairly new; it draws on seventeenth-century and earlier praises of women's beauty and charm, but moralises them by placing them in the context of marriage rather than flirtation. It also draws on the instrumental feminism of the early eighteenth century in its discussion of how education has made women pleasanter and more equal companions. However, Hawkins is very clear that any freedoms women have depend on male permission, and the appearance of equality must not mislead women into forgetting their subordination. Her discussion of modesty makes it clear why Wollstonecraft insists that modesty is compatible with a realistic recognition of one's own talents. Hawkins links the senses of modesty – diffidence, fear of being seen in public, and sexual virtue – which Wollstonecraft is careful to separate, and implies that any self-assertiveness or self-recognition in a woman may compromise her chastity.[30]

One of the most successful books on women of the decade, Thomas Gisborne's *Enquiry into the Duties of the Female Sex*, has points of contact with both Hawkins and Wollstonecraft.[31] Gisborne was an Evangelical clergyman, a friend of Wilberforce and Hannah More, and politically conservative; he wrote in defence of the British Constitution, and opposed extending the franchise.[32] Like Hawkins, he believes that women's subordination is based in Nature, and that men are more proficient than women at concentrated abstract thought.[33] He regards talk of women's rights, and discontent with the limitations of women's sphere, as a way in which women try to excuse their own laziness.[34] Women should be content with the domestic sphere; both their education of their children, and their religious influence on their husbands, are vitally important.[35] However, he shares some of Wollstonecraft's disagreements with earlier conduct books addressed to women. Like her, he criticises John Gregory's views that women should not display their love for their husbands, and should conceal their intellectual abilities, because the concealment will probably make men overestimate them.[36] He says that it is never right for parents to force a daughter into marriage against her will, though they can forbid unsuitable marriages; earlier texts often view this attitude as unusually generous.[37] Like Wollstonecraft, Gisborne disapproves of women fox-hunting, but believes they should take some moderate outdoor exercise; he approves of gardening for girls, and says its advantages make it worth them occasionally getting their clothes dirty.[38] He also says that women should be active in philanthropy, pay special attention to charities providing for poor women, and employ women wherever possible.[39]

Gisborne's emphasis on women's duty to be sensible and contented with the status quo also appears in some writers who have a stronger belief in women's rationality and the need to improve women's education. Maria Edgeworth and Elizabeth Hamilton both satirise rebellious women who demand their rights and criticise conventional sexual morality, but are themselves strong exponents of a rationalist, but politically conservative feminism. Edgeworth believes women should study seriously, and includes chemistry in their curriculum;[40] Hamilton satirises pretentious, self-taught women, who boast about reading books they are not equipped to understand, but has a strong faith in women's capacity and duty to be rational. Both women were very conscious of prejudice against women's writing.[41] They were friends; their views on women, and the comic techniques of their novels, have much in common.[42]

Edgeworth's views on women's education are clearly developed in an early work, *Letters for Literary Ladies*. The longest section of the work is made up of a correspondence between two male writers, one an opponent of women's education, who describes the limitations decorum imposes on women's intellectual development, the other describing the feminist principles which he will apply to the education of his daughter: 'I wish to give her the habit of industry and attention, the love of knowledge, and the power of reasoning; these will enable her to attain excellence in any pursuit of science or of literature.'[43] There is an autobiographical element in this, for it is based on a correspondence between Thomas Day and Edgeworth's father, Richard Lovell Edgeworth.[44] The rest of the book is made up of two cautionary tales, showing what may happen to irrational, uneducated women. *Letters of Julia and Caroline* argues that rational choice is essential for virtuous behaviour. 'In vain, dear Caroline, you urge me to *think*; I profess only to *feel*.'[45] Julia thinks that women's weaknesses make them more lovable: '. . . let us, Caroline, content ourselves to gain in love what we lose in esteem.'[46] The story of Julia's downfall follows: instead of marrying Caroline's brother, she makes a socially more impressive marriage to a peer, neglects her children, separates from her husband, elopes with a lover, and dies of remorse. The *Essay on the Noble Science of Self-Justification* portrays a passive-aggressive wife who always gets her own way by refusing to argue rationally and parading her feminine submissiveness:

> ' . . . you know that it is the duty of a wife to submit; but you hope, however, you may have an opinion of your own.'
> Remember all such speeches as these will lose above half their effect, if you cannot accompany them with the vacant stare, the insipid smile, the passive aspect of the humbly perverse . . .[47]

The *Essay* and the story of Julia both drive home Edgeworth's point that virtuous action in both sexes depends on rational choice.

Elizabeth Hamilton resembles Edgeworth in her emphasis on women's rationality, and her satire against women who are foolishly rebellious or foolishly feminine. She is a strongly Christian writer, and argues that the story of the Fall and the curse on Eve would have been far more misogynist had it been merely a human invention.[48] Her novel *Letters of a Hindoo Rajah* includes a good deal of discussion of women's education, in which ornamental boarding-school education comes in for much severer censure than pedantry or intellectual pretentiousness. The exemplary character, Lady Grey, is just as well-educated as the eccentric learned lady, Miss Ardent, and differs from her only in being less vain, and so less susceptible to new ideas and fads.[49] Hamilton satirises pretentiousness and radical ideas, not intellectual aspirations as such.

Her *Memoirs of Modern Philosophers* makes fun of radical critics of society, intellectual pretentiousness, and self-indulgent illusions about love. It insists on women's rationality, and makes it clear that women's value is independent of their usefulness to husbands and children. Hamilton praises Mary Wollstonecraft's criticism of Rousseau, and makes a sensible character comment on the education of Sophie: 'I wonder . . . what Rousseau would have done with all the ordinary girls, for it is plain his system is adapted only for *beauties*, and should any of these poor beauties fail in getting husbands, God help them, poor things! they would make very miserable old maids.'[50] Hamilton's characters include an exemplary old maid, Mrs Fielding, who writes moral works addressed to women, and founds an Asylum for the Destitute. It is folly in the central character, Bridgetina, to think that she needs a lover to have a purpose in life.[51]

Bridgetina, who parodies Mary Hays' Emma Courtney, is determined to declare her love to a man and enter into a free union with him, but is too ugly to interest anyone. She is vain and self-educated, and parrots fashionable ideas which she does not really understand; eventually she recognises her own folly. Another character, Julia, escapes less easily than Bridgetina. An ill-educated but well-intentioned beauty, she elopes with a hairdresser, out of a principled opposition to marriage, and ends up in Mrs Fielding's Asylum, pregnant and having attempted suicide. Her discussions with Mrs Fielding about what to do next provide an inconclusive debate on the issue of whether fallen women should return to society. Mrs Fielding believes that they should whenever possible, because reputation is a support to virtue, and offers to help Julia and her mother enter good society in Ireland, where no one will know about the scandal. Julia refuses, although Mrs Fielding insists that she will lead a more useful life in this way, because she does not want to lie and is unwilling to abandon her baby. Mrs Fielding is won over.[52] Julia then dies before her child is born, so the practical consequences of this decision are left unexplored.

Mrs Fielding's kindness and willingness to compromise represent the good sense of an earlier generation, which has to be articulated more clearly than earlier in the century, because it is under attack. Julia's sincerity and idealism represent a severer modern attitude. Her initial opposition to marriage, and her later unwillingness to deny her past, are both based on a refusal to tolerate a gap between social appearances and the reality of people's actions and emotions. Hamilton has some distance from this attitude of refusal, but it is common to most reforming writers in this period, from the most radical to the most repressive. Severe and prudish moralists, and exponents of free love, both take it as their starting-point.

Mrs Fielding's philanthropic generosity recalls that of earlier patronesses of good causes, but the idea that women should be more active in charitable work became stronger during this period. It received a powerful stimulus from Sarah Trimmer's *Oeconomy of Charity*, which was first published in 1787. Fear of revolution, and the economic pressures of the war, led to a greater interest in the needs of the poor. Many poor women were left destitute when their husbands went to war, placing an increased burden on the parish rates, and this made people more aware of the need for women to be able to earn a living. Many writers put a new emphasis on upper-class women's responsibility to help poor women. An article printed in *The Times* in 1795 suggested that upper-class women should address the problem of female unemployment, and make more manpower available for the navy by boycotting shops with male shop assistants.[53] This suggestion appears in several other writers, who often connect it with the problem of unemployment among middle-class women, and upper-class women's special charitable duties to poor women. The idea of consumer boycott as a form of political action was familiar from anti-slavery campaigns. Priscilla Wakefield, one of the writers who suggest upper-class women should patronise women workers as much as possible, also suggested that increased use of maple sugar would undermine West Indian slavery.[54]

Realistic discussion of women's economic needs was an important new element in discussions of women's education and women's place in society, which helped to ground such discussions in arguments about society as a whole, and made it more difficult to reduce them to rhapsodies about the value of women in men's lives. Priscilla Wakefield, an active Quaker philanthropist who promoted lying-in charities and female benefit clubs, wrote a book discussing the need for women at all levels of society to be able to earn a living.[55] She also emphasises the value of women's work in her books for children, as in this description of a visit to Coventry:

> At present, they excel in making ribbons; it is supposed that ten thousand people obtain a living by this light, but elegant fabric, which has the advantage, over many others, of giving employment to women. Catharine [aged eleven] was much pleased at seeing them work, and thought she should soon be capable of managing a loom herself.[56]

Wakefield also argues that women should receive equal pay for all work which does not require great physical strength.[57] Increased opportunities for women to work would reduce the numbers of prostitutes.[58] This is the principal theme of Mary Ann Radcliffe's *The Female Advocate*, another plea for women's employment, which also points out that employing women will free men to fight in the war.[59] Radcliffe's book struck one reviewer as worthy but commonplace, which suggests the wide circulation of these ideas.[60] They have much in common with the ideas on women's employment in an unpublished manuscript by a London man, *The Female Protector*. This writer proposes legislation to reserve certain trades for women, as well as legislation to make seduction a criminal offence. He is also interested in women's emotional lives: women do not only love in response to men's love, and if they were freer to express their feelings it would make for more happy marriages, and help bashful men who are too easily rebuffed.[61]

Discussing the issues of love and economic need together was unusual, but not unique. Much discussion of women's economic needs takes place in a context which emphasises women's rationality, plays down their emotional life, and avoids association with political radicalism, but the question of women's work is also discussed by writers who are less concerned to avoid these issues. Two writers who knew Wollstonecraft, and make clear their admiration for her, devote more attention than the *Rights of Woman* does to the place of feeling in women's lives. Mary Robinson, a prolific writer of novels and verse was also famous as a beauty and former mistress of the Prince of Wales.[62] In her *Letter to the Women of England*, published under a pseudonym, she suggests that women are better than men because they love more deeply; she insists on emotional differences between men and women, while arguing for their intellectual equality.[63] Much of the book is taken up with praises of famous and gifted women; however, she makes a strong attack on women's subordination, taking up some ideas which earlier in the century were only formulated in satire. She criticises the subordination of married women, and their lack of control of their own property.[64] She attacks the restraints of decorum, arguing that women should be taught to swim and run; some passages where she complains about women's inability to duel in defence of their own reputations suggest she also thinks women should be taught to use weapons.[65] She claims that French women have benefited intellectually from being less restrained by decorum than women in other countries, argues that women would not be corrupted morally by learning Greek and Latin, and imagines a university for women.[66] She is scathing about the way in which the same actions can attract completely different judgements, depending on whether they are performed by a man or a woman. Discussing the Chevalier D'Eon, Robinson remarks:

> When this extraordinary female filled the arduous occupations of a soldier and an ambassador, her talents, enterprise, and resolution, procured for her distinguished honour. But alas! when she was discovered to be a WOMAN, the highest terms of praise were converted into 'eccentricity, absurd and masculine temerity, at once ridiculous and disgusting.'[67]

Mary Hays is less aggressive and flamboyant than either
Robinson or Wollstonecraft. While she agrees with many
of their demands for reform, she is more pessimistic about
the present condition of women.[68] Her interest in the
influence of environment on human character makes her
pessimistic about the power of individuals to change
themselves. Conservative moralists like Gisborne,
Edgeworth and Hamilton credit women with more power
of decision and moral action than Hays. Hays' feminism
has a strong sense of women's oppression, but does not
have much to say about what women can do to help
themselves; her letters to Godwin suggest that she perceived herself as helpless and damaged. Wollstonecraft
criticised Hays for her apologies for her own work; the
hesitant way in which Hays presents her writings is very
different from Wollstonecraft's professionalism.[69] Her
novels, *Emma Courtney* and *The Victim of Prejudice*, which
both deal with unrequited love, and are static in effect,
despite their melodramatic plots, convey a sense that
single women are utterly helpless. The victim of prejudice
makes a defiant speech of contempt to the man who rapes
her, but the loss of her reputation destroys her life.[70]
The novels express a despairing sense of women's lives,
in spite of polemical passages which argue for women's
rationality, and insist that men should treat them better.
Hay's non-fictional works are less preoccupied with feeling, and argue for a more rational education for women,
and for more opportunities for them to work. In her
Appeal to the Men of Great Britain, published anonymously,
she argues that women's personalities are as varied as
men's, and that wives should be free to criticise their husbands.[71] The conventional moral education of women is
irrational in expecting women who have been trained to
be compliant to be capable of moral firmness; the way
women are treated drives them to behave in the way
misogynists expect of them:

Petty treacheries – mean subterfuge – whining and flattery –
feigned submission – and all the dirty little attendants, which
compose the endless train of low cunning, if not commendable,

cannot with justice be very severely censured, when practised by women. Since alas! – THE WEAK HAVE NO OTHER ARMS AGAINST THE STRONG![72]

Hays herself does not claim there is anything very new in the work, but says she came independently to the ideas expressed in Alexander Jardine's *Letters from Barbary* and Wollstonecraft's *Rights of Woman*.[73]

Hays' rationalist feminism was less controversial than her insistence on the power of women's feelings, and her known interest in political radicalism. Conservative attacks on her usually blame her for irresponsible cultivation of false and inflated emotion, which can have catastrophic results in both political and personal life.[74] This distrust of sentimentalism is an important strand in the conservative propaganda of the period.[75] The most violent attacks on Mary Wollstonecraft criticise her in this way, concentrating on her posthumous novel, *The Wrongs of Woman*, and Godwin's biography of her.

The well-known incidents in Wollstonecraft's life which made her a scandalous figure all occurred after the publication of the *Rights of Woman*. Late in 1792, she went to France, and met an American, Gilbert Imlay, by whom she had a daughter. The couple were never married, although Wollstonecraft sometimes used the name Mary Imlay and, when war broke out between England and France, she registered at the American consulate as Imlay's wife, so as to acquire American nationality and avoid being imprisoned as an enemy alien. In 1795 she returned to England to join Imlay, found that he was living with another woman, and made two suicide attempts. The following year she began an affair with William Godwin, and married him early in 1797; she died a few months later, of complications resulting from the birth of their daughter. The marriage to Godwin was the moment which created the greatest scandal, since it meant that she was either committing bigamy, or unambiguously admitting that she had never been married to Imlay.[76]

Godwin himself described all these events in his biography of her, which was published in 1798, along with her posthumous works and her love-letters to Imlay.[77] Godwin's preface to the love-letters praises their style, and recommends them to admirers of the *Sorrows of Werther*.[78] The biography presents her as a romantic heroine, a 'female Werther', and emphasises her sensibility, her misfortunes, and Imlay's bad behaviour.[79] Godwin's narrative is based on what he had been told by Wollstonecraft herself, and this view of her has affinities with the way in which she presents herself in her most attractive book, the *Letters from Scandinavia*. These letters, written to Imlay during a business trip she undertook on his behalf in the summer of 1795, between her two suicide attempts, portray her as melancholy, deeply concerned about her baby daughter, and apprehensive about bringing her up alone. She describes her sad feelings watching a Swedish peasant family:

> My eyes followed them to the cottage, and an involuntary sigh whispered to my heart, that I envied the mother, much as I dislike cooking, who was preparing their pottage. I was returning to my babe, who may never experience a father's care or tenderness. The bosom that nurtured her, heaved with a pang at the thought which only an unhappy mother could feel.[80]

The self-dramatisation is tempered by a clear-headed realism – 'much as I dislike cooking' – which is never completely absent from her writings, but which could escape readers of Godwin's biography. Wollstonecraft as romantic heroine could seem attractive and admirable; Godwin, like some other writers who treat her in this way, expresses genuine admiration for her work. However, this view of her life could easily lead to more patronising or hostile views: that her life might make a moving story, but her ideas were wrongheaded, or even that her life provided the best refutation of her ideas.[81] One sympathetic writer blamed her for the scandal, on the grounds that her fame as a feminist placed her under a special obligation to lead a blameless private life.[82]

Godwin's biography of Wollstonecraft was a gift to anti-feminist and anti-Jacobin writers. One anti-feminist wrote:

> I cannot but think, that the Hand of Providence is visible, in her life, her death, and the Memoirs themselves. As she was given up to her 'heart's lusts', and let 'to follow her own imaginations', that the fallacy of her doctrines, and the effects of an irreligious conduct, might be manifested to the world; and as she died a death that strongly marked the distinction of the sexes, by pointing out the destiny of women, and the diseases to which they are liable; so her husband was permitted, in writing her Memoirs, to labour under a temporary infatuation, that every incident might be seen without a gloss – every fact exposed without an apology.[83]

Her affairs with Imlay and Godwin, her contempt for her father, and her willingness to abandon her daughter by attempting to commit suicide, were all criticised harshly.[84] The image of Wollstonecraft as suicidal mother was particularly troubling to her contemporaries' imagination. Elizabeth Hamilton makes her Julia die after a suicide attempt; Charles Lloyd shows a rebellious woman committing suicide soon after giving birth to an illegitimate son.[85]

Wollenstonecraft herself used this image in her sketch for the conclusion of her unfinished novel, *The Wrongs of Woman*: pregnant, and abandoned by her lover, the heroine, Maria, attempts suicide, but decides to live when she discovers her daughter is still alive.[86] The novel is primarily concerned with legal and emotional issues Wollstonecraft had left unexamined in the *Rights of Woman*. It is intensely critical of husbands' power over their wives' property, and of the difficulty of ending a loveless marriage: women ought not to be so dependent on their husbands for their own and their children's support that they cannot leave them when they behave badly. The melodramatic plot of the novel disposes of the idea that the indissolubility of marriage protects women; a conservative reviewer was reduced to blaming the heroine for choosing her husband unwisely.[87] Wollstonecraft's defence of Maria's relationship with her lover was topical, because some Evangelicals and severe moralists were scandalised by the fact that divorced women could regain respectability by marrying their lovers. 'The duchess who has violated her marriage oath, who is discarded by her husband and married to her gallant, is but the same degraded creature who is transferred at Smithfield to a new purchaser.'[88] A Bill to make this illegal was almost passed in 1800.[89] *The Wrongs of Woman* is far more critical of marriage than Wollstonecraft's earlier work, and far more controversial. It contributed to caricatures of her, formed from a selective reading of Godwin's life and her own works, which transform her into a monster from misogynist satire, promiscuous, rebellious, and denying basic facts of nature:

> Oh horrid! that Nature did not provide some middle, some stupid, lumpish being, to rear and take care of the human progeny: why not make man an oviparous animal? Then we might have hatched the eggs in tempered stoves, as they do chickens in Egypt.[90]

The image of Wollstonecraft, like the slogan 'Rights of Woman', was often associated with ideas Wollstonecraft herself would have been the first to condemn. The caricatures of Wollstonecraft and Hays as irresponsible and immoral feminists, like their caricatures of conservative oppressors of women, disguise the range of possible views about women, and the subtle differences of tone between writers who say broadly similar things.

One of the most successful and influential women writers of the period, Hannah More, was often contrasted with Wollstonecraft. Some writers treated More as exemplary and Wollstonecraft as a monster; others regarded More as severe and hypocritical, and Wollstonecraft as a heroine and the better writer. A satirist making fun of More remarked:

On poor Mary's errors, she's coldly severe,
Nor drops o'er her wrongs, or her grave, one soft tear.
In vigorous expression, and passion's true tone,
Perhaps she was piqued to be greatly outdone.[91]

More herself was outraged by Wollstonecraft's life and works, but, as contemporaries were amused to note, they were often substantially in agreement on female education.[92] They held utterly opposed religious and political beliefs, but agreed on the importance and dignity of women's role as educators of their children.

More was an Evangelical Christian, and a strong opponent of revolutionary politics. She believed that the influence of the upper classes on society was crucial, and that it was vital to reform them; unlike Wollstonecraft, she had no faith in the superior virtue of the middle classes.[93] For much of her life, More kept a school in Bath with her sisters. More had achieved some success as a playwright during the 1770s and 1780s, and made friends with the Bluestockings and with Dr Johnson. However, she achieved her greatest fame and influence after 1790; her *Cheap Repository Tracts*, directed to a working-class audience, were credited with having helped to prevent revolution in England. She campaigned against slavery, and believed that teaching the poor to read would make them better Christians and more disposed to obey. Her philanthropic activities included the promotion of women's Friendly Societies, whose members paid in a small amount of money weekly, and received benefits when they were ill or in childbirth. She discusses women's inferiority and subordination, but has an extremely strong sense of women's power and influence. Her role in developing the notion that women were subordinate to men, but powerful and probably morally superior in their separate sphere, was very important.[94] She develops the commonplace view that women were more religious than men into the view that women have a special responsibility to resist atheism and exert a good moral influence. More sees the French Revolution and the spread of atheism as intimately connected. The 'apostles of atheism', realising that they have failed to create revolution in England because they concentrated on converting the men, are now using German literature to convert English women to atheism.[95] Another conservative writer, Jane West, expresses similar ideas in the form of a crude conspiracy theory.[96]

More's vision of women's capacities, and of how they should act, is close to Thomas Gisborne's, and has much in common with Wollstonecraft's rationalism. Women are capable of much greater intellectual development than current education allows them though More concedes some innate intellectual difference between the sexes: '. . . women have equal parts, but are inferior in wholeness of mind in the integral understanding'.[97] She uses the standard instrumental feminist argument that developing women's minds will make them better companions to men. Women should avoid religious and political controversy. More argues that women are subordinate to men, but is highly critical of men who despise women, or refuse to discuss serious subjects with them.[98] Her tone is confident, in the same spirit as Jane West's remark: '. . . as, with few exceptions, subservience is claimed from us by all our male relatives, it may not be improper to observe, that whenever they err, either in morals or principles, a mild yet marked disapprobation is not pertinacity but fortitude.'[99]

More's views on women are hard to reconcile with those of the feminists of her day, or with the reality of her own power and influence. However, her rationalism, and her sense of women's philanthropic duties, make her views equally incompatible with those of a writer like Hawkins, who insists on female dependence. In her insistence on women's responsibility, More recalls the feminist writers of the beginning of the century, and her confident tone indicates that some of their ideas about the respect due to women had become common currency. However, her willingness to allow men some intellectual superiority, and her reluctance to deal with the problem of unhappy marriages – More, unlike Astell or Chudleigh, assumes that ill-treated wives can win over their husbands by compliant behaviour – are not in keeping with their views. Because some of the practical recommendations of the early feminists had been adopted, their key argument, that women were fully as rational as men, could be dropped.

A serious argument that women and men were equal was as controversial at the end of the century as at the beginning, but had different implications. Writers at the beginning of the century concentrate on the question of women's rationality, or on the inequality of power between husband and wife, and talk about injustice to individual women. Their practical suggestions were modest enough to be absorbed by an instrumental feminism which aimed at a friendlier, but still unequal, relationship between men and women. Writers at the end of the century often take the achievements of instrumental feminism for granted, and are complacent about the improvements in women's education, the increase in women writers, the greater expressiveness and informality of family relationships, and the decrease in parents' power over children's choice of a marriage partner. They recognise women's oppression as a reality, but one which exists only in the past or in Muslim countries; strong claims for women's equality are obsolete and unnecessary. Often these writers sound confusingly like their feminist comtemporaries in their insistence on the value of improving women's role in society. Feminist writers argue that the improvements which have been made are not enough, and, vague though their proposals for reform often are, they are based on a sense of women as a group in society, and the effects of their position on society as a whole, which goes beyond the earlier concern with justice to individuals. Particular arguments about women's capacities sometimes stay the same throughout the century, but the new ability to see questions about women as questions about a society undergoing change, rather than questions about individuals, gave the arguments a different weight. A mid-century satirist compares the prejudice against women's intelligence to the idea that other peoples are intellectually inferior to Europeans, and develops an analogy suggesting that women's ignorance proves nothing about their capacities:

> Should a man on account of the ignorance which at present prevails in Greece, tell a Grecian that all his countrymen are naturally incapable of studying the sciences; must he not blush if he has any grace left, to hear the Grecian quote him the illustrious names of a Plato, an Aristotle, and many other ancients of equal parts and learning? And what would he have to reply if the Grecian should add, that if his country is not as famous for learning now as it was formerly, it is for want of the same advantages?[100]

This argument does not appear in a serious feminist context; anti-feminists had available the easy response that exemplars like Anne Dacier or Anna Maria van Schurman were not the equals of Plato and Aristotle. At this date, the tragic condition of modern Greece was seen as the result of an irreversible decline; the contrast between ancient and modern Greece inspired meditation on the reverses of history, not nationalist zeal to restore Greece to independence and its former glory.[101] Women's capacities could seem as difficult to bring into present actuality as the former glories of the Greeks.

Hannah More, writing some sixty years later, presents a superficially similar argument from analogy about women's intelligence:

> . . . till the female sex are more carefully instructed, this question will always remain as undecided as to the degree of difference between the understandings of men and women, as the understanding of blacks and whites; for until Africans and Europeans are put nearer on a par in the cultivation of their minds, the shades of distinction between their native powers can never be fairly ascertained. Thus, though in what relates to the actual difference of mind in the sexes, the distinction itself seems

177

clearly marked by the defining finger of the creator, yet of the degree of that native difference a just estimate can never be formed till the understandings of women are made the most of . . . [102]

At first sight this is much weaker than the satirist's argument, as More accepts the inferiority of both blacks and women. However, the slave trade was an object of intense political controversy, in which More herself was active; the passage quoted was written a few years before its abolition. Slavery itself had only been illegal in England since 1772. By comparing women to a group who were benefiting from major legal changes, More suggests that women's position can be affected by the conscious decisions of those in power. If she presents women as passive objects of benevolence, like slaves, rather than rebellious claimants of their rights, she shares with Wollstonecraft the view that the condition of women as a group is important for society as a whole, and can be changed by political decisions. The feminists of the beginning of the century express anger at injustice to individual women, and commitment to the moral and intellectual reform of individual women; they lack this sense of social change, which came from the real shift in women's lives, and from the increasingly sophisticated ways of thinking about society. As debates about women shifted from a context of satire and moralism to a context of social reform, feminist views acquired implications which were more practical and more political.

Notes

Introduction

1. *Analytical Review*, 28 (July/December 1798), in a review of Mary Hays, *Appeal to the Men of Great Britain*, pp. 23-36.
2. Una Birch Pope-Hennessy, *Anna Maria van Schurman* (London: Longmans, Green and Co., 1909); Joyce Irwin, 'Anna Maria van Schurman: From Feminism to Pietism', *Church History*, 46(1) (1977), pp. 48-62. Anna Maria van Schurman, *Dissertatio de ingenii muliebris ad doctrinam et meliores litteras aptitudine* (Leyden, 1641; trans., *The Learned Maid*, London, 1659).
3. Schurman, *Opuscula*, 2nd edn (Leyden, 1650), pp. 338-40.
4. Schurman, *Eukleria*, (Altona, 1673), p. 134.
5. Schurman, *Eukleria*, *passim*; for Labadie, see Michel de Certeau, *La Fable mystique XVIe–XVIIe siècle* (Paris: Gallimard, 1982), pp. 374-405.
6. Alexander Pope, *Epistle to a Lady*, in *Epistles to Several Persons*, ed. F.W. Bateson (London: Methuen, and New Haven, Conn.: Yale University Press, 1951; vol. III.ii of Twickenham edn of *Poems*), p. 70.
7. Robert Bage, *Hermsprong*, 2 vols (Dublin, 1796, vol. 2), p. 28.
8. John Bennett, *Strictures on Female Education*, London, 1788, p. 124.
9. Katharine Rogers, *Feminism in Eighteenth-Century England* (Urbana, Ill.: University of Illinois Press, and Brighton: Harvester Press, 1982).
10. See the discussion in Nancy K. Miller, *The Heroine's Text: Readings in the French and English Novel, 1722–1782* (New York: Columbia University Press, 1980), e.g. at pp. xi, 149-50, 153, 175.
11. John Cleland, *Memoirs of a Woman of Pleasure*, ed. Peter Sabor (Oxford and New York: Oxford University Press (World's Classics), 1985), p. 40; Frances Burney, *Evelina*, ed. Edward A.

Bloom, (London: Oxford University Press, 1968), p. 387.

12. Patricia Meyer Spacks, *Imagining a Self: Autobiography and Novel in Eighteenth-Century England* (Cambridge, Mass. and London: Harvard University Press, 1976), pp. 57-91, 158-92.

13. Robert Halsband, 'Women and Literature in Eighteenth-Century England', in Paul Fritz and Richard Morton (eds.), *Woman in the Eighteenth Century and other Essays* (Toronto and Sarasota: Samuel Stevens Hakkert and Co., 1976) (Publications of the McMaster University Association for Eighteenth-Century Studies, vol. 4), pp. 55-71. For the seventeenth-century background, see Joachim Heinrich, *Die Frauenfrage bei Steele und Addison* (Leipzig: Mayer und Müller, 1930) (Palaestra 168). There are thorough bibliographical essays on the social and literary history of women in the period in Barbara Kanner (ed.), *The Women of England* (London: Mansell, 1980, and Hamden, Conn.: Archon Books, 1979).

14. For analysis of the way in which a period's notion of women is made up of inconsistent ideas from different discourses, see Ian Maclean, *The Renaissance Notion of Woman* (Cambridge: Cambridge University Press, 1980); for an account of a sample of eighteenth-century opinion, see Jean E. Hunter, 'The Eighteenth-Century Englishwoman: According to the *Gentleman's Magazine*', in Fritz and Morton (eds.), *Woman in the Eighteenth Century*, pp. 73-88.

15. Halsband, 'Women and Literature', p. 59.

16. An influential compendium of this sort of knowledge about women was William Alexander, *The History of Women*, 2 vols (London, 1779).

17. See Zillah R. Eisenstein, *The Radical Future of Liberal Feminism* (New York and London: Longman, 1981), pp. 33-112; Susan Moller Okin, *Women in Western Political Thought* (Princeton, NJ: Princeton University Press, 1979), pp. 99-194.

Chapter 1

1. John Locke, *Two Treatises of Government*, ed. Peter Laslett, 2nd edn (Cambridge: Cambridge University Press, 1967), p. 192.

2. Miss R. Roberts, *Sermons Written by a Lady* (London, 1770); Anna Seward, 'Letter to E. Jerningham', *The Gentleman's Magazine*, 71 (1801), p. 196.

3. Sir William Blackstone, *Commentaries on the Laws of England*, 12th edn, 4 vols (London, 1793–95), vol. 1 (1793), p. 445.

4. Blackstone, *Commentaries*, note by Edward Christian, vol. 1, p. 444.

5. Derek Hirst, *The Representative of the People? Voters and Voting*

in England under the Early Stuarts (Cambridge: Cambridge University Press, 1975), p. 18.

6. Karl von den Steinen, 'The Discovery of Women in Eighteenth-Century English Political Life', in Barbara Kanner (ed.), *The Women of England* (London: Mansell, 1980, and Hamden, Conn.: Archon Books, 1979) pp. 229–58, 241.

7. Mary Beth Norton, *Liberty's Daughters: The Revolutionary Experience of American Women, 1750–1800* (Boston and Toronto: Little, Brown and Co., 1980), pp. 191-2. The case against women's suffrage is discussed from a lawyer's point of view in William Griffith, *Eumenes* (Trenton, NJ, 1799).

8. The details are clearly summarised in Lee Holcombe, *Wives and Property: Reform of the Married Women's Property Law in Nineteenth-Century England* (Toronto: University of Toronto Press, 1983), pp. 18-47. For eighteenth-century trusts and settlements generally, see Barbara English and John Savile, *Strict Settlement; A Guide for Historians* (University of Hull Press, 1983) (Hull University Press Occasional Papers in Economic and Social History, no. 10).

9. For the view that these arrangements protected the wife's family rather than the wife herself, see Susan Moller Okin, 'Patriarchy and Married Women's Property in England: Questions on Some Current Views', *ECS* 17(2) (Winter 1983–84), pp. 121-38.

10. Modern writers sometimes attribute the phrase 'kiss or kick' in this context to Lord Chancellor Thurlow (1731–1806); however, it is already attributed to 'one of our present eminent judges', in *The Hardships of the English Laws in Relation to Wives* (London and Dublin, 1735), p. 34.

11. Randolph Trumbach, *The Rise of the Egalitarian Family* (New York: Academic Press, 1978), p. 83.

12. O.R. McGregor, *Divorce in England* (London: William Heinemann, 1957), pp. 10-12.

13. Samuel Pyatt Menefee, *Wives for Sale* (Oxford: Basil Blackwell, 1981).

14. *The Hardships of the English Laws*, pp. 15, 23-8; Leon Radzinowicz, *A History of English Criminal Law and its Administration from 1750* (London: Stevens and Sons, 4 vols, 1948–68), vol. 1 (1948), pp. 209-13.

15. Blackstone, *Commentaries*, vol. 4 (1795), pp. 207-9.

16. Ibid., vol. 3 (1794), p. 140. Edward Christian's note on this passage implies that English law does not protect female chastity enough.

17. Ibid., vol. 4 (1795), pp. 209-15. Blackstone is probably concerned about false accusations of homosexuality by blackmailers and robbers; for a case of this kind, see *Annual Register* (1779), pp. 199, 209. For doubt over whether a

conscious adult woman could be raped by one man without accomplices, see Theodric Romeyn Beck, *Elements of Medical Jurisprudence*, 2nd edn (London, 1825), pp. 57-8.

18. E.A. Wrigley and R.S. Schofield, *The Population History of England 1541–1871* (London: Edward Arnold, 1981), p. 255.

19. Peter C. Hoffer and N.E.H. Hull, *Murdering Mothers: Infanticide in England and New England 1558–1803* (New York and London: New York University Press, 1981) (New York University School of Law Series in Legal History, 2), pp. 65-91.

20. See Guy Williams, *The Age of Agony: The Art of Healing c.1700–1800* (London: Constable, 1975), pp. 24-48; Elizabeth B. Gasking, *Investigations into Generation 1651–1828* (Baltimore: The Johns Hopkins University Press, and London: Hutchinson, 1967); Arthur H. Cash, 'The Birth of Tristram Shandy: Sterne and Dr. Burton', in Paul-Gabriel Boucé (ed.), *Sexuality in Eighteenth-Century Britain* (Manchester: Manchester University Press, and Totowa, NJ: Barnes and Noble, 1982), pp. 198-224.

21. C.A. Seligman, 'Mary Toft – The Rabbit Breeder', *Medical History*, 5 (1961), pp. 349-60; James K. Hopkins, *A Woman to Deliver Her People: Joanna Southcott and English Millenarianism in an Era of Revolution* (Austin: University of Texas Press, 1982), pp. 200-1.

22. Jean Donnison, *Midwives and Medical Men: A History of Inter-Professional Rivalries and Women's Rights* (London: Heinemann, 1977), pp. 41-62; Claire Tomalin, *The Life and Death of Mary Wollstonecraft* (London: Weidenfeld and Nicolson, 1974), pp. 220-7.

23. E.g. Francis Foster, *Thoughts on the Times, but Chiefly on the Profligacy of our Women*, 2nd edn (London, 1779); *The Danger and Immodesty of the present too general custom of unnecessarily employing men-midwives*, 2nd edn (London, 1772).

24. Sarah Stone, *A Complete Practice of Midwifery* (London, 1737), p. xiii; Elizabeth Nihell, *A Treatise on the Art of Midwifery* (London, 1760), pp. xi, 39-52, 78, 163.

25. Louis Lapeyre, *An Enquiry into the Merits of these two Important Questions* (London, 1772); William Clark, *The Province of Midwives in the Practice of their Art* (Bath, 1751). There are numerous horror-stories about ignorant midwives in Stone, *Complete Practice*. For a summary of traditional midwives' harmful interventions, see Edward Shorter, *A History of Women's Bodies* (New York: Basic Books, 1982) pp. 43-7, 58-63.

26. *Danger and Immodesty*, p. 21; Foster, *Thoughts on the Times*, p. 125; Nihell, *Art of Midwifery*, pp. 4, 25, 87-91.

27. Anthony Highmore, *Pietas Londinensis*, 2 vols (London, 1810), vol. 1, pp. 380-92.

28. William Cadogan, *An Essay upon Nursing, and the Management of Children* (London, 1748), p. 3.
29. Tudor and Stuart midwives seem to have been influenced by contemporary textbooks into practices that were more dangerous than those current in the Middle Ages; see Audrey Eccles, *Obstetrics and Gynaecology in Tudor and Stuart England* (London and Canberra: Croom Helm, 1982), pp. 87-8.
30. Cadogan, *Essay*, p. 24.
31. Medical models of womanhood are discussed in Paul Hoffmann, *La Femme dans la pensée des lumières* (Paris: Editions Ophrys, 1977), pp. 42-81.
32. Thomas Seward, 'The Female Right to Literature', in Robert Dodsley (ed.), *A Collection of Poems*, 6 vols (London, 1763), vol. 2, p. 296.
33. Mary Astell, *Reflections upon Marriage*, 3rd edn (London, 1706), Preface, not paginated.
34. For discussion, see Zillah R. Eisenstein, *The Radical Future of Liberal Feminism* (New York and London: Longman, 1981).
35. Locke, *Two Treatises*, ed. Laslett, p. 192; Locke, *The Educational Writings*, ed. James L. Axtell (Cambridge: Cambridge University Press, 1968), p. 117, 122.
36. E.g. Locke, *Two Treatises*, ed. Laslett, pp. 351, 341.
37. Ruth Graham, 'Rousseau's Sexism Revolutionized', in Paul Fritz and Richard Morton (eds.), *Woman in the Eighteenth Century and other essays* (Toronto and Sarasota: Samuel Stevens Hakkert and Co., 1976) (Publications of the McMaster University Association for Eighteenth-Century Studies, vol. 4), pp. 127-39.
38. For discussion, see Susan Moller Okin, *Women in Western Political Thought* (Princeton, NJ: Princeton University Press, 1979), pp. 99-194; and Eisenstein, *Radical Future of Liberal Feminism*, pp. 55-89; for a discussion which is more in sympathy with Rousseau's arguments, see Joel Schwartz, *The Sexual Politics of Jean-Jacques Rousseau* (Chicago and London: University of Chicago Press, 1984).
39. Jean-Jacques Rousseau, *Émile*, ed. Charles Wirz and Pierre Burgelin (Paris: Bibliothèque de la Pléiade, 1969), p. 700.
40. Rousseau, *Émile*, p. 693.
41. E.g. ibid., p. 720; but cf. p. 697.
42. Ibid., pp. 767, 753f.
43. Ibid., p. 746.
44. Marie Jean Antoine Nicolas Caritat, Marquis de Condorcet, 'Lettres d'un bourgeois de New-Haven', in *Oeuvres*, ed. A. Condorcet O'Connor and M.F. Arago, 12 vols (Paris, 1847–49), vol. 9 (1847), p. 20.
45. William Alexander, *The History of Women*, 2 vols (London, 1779), vol. 1, p. 103.

46. Lucy Aikin, *Epistles on Women* (London, 1810), *passim*; John Bennett, *Strictures on Female Education* (London, 1788), pp. 1-65; J. Burton, *Lectures on Female Education and Manners*, 2 vols (Rochester and London, 1793,) vol. 1), pp. 79-80; William Duff, *Letters on the intellectual and moral characters of women* (Aberdeen, 1807), pp. 66-95; S. Hatfield, *Letters on the Importance of the Female Sex* (London, 1803), pp. 15-16; Jane West, *Letters to a Young Lady*, 2nd edn, 3 vols (London, 1806), vol. 1, pp. 35-41.

47. Alexander, *History of Women*, vol. 2, pp. 313-44.

48. *The Annual Necrology for 1797–8* (London, 1800), p. 458.

49. Alexander, *History of Women*, vol. 1, Advertisement to the Reader, not paginated.

50. Betsy Rodgers, *Cloak of Charity* (London: Methuen, 1949), p. 114; Edward Young, Satires 5 and 6, in *Poetical Works*, 2 vols (London, 1741), vol. 1, pp. 224-81.

51. See Marc Angenot, *Les Champions des femmes* (Montreal: Les Presses de l'Université du Québec, 1977).

52. William Walsh, *A Dialogue Concerning Women*, *Works*, (London, 1736) vol. 3, pp. 125-214, 126; Fordyce, *Character and Conduct*, p. 42.

53. Thomas Holcroft, *Anna St Ives*, ed. Peter Faulkner (London: Oxford University Press, 1970), p. 170.

54. See Barbara Brandon Schnorrenburg, 'Education for Women in Eighteenth Century England: An Annotated Bibliography', *Women and Literature*, 4(1) (1976), pp. 49-55; Josephine Kamm, *Hope Deferred: Girls' Education in English History* (London: Methuen, 1965).

55. Richard Steele (or Mary Wray), *The Ladies' Library*, 3 vols (London, 1714); for its sources, see George A. Aitken, 'Steele's "Ladies' Library"', *The Athenaeum*, no. 2958 (5 July 1884), pp. 16-17. The British Library has two compendia with the title *The Whole Duty of a Woman*, one printed in 1700 and one in 1737. These works are similar but not identical in content; both mix moral extracts with household advice and recipes. They should not be confused with William Kenrick's book of this title (London, 1753).

56. Mr Cresswick (i.e. Mary Wollstonecraft), *The Female Reader* (London, 1789); Anna Laetitia Barbauld, *The Female Speaker* (London, 1811); *The Female Miscellany*, 2 vols (Shrewsbury, 1770–1).

57. Richard Allestree, *The Ladies Calling* (Oxford, 1673), Part 1, p. 40, Part 2, p. 81.

58. George Ballard, *Memoirs of Several Ladies of Great Britain* (Oxford, 1752), p. 316; for the importance of his arguments in favour of women's education, see p. 32 of Ruth Perry's introduction to her edition of Ballard (Detroit: Wayne State

University Press, 1985). Cf. Mary Astell, *The Christian Religion as Profess'd by a Daughter of the Church of England* (London, 1705), p. 212. However, George Hickes, who knew Pakington well, is careful to avoid confirming the attribution: George Hickes, *Linguarum Vett. Septentrionalium Thesaurus*, 2 vols (Oxford, 1703), vol. 1, preface to Anglo-Saxon grammar addressed to John Pakington, not paginated.

59. *The Compleat Servant-Maid*, 6th edn (London, 1700), p. 137, quoting Hannah Woolley, *The Gentlewoman's Companion* (London, 1675), p. 215.

60. George Savile, Marquis of Halifax, *The Lady's New-Years Gift: or, Advice to a Daughter* (London, 1688).

61. Isaac Bickerstaffe, *The Sultan* (London, 1787), p. 10.

62. Elizabeth Ogilvie Benger, *The Female Geniad* (London, 1791).

63. Mary Hays, *Female Biography*, 6 vols (London, 1803). The publisher's advertisement for it states: 'This interesting and valuable work is indispensable to the completion of every lady's library, and a suitable companion at school to young ladies, who are finishing their education.' Advertisement at the end of vol. 3 of Mary Robinson, *Poetical Works*, 3 vols (London, 1806).

64. For examples of each response, see Miriam Wilford, 'Bentham on the Rights of Women', *JHI* 36(1) (1975), pp. 167-76, 167; Elizabeth Montagu, *Letters*, ed. Matthew Montagu, 3rd edn, 4 vols (London, 1810–13), vol. 3 (1813), pp. 96-7; *The Anti-Jacobin*, 10 (September–December 1801), pp. 253-9. For discussion of biographical genres, see Donald A. Stauffer, *The Art of Biography in Eighteenth-Century England*, (Princeton, NJ: Princeton University Press, 1941).

65. Harriette Wilson, *Memoirs*, 2nd edn, 4 vols (London, 1825), vol. 1, p. 5.

66. The Hon. Juliana-Susannah Seymour (i.e. John Hill), *The Conduct of Married Life* (London, 1753); John Hill, *Plain and Useful Directions for those afflicted with cancers* (London, 1773); James Boswell, *The Life of Samuel Johnson*, ed. George Birkbeck Hill and L.F. Powell, 6 vols (Oxford: Clarendon Press, 1934–50), vol. 3 (1934), p. 285.

67. Sarah Green, *Mental Improvement for a Young Lady* (London, 1793), p. 2.

68. Wollstonecraft, *A Vindication of the Rights of Woman*, 2nd edn (London, 1792), pp. 168-9.

69. Robert Gould, *Works*, 2 vols (London, 1709), vol. 2, p. 24; cf. Charlotte Charke, *A Narrative of the Life of Mrs. Charlotte Charke* (London, 1755), p. 12.

70. George Colman and Bonnell Thornton (eds.), *Poems by the Most Eminent Ladies of Great-Britain and Ireland*, 2 vols (London, 1773), vol. 1, p. iii.

71. *The Gentleman's Magazine*, 61 (1791), p. 255; Thomas Mathias, *The Shade of Alexander Pope on the Banks of the Thames* (London, 1799), p. 51; Richard Polwhele, *The Unsex'd Females* (London, 1798), pp. 32-4. For the contrary view that critics were biased, see Elizabeth Hamilton, *Memoirs of Modern Philosophers*, 4th edn, 3 vols (Bath, 1804) vol. 1, p. iii.

72. Hays, *Female Biography*, vol. 3, p. 317.

73. See Ford K. Brown, *Fathers of the Victorians* (Cambridge: Cambridge University Press, 1961).

74. Sir Walter Scott, *Letters*, ed. H.J.C. Grierson *et al.*, 12 vols (London: Constable, 1932-37), vol. 10 (1936), pp. 95-7.

75. See Mary Poovey, *The Proper Lady and the Woman Writer: Ideology as Style in the Works of Mary Wollstonecraft, Mary Shelley and Jane Austen* (Chicago and London: University of Chicago Press, 1984); Maurice J. Quinlan, *Victorian Prelude: A History of English Manners 1700–1850* (New York: Columbia University Press, 1941).

76. James Fordyce, *Sermons to Young Women*, 3rd edn, 2 vols (London, 1766), vol. 1, pp. 23-4.

77. Philip Dormer Stanhope, 4th Earl of Chesterfield, *Letters to his Son*, 2 vols (London, 1774), vol. 1, pp. 480, 554, vol. 2, p. 23.

78. Fordyce, *The Character and Conduct of the Female Sex* (London, 1776), pp. 95-6.

79. Maria Edgeworth, *Letters for Literary Ladies* (London, 1795), p. 7.

80. Anne Katherine Elwood, *Memoirs of the Literary Ladies of England*, 2 vols (London, 1843), vol. 2, p. 153; Wollstonecraft, *Rights of Woman*, p. 121.

Chapter Two

1. John Gregory, *A Father's Legacy to his Daughters* (London, 1774), p. 83.

2. M. Dorothy George, *London Life in the Eighteenth Century* (London: Penguin, 1966), p. 171 (1st edn, 1925).

3. Gregory, *Father's Legacy*, p. 39.

4. Launcelot Light and Laetitia Lookabout, *A Sketch of the Rights of Boys and Girls. Part the First* (London, 1792), p. 62.

5. Pierre Fauchery, *La Destinée féminine dans le roman européen du dix-huitième siècle* (Paris: Armand Colin, 1972), p. 198.

6. Gregory, *Father's Legacy*, pp. 50-1.

7. Priscilla Wakefield, *Reflections on the Present Condition of the Female Sex* (London, 1798), p. 14.

8. Samuel Richardson, *Clarissa*, Everyman edn, vol. 2, p. 383.

9. Archibald Arbuthnot, *Memoirs of the Remarkable Life and Surprizing Adventures of Miss Jenny Cameron* (London, 1746),

p. 42.

10. E.g. *The Polite Academy, or School of Behaviour for Young Gentlemen and Ladies*, 3rd edn (London, 1765).

11. Dangers of stays: Thomas Beddoes, *Hygeia*, 3 vols (Bristol, 1802 – 3), vol. 1 (1802), p. 49; William Cadogan, *An Essay upon Nursing* (London, 1748), p. 12; Catharine Macaulay, *Letters on Education*, (London, 1790), p. 42.

12. John Locke, *The Educational Writings*, ed. James L. Axtell (Cambridge: Cambridge University Press), 1968, pp. 123-4.

13. Reginald Blunt (ed.), *Mrs. Montagu 'Queen of the Blues': Her Letters and Friendships from 1762 to 1800*, 2 vols (London: Constable, 1923), vol. 1, p. 182.

14. Sarah Stone, *A Complete Practice of Midwifery* (London, 1737), pp. 126-31.

15. Josephine Kamm, *Hope Deferred* (London: Methuen, 1965), pp. 126-7.

16. Wakefield, *Reflections*, p. 24.

17. *The Lady's Monthly Museum*, 3 (1799), p. 435.

18. J. Burton, *Lectures on Female Education and Manners*, 2 vols (Rochester and London, 1793), vol. 1, p. 16; John Essex, *The Young Ladies' Conduct* (London, 1722), pp. 36-40.

19. Laetitia-Matilda Hawkins, *The Countess and Gertrude*, 2nd edn, 4 vols (London, 1812), vol. 1, p. 7.

20. Mary Cockle, *Important Studies for the Female Sex* (London, 1809), p. 236.

21. Wetenhall Wilkes, *A Letter of Genteel and Moral Advice to a Young Lady* (Dublin, 1740), p. 81.

22. James Fordyce, *Sermons to Young Women*, 3rd edn, 2 vols (London, 1766), vol. 1, p. 69.

23. Alexander Pope, *Epistle to a Lady*, lines 51-2, in *Epistles to Several Persons*, ed. F.W. Bateson (London: Methuen, and New Haven, Conn.: Yale University Press, 1951) (vol. III.ii of Twickenham edn of *Poems*), p. 53.

24. Edward Ward, *A Compleat and Humorous Account of the Remarkable Clubs and Societies in the Cities of London and Westminster* (London, 1745), pp. 265, 267-8.

25. Fordyce, *Sermons*, vol. 1, pp. 46-7.

26. J. Jean Hecht, *The Domestic Servant Class in Eighteenth-Century England* (London: Routledge and Kegan Paul, 1956), p. 122; Hawkins, *Letters on the Female Mind*, 2 vols (London, 1793), vol. 2, pp. 146-7.

27. George Anne Bellamy, *An Apology for the Life of George Anne Bellamy*, 3rd edn, 6 vols (London, 1785), vol. 3, p. 1; Robert D. Bass, *The Green Dragoon: The Lives of Banastre Tarleton and Mary Robinson* (New York: Henry Holt and Co., 1957), p. 204.

28. Frances Burney, *Evelina*, ed. Edward A. Bloom (London: Oxford University Press, 1968), pp. 193-206.

29. Erasmus Darwin, *A Plan for the Conduct of Female Education in Boarding-Schools* (Derby and London, 1797), pp. 33-7; Fordyce, *Sermons*, vol. 1, pp. 145-50.
30. Clara Reeve discusses this view in *The Progress of Romance*, 2 vols (Colchester and London, 1785), vol. 2, pp. 86-7.
31. Sarah Maese, *The School*, 3 vols (London, 1766), vol. 2, p. 323.
32. Reeve *Progress of Romance*, is the fullest defence of novels.
33. Mary Hays, *Memoirs of Emma Courtney*, 2 vols (London, 1796), vol. 1, p. 26.
34. For a discussion of one of the publishers specialising in romances, see Dorothy Blakey, *The Minerva Press, 1790 – 1820* (London: for the Bibliographical Society at the University Press, Oxford, 1939).
35. George Colman, the elder, *Polly Honeycombe*, 4th edn (London, 1778), p. xii.
36. Mary Wollstonecraft, *Mary: A Fiction*, in *Mary, and The Wrongs of Woman*, ed. James Kinsley and Gary Kelly (Oxford: Oxford University Press, 1976), p. 3.
37. *The Spectator*, ed. Donald Bond, 5 vols (Oxford: Clarendon Press, 1965), vol. 1, no. 37, pp. 152-9.
38. J.-L. Chirol, *An Enquiry into the Best System of Female Education* (London, 1809), pp. 38-40.
39. R.P. Neuman, 'Masturbation, Madness, and the Modern Concepts of Childhood and Adolescence', *Journal of Social History* 8 (3) (1975), pp. 1-27; Robert H. MacDonald, 'The Frightful Consequences of Onanism: Notes on the History of a Delusion', *JHI* 28(3) (1967), pp. 423-31.
40. Essex, *The Young Ladies Conduct*, p. 61.
41. Anne Donnellan to Elizabeth Montagu, April 1740, in Elizabeth Montagu, *Letters*, ed. Matthew Montagu, 3rd edn, 4 vols (London, 1810–13), vol. 1 (1810), p. 105.
42. Thomas Gisborne, *An Enquiry into the Duties of the Female Sex* (London, 1797), p. 168.
43. Terry Castle, 'Eros and Liberty at the English Masquerade, 1710–90', *ECS* 17(2) (1983–84), pp. 156-76; Castle, 'The Carnivalization of Eighteenth-Century English Narrative', *PMLA* 99(5) (1984), pp. 903-16.
44. Elizabeth Carter, *Letters from Mrs. Elizabeth Carter to Mrs. Montagu, between the years 1755 and 1800*, ed. Montagu Pennington, 3 vols (London, 1817), vol. 2, p. 135.
45. Fordyce, *Sermons*, vol. 1, p. 144; Richard Allestree, *The Ladies Calling*, 2nd imp. (Oxford, 1673), Part 2, p. 11.
46. Fordyce, *Sermons*, vol. 1, p. 132.
47. Lady Mary Wortley Montagu, 'The Lady's Resolve', in George Colman and Bonnell Thornton (eds.), *Poems by the Most Eminent Ladies of Great-Britain and Ireland*, 2 vols (London,

1773), vol. 2, p. 178; cf. Jane West, *Letters to a Young Lady*, 2nd edn, 3 vols (London, 1806), vol. 1, p. 238.

48. Fordyce, *Sermons*, vol. 1, p. 86.

49. Elizabeth Montagu, *Letters*, vol. 4, p. 19.

50. Elizabeth Carter felt it was necessary to assure Elizabeth Montagu that she was not harming herself by sewing: Carter, *Letters to Mrs. Montagu*, vol. 1, pp. 132, 143.

51. Sarah, Lady Pennington, *A Mother's Advice to her Absent Daughters*, (London, 1761), pp. 40-1.

52. John Bennett, *Letters to a Young Lady*, 2nd edn, 2 vols (London, 1795), vol. 1, p. xi.

53. Burton, *Lectures*, vol. 1, p. 127; Fordyce, *Sermons*, vol. 1, p. 255; H. Cartwright, *Letters on Female Education* (London, 1787), p. 47.

54. George C. Brauer, Jr, *The Education of a Gentleman* (New York: Bookman Associates, 1959), pp. 74-5.

55. Maria Edgeworth, *Letters for Literary Ladies* (London, 1795), pp. 48-50; Hannah More, *Strictures on the Modern System of Female Education*, 2 vols (London, 1799), vol. 1, pp. 32-3.

56. Darwin, *Female Education in Boarding-Schools*, pp. 115-18.

57. Beddoes, *Hygeia*, vol. 1 (1802), Essay 3, pp. 12-82; Chirol, *Enquiry, passim*.

58. Wollstonecraft, *A Vindication of the Rights of Woman*, 2nd edn (London, 1792), pp. 287-8.

59. The Society for the Suppression of Vice, *Report*, 1825, pp. 29-31, 39. The case in question took place in 1802.

60. Elizabeth Hamilton, *Memoirs of Modern Philosophers*, 3 vols (Bath, 1800), vol. 1, p. 15.

61. Gregory, *Father's Legacy*, p. 70.

62. Hester Chapone, *Letters on the Improvement of the Mind*, 4th edn, 2 vols (London, 1774), vol. 1, p. 140.

63. Burton, *Lectures*, vol. 2, p. 260.

64. Jeremy Taylor, *A Discourse of the Measures and Offices of Friendship* (London, 1657).

65. Henry Mackenzie, *Julia de Roubigné*, 2 vols (London, 1777), vol. 1, p. 58-9.

66. West, *Letters to a Young Lady*, vol. 3, pp. 66-76.

67. Blunt, *Mrs. Montagu*, p. 99.

68. Richardson, *Clarissa*, vol. 3, p. 517.

69. Anna Seward, *Letters*, 6 vols (Edinburgh, 1811), vol. 4, p. 100.

70. Maese, *The School*, vol. 3, p. 23.

71. Anna Seward, *Llangollen Vale* (London, 1796), p. 9.

72. Elizabeth Mavor, *The Ladies of Llangollen* (London: Michael Joseph, 1971), pp. 81-3.

73. William Godwin, *Memoirs of the Author of A Vindication of the*

Rights of Woman, ed. W. Clark Durant (London: Constable, and New York: Greenberg, 1927), pp. 18-19.

74. A relatively benign example is William Hayley, *A Philosophical, Historical and Moral Essay on Old Maids*, 3 vols (London, 1785). John Bennett recommends it to young women: *Letters to a Young Lady*, vol. 2, p. 24.

75. Allestree, *The Ladies Calling*, Part 2, pp. 3-4; cf. Jeremy Taylor, *Holy Living*, in *Works*, ed. Reginald Heber and Charles Page Eden, 10 vols (London, 1854), vol. 3, pp. 56-62; William Law, *A Serious Call to a Devout and Holy Life* (London, 1729), pp. 95-139.

76. Montagu Pennington, *Memoirs of the Life of Mrs. Elizabeth Carter*, 3rd edn, 2 vols (London, 1816), vol. 1, p. 28.

77. Pennington, *Life of Carter*, vol. 1, p. 33.

78. William Duff, *Letters on the Intellectual and Moral Characters of Women* (Aberdeen, 1807), p. 262; Gisborne, *Duties of the Female Sex*, p. 405.

79. Bennett, *Letters to a Young Lady*, vol. 2, pp. 207-8.

80. E.g. Fribble in David Garrick, *Miss in her Teens* (London, 1747); Sophia, *Woman's Superior Excellence over Man* (London, 1740), pp. 35-7.

81. Richardson, *Clarissa*, vol. 1, p. xv.

82. Bennett, *Letters to a Young Lady*, vol. 2, pp. 173-4: West, *Letters to a Young Lady*, vol. 3, p. 103.

83. Sir Frederic Morton Eden, *The State of the Poor*, 3 vols (London, 1797), vol. 1, pp. 625-30.

84. *The Gentleman's Magazine*, 59 (1789), pp. 766-7.

85. Lee Holcombe, *Wives and Property* (Toronto: University of Toronto Press, 1983), p. 30.

86. Sir William Blackstone, *Commentaries on the Laws of England*, 12th edn, 4 vols (London, 1793–95), vol. 1 (1793), pp. 444-5.

87. James Gillray, *The Caricatures of Gillray* (London, 1818), frontispiece.

88. Allestree, *The Ladies Calling*, Part 2, p. 30.

89. Isabella Howard, Countess Dowager of Carlisle, *Thoughts in the Form of Maxims: Addressed to Young Ladies*, 2nd edn (London, 1790), p. 27.

90. *The Gentleman's Magazine*, 30 (1760), pp. 130-1; Hannah More, *Coelebs in Search of a Wife*, 2 vols (London, 1808), vol. 1, pp. 245-64; Daniel Bellamy, *The Young Ladies Miscellany* (London, 1723), pp. 204-7.

91. Jane Collier, *An Essay on the Art of Ingeniously Tormenting* (London, 1753), pp. 107-34; Maria Edgeworth, *Essay on the Noble Science of Self-Justification*, in *Letters for Literary Ladies* (London, 1795); Blunt, *Mrs. Montagu*, vol.1, pp. 265-6.

92. Eugenia, *The Female Advocate* (London, 1700), p. 20.

93. Fordyce, *The Character and Conduct of the Female Sex* (London,

1776), pp. 84-5.

94. Gregory, *Father's Legacy*, p. 88; West, *Letters to a Young Lady*, vol. 3, p. 104.

95. Wollstonecraft, *Thoughts on the Education of Daughters* (London, 1787), pp. 97-8; Wollstonecraft, *Rights of Woman*, p. 56.

96. Duff, *Characters of Women*, p. 188; Gisborne, *Duties of the Female Sex*, p. 254.

97. Cockle, *Important Studies*, p. 188; Keith Thomas, 'The Double Standard', *JHI*, 20(2) (1959), pp. 195-216.

98. Taylor, *Holy Living*, in *Works*, vol. 3, pp. 59-60.

99. Ibid., p. 60; William Nicholls, *The Duty of Inferiours towards their Superiours* (London, 1701), pp. 107-8.

100. Gregory, *Father's Legacy*, p. 125.

101. For full discussion, see Randolph Trumbach, *The Rise of the Egalitarian Family* (New York and London: Academic Press, 1978).

102. *Encyclopédie* (Paris, 1756), art. 'Femme en couche'.

103. Richard Griffith, *The Triumvirate*, 2 vols (London, 1764), vol. 2, p. 68.

104. Trumbach, *Egalitarian Family*, pp. 197-224.

105. Cockle, *Important Studies*, p. 139.

106. Martha Mears, *The Pupil of Nature* (London, 1797), p. 140.

107. Hugh Smith, *Letters to Married Women*, 4th edn (Dublin, 1777), p. 76.

108. Anthony Highmore, *Pietas Londinensis*, 2 vols (London, 1810), vol. 1, pp. 188, 210.

109. More, *Strictures on the Modern System of Female Education*, 2 vols (London, 1799), vol. 1, p. 141.

110. Collier, *Essay*, p. 196.

111. George Otto Trevelyan, *The Early History of Charles James Fox* (New York, 1880), p. 40.

112. Sarah Trimmer, *The Oeconomy of Charity* (London, 1787), pp. 87-98; cf. Wakefield, *Reflections*, p. 83.

113. Highmore, *Pietas Londinensis*, vol. 1, pp. 184-214; Society for Bettering the Condition of the Poor, *Reports*, vol. 2 (London, 1800), pp. 179-86, vol. 4 (London, 1805), pp. 52-7, 193-9.

114. Lawrence Stone, *The Family, Sex, and Marriage in England 1500 -1800* (London: Weidenfeld and Nicholson, 1977), p. 639; Dorothy Marshall, *The English Poor in the Eighteenth Century* (London: George Routledge and Sons Ltd, 1926), pp. 212-13.

115. Ruth K. McClure, *Coram's Children* (New Haven and London: Yale University Press, 1981), p. 30.

116. S. Glasse, *Advice from a Lady of Quality to her Children*, 2 vols (Gloucester, 1778), vol. 1, p. 27.

117. Blackstone, *Commentaries*, vol. 1 (1793), p. 461.

118. Sir George Wheeler, *The Protestant Monastery* (London, 1698),

pp. 39-45.
119. Blackstone, *Commentaries*, vol. 1 (1793), p. 440.
120. Allestree, *The Ladies Calling*, Part 2, p. 73.
121. Mary Ann Radcliffe, *The Memoirs of Mrs. Mary Ann Radcliffe* (Edinburgh, 1810), p. 125.
122. Reeve, *The School for Widows*, 3 vols (London, 1791), vol. 2, p. 61.
123. Law, *Serious Call*, pp. 95-139, anthologised in Anna Laetitia Barbauld, *The Female Speaker* (London, 1811).
124. Wollstonecraft, *Rights of Woman*, pp. 99-106; cf. Reeve, *The School for Widows, passim*.

Chapter Three

1. Pierre Fauchery, *La Destinée féminine dans le roman européen du dix-huitième siècle* (Paris: Armand Colin, 1972), pp. 841-51. For other discussions of the eighteenth-century heroine-centred novel, and of eighteenth-century women novelists, see Marilyn Butler, *Jane Austen and the War of Ideas* (Oxford: Clarendon Press, 1975); Joyce M. Horner, *The English Women Novelists and their Connection with the Feminist Movement (1688–1797)* (Smith College Studies in Modern Languages, XI (1,2,3)) (Northampton, Mass., 1929 –30); B.G. MacCarthy, *The Later Women Novelists 1744–1818* (Cork: Cork University Press and Oxford: Basil Blackwell, 1947); Nancy K. Miller, *The Heroine's Text: Readings in the French and English Novel, 1722–1782* (New York: Columbia University Press, 1980); Philippe Séjourné, *Aspects géneraux du roman féminin en Angleterre de 1740 à 1800*, Publications des Annales de la Faculté des Lettres (Aix-en-Provence, nouvelle série no. 52, 1966); Patricia Meyer Spacks, *Imagining a Self: Autobiography and Novel in Eighteenth-Century England* (Cambridge, Mass. and London: Harvard University Press, 1976), pp. 57-91.
2. George Colman, *Polly Honeycombe*, 4th edn (London, 1778), p. xii.
3. Robert Darnton, 'Readers Respond to Rousseau: The Fabrication of Romantic Sensitivity', in *The Great Cat Massacre and Other Episodes in French Cultural History* (New York: Basic Books, 1984), pp. 215-56.
4. E.g. Lady Mary Wortley Montagu, *Complete Letters*, ed. Robert Halsband, 3 vols (Oxford: Clarendon Press, 1965–67), vol. 3 (1967), p. 8 f.
5. Portia, *The Polite Lady* (London, 1760), p. 200; Jane West, *Letters to a Young Lady*, 2nd edn, 3 vols (London, 1806), vol. 1, p. 123; William Paley, *The Principles of Moral and Political Philosophy* (London, 1785), p. 252.

6. Ronald Paulson, *Hogarth's Graphic Works*, revised edn, 2 vols (New Haven and London: Yale University Press, 1970), vol. 1, p. 144.

7. *Clarissa* was first published in four instalments during 1747–48; this text is now available in the edition of the novel by Angus Ross (London: Penguin, 1985). Richardson made significant additions and changes in the third edition of 1751; other modern editions, including the Everyman, are based on this text. Ross's introduction includes a bibliography of the critical literature on the novel.

8. Margaret Doody, *A Natural Passion: A Study of the Novels of Samuel Richardson* (Oxford: Clarendon Press, 1974), p. 130.

9. Richardson, *Clarissa*, Everyman edn, vol. 1, p. xiv (not in 1st edn). Subsequent references will be incorporated into the text; unless otherwise stated, there are no significant differences between editions in the passages quoted.

10. Theodric Romeyn Beck, *Element of Medical Jurisprudence*, 2nd edn (London, 1825), pp. 57-8.

11. E.H. East, *A Treatise of the Pleas of the Crown*, 2 vols (London, 1803), vol. 1, p. 445, treats this as a view which has only recently been disproved; cf. Beck, *Medical Jurisprudence*, p. 70, William A. Guy, *Principles of Forensic Medicine* (London, 1844), p. 64, and *A Treatise of Feme Coverts* (London, 1732), p. 48. For general discussion of eighteenth-century beliefs about conception, see Elizabeth B. Gasking, *Investigations into Generation 1651–1828* (Baltimore: The Johns Hopkins University Press, and London: Hutchinson, 1967).

12. Elizabeth Carter, *A Series of Letters between Mrs. Elizabeth Carter and Miss Catherine Talbot, from the year 1741 to 1770*, ed. Montagu Pennington, 4 vols (London, 1809), vol. 1, p. 315; Elizabeth Montagu, *Letters*, ed. Matthew Montagu, 3rd edn, 4 vols (London, 1810–13), vol. 3 (1813), pp. 100-1. Carter's judgement was written with only the first four volumes available, and internal evidence suggests Montagu's undated letter was too.

13. Lady Mary Wortley Montagu, *Complete Letters*, ed. Robert Halsband, 3 vols (Oxford: Clarendon Press, 1965–67), vol. 3 (1967), p. 9.

14. *Critical Review*, 12 (September 1761), p. 204.

15. Lady Mary Wortley Montagu, *Complete Letters*, vol. 3, p. 96.

16. G. Birkbeck Hill, *Johnsonian Miscellanies*, 2 vols (Oxford, 1897), vol. 1, p. 297.

17. Catharine Macaulay, *Letters on Education* (London, 1790), p. 146.

18. John Bennett, *Letters to a Young Lady*, 2nd edn, 2 vols (London, 1795), vol. 2, p. 102.

19. Sarah Fielding, *Remarks on Clarissa* (London, 1749),

pp. 13-14, 41.

20. George Colman, *Polly Honeycombe*, 4th edn (London, 1778), p. 13, 20; Elizabeth Hamilton, *Memoirs of Modern Philosophers*, 3 vols (Bath, 1800), vol. 2, p. 265.

21 Lady Mary Wortley Montagu, *Complete Letters*, vol. 3 (1967), p.96.

22. Sarah Maese, *The School*, 3 vols (London, 1766), vol. 1, p. 209.

23. *The Gentleman's Magazine*, 19 (1749), p. 346.

24. Carter, *Letters between Carter and Talbot*, vol. 1, p. 243.

25. William Merritt Sale, Jr, *Samuel Richardson: A Bibliographical Record of his Literary Career* (New Haven: Yale University Press, and London: Oxford University Press, 1936), pp. 96-7.

26. Elizabeth Montagu, *Letters*, vol. 3, p. 134; Clara Reeve, *The Progress of Romance*, 2 vols (Colchester and London, 1785), vol. 1, p. 137.

27. Mary Hays, *Letters and Essays* (London, 1793), p. 95.

28. Samuel Richardson, *Correspondence*, ed. Anna Laetitia Barbauld, 6 vols (London, 1804), vol. 1, p. xcix.

29. Jean-Jacques Rousseau, *Julie, ou la nouvelle Héloïse*, was first published in 1761; an English translation, by William Kenrick, appeared in the same year. There are modern editions of the French text by René Pomeau (Paris: Garnier, 1960, and Bernard Guyon, Paris: Gallimard, 1961).

30. Rousseau, *Julie, Préface*. Subsequent references to the novel are by part and letter number, and are incorporated into the text.

31. Anna Seward, *Poetical Works: with extracts from her literary correspondence*, 3 vols (Edinburgh, 1810), vol. 1, p. xlviii.

32. Lester G. Crocker, 'Julie ou la nouvelle duplicité', *Annales de la société Jean-Jacques Rousseau*, 36 (1963 – 65), pp. 105-52.

33. Seward, *Poetical Works*, vol. 1, p. lxiv-v.

34. Seward, *Letters*, 6 vols (Edinburgh and London, 1811), vol. 1, pp. 15-16; cf. Rousseau, *La nouvelle Héloïse*, ed. Daniel Mornet (Paris: Hachette, 1925), 4 vols, vol. 1, p. 265.

35. James H. Warner, 'Eighteenth-Century English reactions to the *Nouvelle Héloïse*', *PMLA*, 52 (1937), pp. 803-19.

36. Carter, *Letters from Mrs. Elizabeth Carter to Mrs. Montagu*, ed. Montagu Pennington, 3 vols (London, 1817), vol. 2, p. 330.

37. Reginald Blunt (ed.), *Mrs Montagu 'Queen of the Blues'*, 2 vols (London: Constable, 1923), vol. 1, p. 15.

38. *Critical Review*, 12 (September 1761), p. 205.

39. Mary Hays, *Memoirs of Emma Courtney*, 2 vols (London, 1796), vol. 1, p. 41; Amelia Opie, *Adeline Mowbray*, 2 vols, 1st US edn (Georgetown, 1808), vol. 1, pp. 95-6.

40. Edmund Burke, *A Letter from Mr. Burke to a Member of the National Assembly* (Paris and London, 1791), pp. 31-44.

41. Ibid., pp. 39-40.

42. Reeve, *Progress of Romance*, vol. 2, pp. 17-18; cf. Jane West, *Letters to a Young Man*, 3 vols (London, 1801), vol. 3, p. 188.
43. Bennett, *Letters to a Young Lady*, vol. 2, p. 182.
44. Hannah More, *Coelebs in Search of a Wife*, 2 vols (London, 1808), vol. 1, pp. 245-64.
45. E.g. Hamilton, *Memoirs of Modern Philosophers*; George Walker, *The Vagabond*, 2 vols (London, 1799).
46. Reeve, *The School for Widows*, 3 vols (London, 1791), vol. 2, p. 134.
47. West, *Letters to a Young Man*, vol. 3, p. 193.
48. T.C. Duncan Eaves and Ben D. Kimpel, *Samuel Richardson: A Biography* (Oxford: Clarendon Press, 1971), p. 287.
49. William Godwin, *Memoirs of the Author of a Vindication of the Rights of Woman*, ed. W. Clark Durant (London: Constable: and New York: Greenberg, 1927), pp. 112-23.
50. See Warner, 'English reactions to the *Nouvelle Héloïse*'.
51. Hays, *Emma Courtney*, vol. 1, p. 113.
52. Jean-Jacques Rousseau, *Émile*, ed. Charles Wirz and Pierre Burgelin (Paris: Bibliothèque de la Pléiade, 1969), p. 864; Rousseau, *Julie*, 6.11 and 6.13.
53. Fauchery, *Destinée féminine*, p. 70.
54. Henry Mackenzie, *Julia de Roubigné*, 2 vols (London, 1777).
55. Helen Maria Williams, *Julia*, 2 vols (London, 1790).
56. Thomas Holcroft, *Anna St Ives*, ed. Peter Faulkner (London: Oxford University Press, 1970). Page references in the text are to Faulkner's edition.
57. Rousseau, *Émile*, pp. 753-4.
58. Richardson, *Correspondence*, ed. Barbauld, vol. 1, p. lxxxvii.
59. Eaves and Kimpel, *Samuel Richardson*, pp. 463-5.
60. Rousseau, *Émile*, p. 694.

Chapter Four

1. François Poulain de la Barre, *De l'excellence des hommes contre l'égalité des deux sexes* (Paris, 1675), pp. 76-7; for discussion, see Michael A. Seidel, 'Poulain de la Barre's *The Woman as Good as the Man*', *JHI*, 35(3) (1974), pp. 499-508.
2. See David Foxon, *Libertine Literature in England 1660-1745* (London), reprinted from *The Book Collector* (1964); Dudley W.R. Bahlman, *The Moral Revolution of 1688* (London and New Haven: Yale University Press, 1957).
3. Edward Stephens, *A Christian Admonition to the Grecians* (London, 1701), p. 2; Alan Bray, *Homosexuality in Renaissance England* (London: Gay Men's Press, 1982), pp. 81-114.
4. William C. Braithwaite, *The Beginnings of Quakerism*, 2nd edn (Cambridge. Cambridge University Press, 1955), pp. 340-1;

Braithwaite, *The Second Period of Quakerism*, 2nd edn (Cambridge: Cambridge University Press, 1955), pp. 269-89; Arnold Lloyd, *Quaker Social History 1669–1738* (London: Longmans, Green and Co., 1951), pp. 107-20.

5. See Philip Webster Souers, *The Matchless Orinda* (Cambridge: Harvard University Press, 1931).

6. Robert Gould, *Works*, 2 vols (London, 1709), vol. 1, p. 101.

7. Compare *An Essay in Defence of the Female Sex* (London, 1696), p. 56; and Timothy Rogers, *The Character of a Good Woman* (London, 1697), sig. d2.

8. Felicity A. Nussbaum, *The Brink of All We Hate* (Lexington: University Press of Kentucky, 1984), pp. 8-42.

9. Richard Ames, *Sylvia's Revenge* (London, 1688), p. 21.

10. William Fleetwood, *The Relative Duties of Parents and Children, Husbands and Wives, Masters and Servants* (London, 1705), pp. 184-9; William Nicholls, *The Duty of Inferiours towards their Superiours* (London, 1701), pp. 98, 109-11.

11. Jeremy Collier, *A Short View of the Immorality and Profaneness of the English Stage*, 3rd edn (London, 1698), p. 83.

12. E.A. Wrigley and R.S. Schofield, *The Population History of England 1541–1871* (London: Edward Arnold, 1981), pp. 257-65.

13. Lawrence Stone, *The Family, Sex and Marriage in England 1500–1800* (London: Weidenfeld and Nicolson, 1977), p. 330; Stone, *The Crisis of the Aristocracy 1558–1641* (Oxford: Clarendon Press, 1965), pp. 637-45.

14. Natalie Zemon Davis, 'Women on Top', in Davis, *Society and Culture in Early Modern France* (London: Duckworth, and Stanford: Stanford University Press, 1975), pp. 124-51 (in Stanford edn).

15. See J.P. Kenyon, *Revolution Principles: The Politics of Party 1689–1720* (Cambridge: Cambridge University Press, 1977).

16. William Sherlock, *The Case of the Allegiance due to Soveraign Powers*, 3rd edn (London, 1691), pp. 20-1.

17. Mary, Lady Chudleigh, *The Ladies Defence* (London, 1701), Preface to the Reader, not paginated, and p. 3; Shirley Strum Kenny, 'Marriage in English Comedy 1690–1720', *South Atlantic Quarterly*, 78(1) (1979), pp. 84-106, 95.

18. See Gordon J. Schochet, *Patriarchalism in Political Thought* (Oxford: Basil Blackwell, 1975).

19. John Locke, *Two Treatises of Government*, ed. Peter Laslett, 2nd edn (Cambridge: Cambridge University Press, 1967), pp. 191-2.

20. Locke, *The Educational Writings*, ed. James L. Axtell (Cambridge: Cambridge University Press, 1968), pp. 5, 8, 117.

21. Nicholls, *Duty of Inferiours*, pp. 87-90; Fleetwood, *Relative Duties*, pp. 168-70.

22. Fleetwood, *Relative Duties*, p. 169.
23. John Sprint, *The Bride-Woman's Counsellor* (London, 1699).
24. *Conjugal Duty: set forth in a Collection of Ingenious and Delightful Wedding-Sermons*, 2 vols (London, 1732).
25. Eugenia, *The Female Advocate* (London, 1700), p. iii. There is an earlier edition of this work, without the preface: *The Female Preacher*, London, 1699.
26. Ibid., p. vi, 28.
27. Ibid., p. vii, 7.
28. Ibid., p. 20.
29. Ibid., p. 26.
30. Sprint, *Bride-Woman's Counsellor*, p. 11; Eugenia, *The Female Advocate*, p. 40.
31. Sprint, *The Bride-Woman's Counsellor*, p. 13; Eugenia, *The Female Advocate*, p. 43.
32. Mary, Lady Chudleigh, *The Ladies Defence* (London, 1701).
33. Ibid., Epistle Dedicatory, not paginated.
34. Ibid., Preface to the Reader, not paginated.
35. Ibid., p. 16.
36. Ibid., p. 18.
37. Chudleigh, *Essays upon several subjects in Prose and Verse* (London, 1710), To the Reader, not paginated.
38. Chudleigh, *Poems on Several Occasions*, 2nd edn (London, 1713), p. 40.
39. Mary Astell, *Some Reflections upon Marriage, occasion'd by the Duke and Dutchess Mazarine's Case*, 3rd edn (London, 1706), Preface, not paginated. The definitive work on Astell is now Ruth Perry, *The Celebrated Mary Astell: An Early English Feminist* (Chicago and London: University of Chicago Press, 1986), which reached me too late to be used in writing this chapter.
40. Claude Érard and C. Marguetel de Saint-Denis, Seigneur de Saint-Évremond, *The Arguments of Monsieur Erard, for Monsieur the Duke of Mazarin . . . And the Factum for Madam the Dutchess of Mazarin . . . by Monsieur de St. Evremont* (London, 1699).
41. C.H. Hartmann, *The Vagabond Duchess* (London: G. Routledge and Sons, 1926).
42. Saint-Évremond, *Factum*, pp. 148-9.
43. Sir John Vanbrugh, *The Provok'd Wife*, in *Complete Works*, ed. Geoffrey Webb and Bonamy Dobrée, 4 vols (London: Nonesuch Press, 1927–28), vol. 1 (ed. Dobrée, 1927), p. 116.
44. Astell, *The Christian Religion, as Profess'd by a Daughter of the Church of England* (London, 1705), pp. 133, 304-7.
45. Astell, *Reflections*, 1st edn (London, 1700), pp. 66-7.
46. Ibid., p. 63. This looks like an answer to Chudleigh; *The Ladies Defence* was not printed till 1701, but Astell may have had

access to Chudleigh's manuscript. Both women knew John Norris, and he could have informed them about each other's work; see Richard Acworth, *The Philosophy of John Norris of Bemerton (1657 – 1712)* (Hildesheim and New York: Georg Olms Verlag, 1979), p. 10.

47. Astell, *Reflections* (1706), Preface, sig. A2; she refers to William Whiston, *A New Theory of the Earth* (London, 1696), p. 170.
48. Astell, *Reflections* (1706), Preface, sig. A2.
49. Nicholls, *Duty of Inferiours*, pp. 87-90; Fleetwood, *Relative Duties*, pp. 168-70.
50. Astell, *Reflections* (1700), pp. 91, 15.
51. Astell, *An Impartial Inquiry into the Causes of Rebellion and Civil War in this Kingdom* (London, 1704), pp. 59-60.
52. Ruth Perry, 'A seventeenth-century feminist poet', *TLS* (20 August 1982), p. 911.
53. Florence M. Smith, *Mary Astell* (New York: Columbia University Press, 1916), p. 117.
54. Astell, *Impartial Enquiry*; Astell, *A Fair Way with the Dissenters and their Patrons* (London, 1704); Astell, *Moderation truly Stated* (London, 1704).
55. For Astell's praise of Lady Catherine, see Astell, *Christian Religion*, p. 3; Astell and John Norris, *Letters Concerning the Love of GOD* (London, 1695), Dedication and Preface, not paginated.
56. Smith, *Mary Astell*, pp. 7, 32.
57. Astell, *Reflections* (1700), pp. 40-1; Astell, *A Serious Proposal to the Ladies* (London, 1694), p. 158.
58. Ibid., pp. 77-8.
59. Ibid., pp. 85-6.
60. George Ballard, *Memoirs of Several Ladies of Great Britain* (Oxford, 1752), p. 446.
61. Astell, *A Serious Proposal to the Ladies*, Part II (London, 1697), Dedication, not paginated; and Astell, *Christian Religion*, pp. 142-3.
62. Astell, *Serious Proposal*, pp. 160-1.
63. Charlotte Fell-Smith, *Mary Rich, Countess of Warwick* (London: Longmans, Green and Co., 1901), pp. 315-16.
64. Reginald Blunt (ed.), *Mrs Montagu 'Queen of the Blues'*, 2 vols (London: Constable, 1923), vol. 2, p. 126; Edward Chamberlayne, *An Academy or Colledge* (London, 1671), p.3.
65. John Duncon, *The Returns of Spiritual Comfort and Grief in a Devout Soul* (London, 1649), p. 196.
66. Richard Allestree, *The Ladies Calling*, 2nd imp. (Oxford, 1673), Part II, p. 3. Cf. *The Whole Duty of a Woman* (London, 1700), p. 38; *The Whole Duty of a Woman* (London, 1737) pp. 69-70 ; Mary Wray (ed.), *The Ladies Library*, 3 vols (London, 1714), vol. 2, p. 26.

67. Chamberlayne, *An Academy or Colledge*, pp. 5-7; Chamberlayne, *England's Wants* (London, 1667), pp. 8-9.
68. Sir George Wheeler, *The Protestant Monastery* (London, 1698), pp. 14-18; Daniel Defoe, *An Essay upon Projects* (London, 1697), pp. 285-93.
69. Wheeler, *Protestant Monastery*, p. 13.
70. Astell, *A Serious Proposal to the Ladies, Part II* (London, 1697).
71. Ibid., p. 119; *Logic; or, the Art of Thinking* (London, 1685), a translation of Antoine Arnauld and Pierre Nicole, *L'art de penser. La logique de Port-Royal* (Paris, 1662). For discussion of the *Port-Royal Logic* in England, see Wilbur Samuel Howell, *Logic and Rhetoric in England 1500–1700* (Princeton, NJ; Princeton University Press, 1956), pp. 350-63.
72. *Art of Thinking*, Preface, not paginated.
73. Astell, *Serious Proposal, Part II*, pp. 30-1.
74. Ibid., pp. 164, 175, 180.
75. On Norris, see Acworth, *The Philosophy of John Norris*.
76. Astell and Norris, *Letters Concerning the Love of GOD* (London, 1695).
77. Damaris, Lady Masham, *A Discourse concerning the Love of God* (London, 1696).
78. Locke, *Educational Writings*, ed. Axtell, p. 288.
79. Elizabeth Thomas, *The Honourable Lovers: Or, the Second and Last Volume of Pylades and Corinna* (London, 1732), pp. 202-5.
80. Astell, *Serious Proposal*, p. 78, quoting William Wotton, *Reflections upon Ancient and Modern Learning* (London, 1694), pp. 349-50.
81. François Salignac de la Mothe Fénelon, *Instructions for the education of a daughter*, trans. George Hickes (London, 1707).
82. Elizabeth Elstob,*An English-Saxon Homily on the Birth-Day of St. Gregory* (London, 1709), p. vii.
83. Elstob, *The Rudiments of Grammar for the English-Saxon Tongue* (London, 1715), p. ii.
84. Elstob, *English-Saxon Homily*, pp. iii-iv.
85. Elstob, *Rudiments*, pp. xxxiii-iv.
86. Elstob, *English-Saxon Homily*, pp. iii-iv; Astell, Preface (written 1724), to Lady Mary Wortley Montagu, *Letters*, 3 vols (London, 1763), vol 1, pp. x-xi.
87. George A. Aitken, 'Steele's "Ladies' Library"', *The Athenaeum* (5 July 1884), pp. 16-17.
88. *The Tatler*, 32.

Chapter Five

1. John Locke, *The Educational Writings*, ed. James L. Axtell (Cambridge: Cambridge University Press, 1968), p. 117;

Pierre Burgelin, 'L' éducation de Sophie', *Annales de la société Jean-Jacques Rousseau*, 35 (1959–62), pp. 113-30.

2. Mary Wollstonecraft, *A Vindication of the Rights of Woman*, 2nd edn (London, 1792), pp. 170-206.

3. M.G. Jones, *The Charity School Movement: A Study of Eighteenth-Century Puritanism in Action* (Hamden, Conn.: Archon Books, 1964), p. 5 (reprint of Cambridge: Cambridge University Press, 1938).

4. John Bennett, *Letters to a Young Lady*, 2nd edn, 2 vols (London, 1795), vol. 1, p. 200 (1st edn, Warrington, 1789).

5. Catherine Trotter Cockburn, *A Defence of the 'Essay of Human Understanding', written by Mr Lock*, (London, 1702).

6. Bennett, *Letters to a Young Lady*, vol. 1, p. 168; Hannah More, *Strictures on the Modern System of Female Education*, 2 vols (London, 1799), vol. 1, p. 164.

7. Charlotte Charke, *A Narrative of the Life of Mrs. Charlotte Charke* (London, 1755), p.26.

8. Wetenhall Wilkes, *A Letter of Genteel and Moral Advice to a Young Lady* (Dublin, 1740), p. 102; Sarah Maese, *The School*, 3 vols (London, 1766), vol. 1, p. 190; cf. Susie I. Tucker, *Protean Shape: A Study in Eighteenth-Century Vocabulary and Usage* (London: The Athlone Press, 1967), pp. 78-80.

9. Samuel Richardson, *Correspondence*, ed. Anna Laetitia Barbauld, 6 vols (London, 1804), vol. 1, pp. clxiii-iv.

10. More, *Strictures*, vol. 1, p. 172.

11. George Ballard, *Memoirs of Several Ladies of Great Britain*, ed. Ruth Perry (Detroit: Wayne State University Press, 1985), p. 25; Montagu Pennington, *Memoirs of the Life of Mrs. Elizabeth Carter*, 3rd edn, 2 vols (London, 1816), vol. 1, p. 443; cf. pp. 447-8.

12. George Colman and Bonnell Thornton (eds.), *Poems by the Most Eminent Ladies of Great Britain and Ireland*, 2 vols (London, 1773), vol. 1, p. 236.

13. Mary Scott, *The Female Advocate* (London, 1774), pp. 14-15.

14. Ibid., p.vi.

15. Ibid., p. viii.

16. Mary Hays, *Female Biography*, 6 vols (London, 1803), vol. 1, p. iv; cf. Maese, *The School*, vol. 3, p. 83.

17. Bennett, *Strictures on Female Education* (London, 1788), p. 102.

18. J. Burton, *Lectures on Female Education and Manners*, 2 vols (Rochester and London, 1793), vol. 1, pp. 185-6; Thomas Gisborne, *An Enquiry into the Duties of the Female Sex* (London, 1797), pp. 10-11.

19. Wollstonecraft, *Rights of Woman*, pp. 168-9.

20. Ibid., p. 112.

21. Philautus, *The Pretty Gentleman: or, Softness of Manners Vindicated from the false Ridicule Exhibited under the Character of*

William Fribble, Esq. (London, 1747), pp. 15-16.

22. More, *Coelebs in Search of a Wife*, 2 vols (London, 1808), vol. 1, p. 23.
23. John Moir, *Female Tuition* (London, 1784), pp. 295, 299, 306; *European Magazine*, 33 (1798), p. 247.
24. Alexander Jardine, *Letters from Barbary*, 2 vols (London, 1788), vol. 1, p. 312.
25. A Lady, *The Unhappy Wife*, 2 vols (London, 1770), vol. 1, p. 50.
26. Wollstonecraft, *Rights of Woman*, p. 235, making fun of Wilkes, *Genteel and Moral Advice*, p. 126.
27. Jardine, *Letters from Barbary*, vol. 2, p. 495.
28. Catharine Macaulay, *Letters on Education* (London, 1790), p. 203.
29. Hays, undated letter to William Godwin, perhaps January 1796, ms. MH 24, The Carl H. Pforzheimer Library, New York. Quoted by permission of the Carl H. Pforzheimer Library. Cf. Hays, *Memoirs of Emma Courtney*, 2 vols (London, 1796), vol. 2, pp. 16, 53.
30. Jardine, *Letters from Barbary*, vol. 1, p. 324.
31. Burton, *Lectures on Female Education*, vol. 1, p. 28; Hays, *Letters and Essays, Moral, and Miscellaneous* (London, 1793), pp. 21-2; S. Hatfield, *Letters on the Importance of the Female Sex* (London, 1803), p. 52; Jane West, *Letters to a Young Lady*, 2nd edn, 3 vols (London, 1806), vol. 1, p. 160.
32. Philip Dormer Stanhope, 4th Earl of Chesterfield, *Letters to his Son*, 2 vols (London, 1774), vol. 2, p. 330; Macaulay, *Letters on Education*, p. 209.
33. Hays, *Appeal to the Men of Great Britain in behalf of women* (London, 1798), p. 97.
34. Hays, *Emma Courtney*, vol. 2, pp. 43-4.
35. Maese, *The School*, vol. 3, p. 142.
36. Isabella Howard, Countess Dowager of Carlisle, *Thoughts in the Form of Maxims*, 2nd edn (London, 1790), pp. 123, 128.
37. *Old England to Her Daughters: Address to the Females of Great Britain*, quoted from Frank J. Klingberg and Sigurd B. Hustvedt (eds.), *The Warning Drum: The British Home Front Faces Napoleon: Broadsides of 1803* (Berkeley and Los Angeles: University of California PRess, 1944), p. 78.
38. Hays, *Female Biography*, vol. 3, p. 317.
39. Elizabeth Montagu, *Letters*, ed. Matthew Montagu, 3rd edn, 4 vols (London, 1810–13), vol. 1 (1810), pp. 6-7.
40. Bathsua Makin, *An Essay to Revive the Ancient Education of Gentlewomen* (London, 1673).
41. Elizabeth Montagu, *Letters*, vol. 2 (1810), pp. 55, 59, 65.
42. Elizabeth Montagu, *Letters*, vol. 2, pp. 282-3.
43. Sarah Scott, *A Description of Millennium Hall*, ed. Walter M. Crittenden (New York: Bookman Associates, 1955), p. 10 (1st

edn, 1762).

44. Reginald Blunt (ed.), *Mrs. Montagu 'Queen of the Blues'*, 2 vols (London: Constable, 1923), vol. 2, p. 304. On Opie, see Margaret Eliot MacGregor, *Amelia Alderson Opie: Worldling and Friend* (Northampton, Mass, 1933) (Smith College Studies in Modern Languages, vol. 14, nos 1–2 (October 1932–January 1933).

Chapter Six

1. A Lady, *Female Rights Vindicated; or the Equality of the Sexes Morally and Physically Proved* (London, 1758), p. 43.

2. François Poulain de la Barre, *De l'égalité des deux sexes* (Paris, 1673) (translation: *The Woman as Good as the Man*, London, 1677); *De l'excellence des hommes contre l'égalité des sexes* (Paris, 1675); *Dissertation ou discours, pour servir de troisième partie au livre de l'égalité des deux sexes* (Paris, 1690); for discussion, see Michael A. Seidel, 'Poulain de la Barre's *The Woman as Good as the Man*', *JHI*, 35 (1974), pp. 499-508.

3. Sophia, *Woman not Inferior to Man* (London, 1739); A Gentleman, *Man Superior to Woman: or, a Vindication of Man's Natural Right of sovereign Authority over the Woman* (London, 1739); Sophia, *Woman's Superior Excellence over Man* (London, 1740); the trilogy reprinted in 1751, under the title *Beauty's Triumph*, and in 1780 under the title *Female Restoration*. A Lady, *Female Rights Vindicated*, uses some material from Sophia.

4. Sophia, *Woman not Inferior to Man*, pp. 36-7.

5. John Bennett, *Letters to a Young Lady*, 2nd edn, 2 vols (London, 1795), vol. 1, pp. 168-9.

6. Richard Allestree, *The Gentleman's Calling* (London, 1660), p. 31.

7. Sophia, *Woman's Superior Excellence*, p.37.

8. James Fordyce, *Sermons to Young Women*, 3rd edn, 2 vols. (London, 1766), vol. 2, p. 163.

9. Mary Wollstonecraft, *A Vindication of the Rights of Woman*, 2nd edn (London, 1792), p. 211.

10. Hester Lynch Thrale, *Thraliana*, ed. Katharine C. Balderston, 2 vols (Oxford: At the Clarendon Press, 1942), vol. 1, p. 547.

11. Wollstonecraft, *Rights of Woman*, p. 313.

12. Helen Maria Williams, *A Residence in France during the Years 1792, 1793, 1794 and 1795; described in a series of letters from an English Lady*, 3rd edn, 2 vols (London, 1797), vol. 1, pp. 270, 271-2.

13. Hannah More, *Strictures on the Modern System of Female Education*, 2 vols (London, 1799), vol. 1, p. 118; *Reports of the*

Society for Bettering the Condition of the Poor, vol. 4 (1805), pp. 61-80, 181-92.

14. Martha Mears, *The Pupil of Nature* (London, 1797), p. 69.
15. Sarah Trimmer *The Oeconomy of Charity* (London, 1787), p. 67; Hannah More, *Coelebs in Search of a Wife*, 2 vols (London, 1808), vol. 2, p. 327-8.
16. Ivy Pinchbeck, *Women Workers and the Industrial Revolution 1750–1850* (London: Routledge, 1930); R. Campbell, *The London Tradesman* (London, 1747), pp. 152, 208, 257, 258.
17. *The Histories of Some of the Penitents in the Magdalen-House*, 2 vols (London, 1760); Samuel Richardson, *Clarissa*, Everyman edn, 4, pp. 536-47; *The Times*, 31 December 1785; *The Gentleman's Magazine*, 2 (1732), pp. 709-10.
18. Campbell, *London Tradesman*, p. 209.
19. Saunders Welch, *A Proposal to render effective a Plan, to remove the Nuisance of Common Prostitutes from the Streets of this Metropolis* (London, 1758), p. 4.
20. John Moir, *Female Tuition* (London, 1784), p. 250.
21. E.g. *The Life and Adventures of Mrs. Christian Davies, The British Amazon* (London, 1740); *The Female Soldier; or the surprising Life and Adventures of Hannah Snell* (London, 1750).
22. Dianne Dugaw, 'Balladry's Female Warriors: Women, Warfare and Disguise in the Eighteenth Century', *Eighteenth-Century Life*, 9 (2) n.s. (1985), pp. 1-20, 8.
23. *The Annual Register* (1766), p.144; cf. p. 116.
24. More, *Strictures*, vol. 2, p. 28.
25. Mary Ann Radcliffe, *The Female Advocate*, (pp. 393-471 in *The Memoirs of Mrs. Mary Ann Radcliffe*, Edinburgh, 1810), p. 469 (1st edn of *The Female Advocate*, 1799). Cf. Clara Reeve, *Plans of Education* (London, 1792), p. 79.
26. Wylie Sypher, *Guinea's Captive Kings: British Anti-Slavery Literature of the XVIIIth Century* (Chapel Hill: University of North Carolina Press, 1942), p. 169; David Brion Davis, *The Problem of Slavery in Western Culture* (Ithaca NY: Cornell University Press, 1966), p. 357.
27. Mary Robinson, *Poetical Works*, 3 vols (London, 1806), vol. 2, pp. 170-5; Robert D. Bass, *The Green Dragoon: The Lives of Banastre Tarleton and Mary Robinson* (New York: Henry Holt and Co., 1957), pp. 381, 398.
28. *A Treatise of Feme Coverts: or, the Lady's Law* (London, 1732), p. 52. *The Laws respecting Women* (London, 1777), devotes a good deal of space to the recent trial for bigamy of the Duchess of Kingston.
29. Courtney Stanhope Kenny, *The History of the Law of England as to the Effects of Marriage on Property and on the Wife's Legal Capacity* (London, 1879), pp. 103-11.
30. Kenny, *Effects of Marriage*, pp. 147-9.

31. *The Hardships of the English Laws in Relation to Wives*, London and Dublin, 1735; extracts in *The Gentleman's Magazine*, 5 (1735).

32. Ibid., p. 50.

33. Ibid., pp. 59-66.

34. Ibid., p. 12; *The Laws respecting Women*, p. 173; Kenny, *Effects of Marriage*, p. 146.

35. Susan Moller Okin, 'Patriarchy and Married Women's Property in England: Questions on Some Current Views,' *ECS*, 17 (2) (1983 – 84), pp. 121-38.

36. William Paley, *The Principles of Moral and Political Philosophy* (London, 1785), pp. 292-3.

37. Thomas Gisborne, *An Enquiry into the Duties of Men in the Higher and Middle Classes of Great Britain* (London, 1794), p. 619.

38. Elizabeth Carter, *Letters from Mrs. Elizabeth Carter to Mrs. Montagu between the years 1755 and 1800*, ed. Montagu Pennington, 3 vols (London, 1817), vol. 2, pp. 16, 201; Thrale, *Thraliana*, vol. 2, p. 868.

39. Thomas Sharp, *The Life of John Sharp, D.D. Lord Archbishop of York*, 2 vols (London, 1825), vol. 2, pp. 281-302.

40. Samuel Richardson, *The History of Sir Charles Grandison*, Shakespeare Head edn, 6 vols (1931), vol. 3, pp. 384-5.

41. Reeve, *Plans of Education*, pp. 130-64; Helena Wells Whitford, *Thoughts and Remarks on Establishing an Institution for the Support and Education of Unportioned Respectable Females* (London, 1809).

42. Radcliffe, *Female Advocate*, p. 442.

43. Susan Staves, 'British Seduced Maidens', *ECS*, 14 (2) (1980 – 81), pp. 109-34.

44. Sir William Blackstone, *Commentaries on the Laws of England*, 12th edn, 4 vols (London, 1793–95), vol. 1 (1793), pp. 444-5, note by Edward Christian.

45. Martin Madan, *Thelyphthora: or, a Treatise on Female Ruin*, 3 vols (London, 1780–81).

46. Madan, *Thelyphthora*, vol. 3 (1781), pp. 321-4.

47. *The Female Protector. Written in the Year 1800*, ms. in the Fawcett Library, London, not paginated.

48. Peter C. Hoffer and N.E.H. Hull, *Murdering Mothers: Infanticide in England and New England 1558–1803* (New York University School of Law Series in Legal History, 2) (New York and London: New York University Press, 1981), pp. 85-6.

49. Blackstone, *Commentaries*, vol. 1 (1793), p. 461.

50. *Hardships of the English Laws*, pp. 18-23.

51. Ivy Pinchbeck and Margaret Hewitt, *Children in English*

Society, 2 vols (London: Routledge and Kegan Paul, and Toronto: University of Toronto Press, 1969–73), vol. 1 (1969), p. 219.

52. James Lawrence, *An Essay on the Nair System of Gallantry and Inheritance* (London, 1800), p. 28.
53. Karl von den Steinen, 'The Discovery of Women in Eighteenth-Century English Political Life,' in Barbara Kanner (ed.), *The Women of England* (London: Mansell, 1980), pp. 229-58 (US edn, Hamden, Conn.: Archon Books, 1979).
54. Catharine Macaulay, *Letters on Education* (London, 1790), p. 215.
55. *The Lady's Choice of a New Standing Member, A New Ballad* (London, 1747); Paley, *Moral and Political Philosophy*, p. 487.
56. *The Gentleman's Magazine*, 58 (1788), pp. 99-101, 222-4.
57. Sir Frederic Morton Eden, *The State of the Poor*, 3 vols (London, 1797), vol. 1, p. 629.
58. Alexander Jardine, *Letters from Barbary*, 2 vols (London, 1788), vol. 1, pp. 331, 345.
59. Wollstonecraft, *Rights of Woman*, pp. 337-8; Pinchbeck, *Women Workers*, pp. 300-5.
60. Mary Hays, *Appeal to the men of Great Britain in behalf of women* (London, 1798), p. 199.
61. *The Female Protector*, not paginated.
62. Mary Robinson, *A Letter to the Women of England, on the Injustice of Mental Subordination* (London, 1799), p. 18-19.
63. Jean-Jacques Rousseau, *Émile*, ed. Charles Wirz and Pierre Burgelin (Paris: Bibliothèque de la Pléiade, 1969), p. 476.
64. Hays, *Appeal*, p. 200; John Bennett, *Letters to a Young Lady*, 2nd edn, 2 vols (London, 1795), vol. 1, p. 240.
65. Priscilla Wakefield, *Reflections on the Present Condition of the Female Sex* (London, 1798), pp. 165-6.
66. Wakefield, *Reflections*, pp. 153-4; *The Times*, 11 March 1795; *Reports of the Society for Bettering The Condition of the Poor*, vol. 4 (1805), pp. 188-9; Gisborne, *An Enquiry into the Duties of the Female Sex* (London, 1797), p. 319.
67. Ruth K. McClure, *Coram's Children: The London Foundling Hospital in the Eighteenth Century* (New Haven and London: Yale University Press, 1981), p. 23.
68. Ford K. Brown, *Fathers of the Victorians: The Age of Wilberforce* (Cambridge: Cambridge University Press, 1961), p. 4.
69. *Reports of the Society for Bettering the Condition of the Poor*, vol. 4 (London, 1805), Appendix, p. 61.
70. For discussion, see Mary Poovey, *The Proper Lady and the Woman Writer: Ideology as Style in the works of Mary Wollstonecraft, Mary Shelley, and Jane Austen* (Chicago: University of Chicago Press, 1984).

Chapter Seven

1. Keith Thomas, 'The Double Standard', *JHI* 20 (2) (1959), pp. 195-216.
2. Jean-Jacques Rousseau, *Émile*, Pléïade edn, p. 698.
3. *Critical Review* (12 September 1761), p. 205; Catharine Macaulay, *Letters on Education* (London, 1790), pp. 212, 222.
4. Mary Hays, *La Victime du préjugé*, 2 vols (Paris, 1799), vol. 2, p. 83; Helena Wells Whitford, *Letters on subjects of importance to the happiness of young females* (London, 1799), pp. 132-48.
5. Archibald Hamilton Rowan, *Autobiography* (Dublin, 1840), p. 253.
6. William Duff, *Letters on the intellectual and moral characters of women* (Aberdeen, 1807), p. 171.
7. James Fordyce, *Sermons to Young Women*, 3rd edn, 2 vols (London, 1766), vol. 1, pp. 46-7, 98, 99; vol. 2, p. 71.
8. Sarah Trimmer, *The Oeconomy of Charity* (London, 1787), p. 40.
9. Whitford, *Thoughts and Remarks on Establishing an Institution, for the Support and Education of Unportioned Respectable Females* (London, 1809), pp. 2, 205-6.
10. Reginald Blunt (ed.), *Mrs Montagu 'Queen of the Blues'*, 2 vols (London: Constable, 1923), vol. 2, p. 64.
11. Elizabeth Carter, *Letters from Mrs. Elizabeth Carter to Mrs. Montagu*, ed. Montagu Pennington, 3 vols (London, 1817), vol. 2, p. 176.
12. William Paley, *Principles of Moral and Political Philosophy*, 3.9, 3.2.
13. John Campbell, *The Lives of the Lord Chancellors*, 5 vols (London, 1845–46), vol. 4 (1846), pp. 667-8.
14. Lady Mary Wortley Montagu, *Complete Letters*, ed. Robert Halsband, 3 vols (Oxford: Clarendon Press, 1965–67), vol. 3 (1967), p. 48; Elizabeth Sarah Villa-Real Gooch, *The Life of Mrs. Gooch, written by herself*, 3 vols (London, 1792), vol. 3, p. 139.
15. Martin Madan, *Thelyphthora; or, a Treatise on Female Ruin*, 3 vols (London, 1780–81); the British Library catalogue lists a large number of responses. John Locke, *Two Treatises of Government*, ed. Peter Laslett, 2nd edn (Cambridge: Cambridge University Press, 1967), p. 339 note.
16. See Robert Dingley, *Proposals for establishing a public place of reception for penitent prostitutes* (London, 1758); *The Plan of the Magdalen House for the Reception of Penitent Prostitutes* (London, 1758); H.F.B. Compston, *The Magdalen Hospital: The Story of a Great Charity* (London: SPCK, 1917).
17. The Times, 31 December 1785; Patrick Colquhoun, *A Treatise on the Police of the Metropolis*, 4th edn (London, 1797), p. 421; Anthony Highmore, *Pietas Londinensis*, 2 vols (London, 1810),

vol. 1, p. 237.

18. Saunders Welch, *A Proposal to render effectual a Plan, to remove the Nuisance of Common Prostitutes from the Streets of the Metropolis*, London (1758), p. 6; *The Histories of Some of the Penitents in the Magdalen-House*, 2 vols (London, 1760), vol. 1, pp. xii-xiv; Ford K. Brown, *Fathers of the Victorians: The Age of Wilberforce* (Cambridge: Cambridge University Press, 1961), p. 347.

19. Horace Walpole, *Correspondence*, ed. W.S. Lewis and Ralph S. Brown Jr (New Haven: Yale University Press and London: Oxford University Press), 48 vols (1937–85), vol. 9 (1941), pp. 273-4.

20. Portia, *The Polite Lady* (London, 1760), pp. 197-8.

21. *The Magdalen, or History of the first Penitent received into that charitable asylum* (London, 1780), pp. xvi-xvii; Highmore, *Pietas Londinensis*, vol. 1, p. 217.

22. Blunt, *Mrs. Montagu,*. vol. 1, p. 93.

23. Richard Ames, *Sylvia's Complaint, of her Sexes Unhappiness* (London, 1692), p. 18.

24. Lady Mary Wortley Montagu, *Complete Letters*, vol. 3, p. 98.

25. Fordyce, *Sermons to Young Women*, vol. 1, p. 17.

26. Alexander Pope, *Epistle to a Lady*, in *Poems*, Twickenham edn, III.ii, p. 65.

27. Laetitia Pilkington, *Memoirs*, 3 vols (Dublin, 1748–54), vol. 1 (1748), p. 167.

28. Ann Batten Cristall, *Poetical Sketches* (London, 1795), pp. 156-82.

29. Elizabeth Griffith, *Essays Addressed to Young Married Women* (London, 1782), p. 93.

30. Macaulay, *Letters on Education*, p. 222.

31. Ibid., p. 220.

32. Thomas Beddoes, *Hygeia*, 3 vols (Bristol, 1802 – 3), vol. 1 (1802), p. 63.

33. George Colman and Bonnell Thornton (eds.), *Poems by the Most Eminent Ladies of Great-Britain and Ireland*, 2 vols (London, 1773), vol. 1, pp. 232-3.

34. Mary Hays to William Godwin, 6 February 1796, ms. in the Carl H. Pforzheimer Library, New York. Quoted by permission of the Carl H. Pforzheimer Library.

35. Mary Hays, *Memoirs of Emma Courtney*, 2 vols (London, 1796), vol. 2, p. 108.

36. Mary Hays to William Godwin, 1 March 1796, ms. in the Carl H. Pforzheimer Library, New York. Summarised by permission of the Carl H. Pforzheimer Library.

37. Charles Lloyd, *Edmund Oliver*, 2 vols (Bristol, 1798); Elizabeth Hamilton, *Memoirs of Modern Philosophers*, 3 vols (Bath, 1800).

38. Griffith, *Essays*, pp. 15-16; for fictional sympathy for lovers

married to other people, see e.g. A Lady, *The Unhappy Wife*, 2 vols (London, 1770).

39. Rowan, *Autobiography*, p. 259; William Godwin, *An Enquiry concerning Political Justice*, 2 vols (London, 1793), vol. 2, pp. 850-2.
40. James Lawrence, *The Empire of the Nairs; or, the Rights of Women*, 4 vols (London, 1811), vol. 2, p. 91. For the Nayar of Kerala, Lawrence's inspiration, see David M. Schneider and Kathleen Gough, *Matrilineal Kinship* (Berkeley and Los Angeles: University of California Press, 1961), pp. 298-404.
41. Lawrence, *Empire of the Nairs*, vol. 1, p. vii; Lawrence, *An Essay on the Nair System of Gallantry and Inheritance* (London, 1800), pp. 1, 31-2.
42. Lawrence, *Nair System*, pp. 5-7, 28-9; Lawrence, *Empire of the Nairs*, vol. 2, p. 194.
43. Hays, *Appeal to the men of Great Britain in behalf of women* (London, 1798), p. 174; Macaulay, *Letters on Education*, p. 211.
44. Laetitia-Matilda Hawkins, *Letters on the female mind*, 2 vols (London, 1793), vol. 1 pp. 84-7; cf. the caricature of Wollstonecraft in George Walker, *The Vagabond*, 2 vols (London, 1799).
45. Mary Robinson, *The False Friend*, 4 vols (London, 1799), vol. 2, p. 77.

Chapter Eight

1. Edmund Burke, *Reflections on the Revolution in France* (London, 1790), p. 114.
2. Mary Wollstonecraft, *An Historical and Moral View of the Progress of the French Revolution* (London, 1794), p. 509.
3. Lillian Faderman, *Surpassing the Love of Men* (London: Junction Books, 1982), pp. 42-3; Hester Lynch Thrale, *Thraliana*, ed. Katharine C. Balderston, 2 vols (Oxford: Clarendon Press, 1942), vol. 2, pp. 740, 949.
4. Jane Abray, 'Feminism in the French Revolution', *AHR* 80 (1975), pp. 43-62; Ruth Graham, 'Rousseau's Sexism Revolutionized', in Paul Fritz and Richard Morton (eds.), *Woman in the Eighteenth Century* (Toronto and Sarasota: Samuel Stevens Hakkert and Co., 1976) (Publications of the McMaster University Association for Eighteenth-Century Studies, vol. 4), pp. 127-39; Ruth Graham, 'Loaves and Liberty: Women in the French Revolution', in Renate Bridenthal and Claudia Koonz (eds.), *Becoming Visible: Women in European History*, (Boston: Houghton Mifflin Co., 1977), pp. 236-54.
5. Launcelot Light and Laetitia Lookabout, *A Sketch of the Rights of Boys and Girls. Part the First* (London, 1792); Thomas Taylor,

A Vindication of the Rights of Brutes (London, 1792).

6. Wollstonecraft, *A Vindication of the Rights of Men, in a letter to the Right Honourable Edmund Burke* (London, 1790); for discussion of this work, see James T. Boulton, *The Language of Politics in the Age of Wilkes and Burke* (London: Routledge and Kegan Paul, and Toronto: University of Toronto Press, 1963), pp. 167-76.

7. A Lady, *Female Rights Vindicated* (London, 1758); Thomas Seward, 'The Female Right to Literature', in Robert Dodsley, *A Collection of Poems*, 6 vols (London, 1763), pp. 294-300.

8. Wollstonecraft, *A Vindication of the Rights of Woman*, 2nd edn (London, 1792), pp. iii-xiv.

9. Wollstonecraft, *Rights of Woman*, pp. 335, 320.

10. Ibid., p. 367.

11. Ibid., pp. 423-4, 173-4.

12. R.M. Janes, 'On the Reception of Mary Wollstonecraft's *A Vindication of the Rights of Woman*', *JHI* 39 (2) (April/June 1978), pp. 293-302.

13. Elizabeth Hamilton, *Memoirs of Modern Philosophers*, 3 vols (Bath, 1800), vol. 1, p. 196; cf. Anne Katharine Elwood, *Memoirs of the Literary Ladies of England*, 2 vols (London, 1843), vol. 2, p. 153.

14. Wollstonecraft, *Rights of Woman* (p. 234); cf. her translation of Christian Gotthilf Salzmann's *Moralisches Elementarbuch*, *Elements of Morality for the Use of Children*, 2 vols (London, 1790), vol. 1, pp. xii-xiii; Taylor, *Rights of Brutes*, pp. 81-3. James Lawrence, in *An Essay on the Nair System of Gallantry and Inheritance* (London, 1800), argues that co-educational schools would only be possible in a society which allowed women greater freedom in their choice of sexual partners.

15. Wollstonecraft, *Rights of Woman*, pp. 154-5; cf. William Paley, *The Principles of Moral and Political Philosophy* (London, 1785), pp. 286, 288-9.

16. Wollstonecraft, *Rights of Woman*, pp. 335, 338-9, 426.

17. Ibid., pp. 159-60.

18. Hannah More, *Coelebs in Search of a Wife*, 2 vols (London, 1808), vol. 1, p. vii.

19. Wollstonecraft, *Rights of Woman*, p. 234-5.

20. Ibid., pp. 168-9; cf. Mary Robinson, *A Letter to the Women of England, on the Injustice of Mental Subordination* (London, 1799), p. 71; James Armstrong Neal, *An Essay on the Education and Genius of the Female Sex* (Philadelphia, 1795), p. 17; Theodor Gottlieb von Hippel, *Über die bürgerliche Verbesserung der Weiber* (Frankfurt and Leipzig, 1794), p. 327; Lawrence, *Nair System*, p. 6.

21. Wollstonecraft, *Rights of Woman*, p. 26-7, 42-5; George Walker, *The Vagabond*, 2nd American, from the 4th English edn

(Harrisonburg, 1814), p. 98.

22. Robinson, *Letter to the Women of England*, p. 18; Hamilton, *Memoirs of Modern Philosophers*, vol. 1, p. 257.

23. Laetitia-Matilda Hawkins, *Letters on the female mind, its powers and pursuits*, 2 vols (London, 1793); cf. Helen Maria Williams, *Letters Written in France in the Summer of 1790* (Dublin, 1791).

24. Hawkins, *Letters on the female mind*, vol. 2, p. 197.

25. Ibid., pp. 43-5; vol. 1, p. 34.

26. Ibid., vol. 1, pp. 79-81.

27. Wollstonecraft, *Rights of Woman*, pp. 20, 123-4, 244-5.

28. Hawkins, *Letters on the female mind*, vol. 2, p. 14.

29. Ibid., vol. 1, p. 7.

30. Ibid., p. 29, vol. 2, p. 171; cf. Wollstonecraft, *Rights of Woman*, p. 274.

31. Thomas Gisborne, *An Enquiry into the Duties of the Female Sex* (London, 1797); numerous subsequent editions. *The Female Aegis* (London, 1798), is an abridged version of Gisborne, with a little additional material.

32. Gisborne, *An Enquiry into the Duties of Men in the Higher and Middle Classes of Society in Great Britain* (London, 1794), pp. 13-15.

33. Gisborne, *Duties of Men*, p. 601; Gisborne, *Duties of the Female Sex*, p. 21.

34. Gisborne, *Duties of the Female Sex*, p. 19.

35. Ibid., pp. 361-95, 250, 346.

36. Ibid., pp. 254, 263; John Gregory, *A Father's Legacy to his Daughters* (London, 1774), pp. 88, 31-2; Wollstonecraft, *Rights of Woman*, pp. 283-4, 218-19.

37. Gisborne, *Duties of the Female Sex*, p. 241; cf. *Almeria: or, Parental Advice . . . By a Friend to the Sex*, 2nd edn (London, 1775), p. 32.

38. Gisborne, *Duties of the Female Sex*, pp. 199-200, 222, 91; Wollstonecraft includes a passage by Thomson criticising women fox-hunters in her anthology *The Female Reader* (London, 1789), pp. 332-3.

39. Gisborne, *Duties of the Female Sex*, p. 319.

40. Maria Edgeworth, *Letters for Literary Ladies* (London, 1795), p. 66; for women learning chemistry, cf. Erasmus Darwin, *A Plan for the Conduct of Female Education in Boarding-Schools* (London, 1797), p. 41.

41. Edgeworth, *Letters for Literary Ladies*, pp. 1-43; Hamilton, *Memoirs of Modern Philosophers*, 4th edn, 3 vols (Bath, 1804), vol. 1, p. iii.

42. Elizabeth Ogilvie Benger, *Memoirs of the late Mrs. Elizabeth Hamilton*, 2 vols (London, 1818), pp. 164, 210-11; Marilyn Butler, *Maria Edgeworth: A Literary Biography* (Oxford: Oxford University Press, 1972), pp. 199, 220.

43. Edgeworth, *Letters for Literary Ladies*, pp. 73-4.

44. Butler, *Maria Edgeworth*, p. 149.

45. Edgeworth, *Letters of Julia and Caroline* (London, 1795), p. 3 (bound with *Letters for Literary Ladies*).

46. Ibid., p. 9.

47. Edgeworth, *Essay on the Noble Science of Self-Justification* (London, 1795), pp. 46-7 (bound with *Letters for Literary Ladies*).

48. Hamilton, *Letters addressed to the Daughter of a Nobleman*, 3rd edn, 2 vols (London, 1814), vol. 2, pp. 28-30.

49. Hamilton, *Translation of the Letters of a Hindoo Rajah*, 2 vols (London, 1796), vol. 2, pp. 107-9.

50. Hamilton, *Memoirs of Modern Philosophers*, 1st edn, vol.1, p. 195.

51. Ibid., vol. 2, p. 92.

52. Ibid., vol. 3, pp. 303-25.

53. *The Times*, 11 March 1795.

54. Priscilla Wakefield, *Reflections on the Present Condition of the Female Sex* (London, 1798), pp. 153-4, 164; Wakefield, *Mental Improvement*, 2 vols (London, 1794), vol. 1, pp. 177-80.

55. Wakefield, *Reflections*; cf. Society for Bettering the Condition of the Poor, *Reports*, vol. 2 (London, 1800), pp. 179-86, and vol. 3 (London, 1802), pp. 186-91.

56. Wakefield, *A Family Tour through the British Empire* (London, 1804), p. 27.

57. Wakefield, *Reflections*, pp. 151-2.

58. Ibid., p. 166.

59. Mary Ann Radcliffe, *The Female Advocate*, pp. 393-471 of *The Memoirs of Mrs. Mary Ann Radcliffe* (Edinburgh, 1810), p. 434 (1st edn of *The Female Advocate*, London, 1799).

60. Janes, 'Reception of Wollstonecraft's *Rights of Woman*', p. 302.

61. *The Female Protector: Written in the Year 1800*. MS., not paginated, The Fawcett Library, London.

62. Robert D. Bass, *The Green Dragoon: The Lives of Banastre Tarleton and Mary Robinson* (New York: Henry Holt and Co., 1957); see also Robinson, *Memoirs*, 2 vols (London, 1801).

63. Robinson, *Letter to the Women of England*, p. 10.

64. Ibid., p. 76.

65. Ibid., pp. 62, 88, 5, 71, 74.

66. Ibid., pp. 60-1, 68, 92-3.

67. Ibid., p. 71.

68. Gina M. Luria, *Mary Hays: A Critical Biography*, PhD thesis (New York University, 1972).

69. Wollstonecraft, *Collected Letters*, ed. Ralph M. Wardle (Ithaca, NY and London: Cornell University Press, 1979), pp. 219-20 (12 November 1792), criticising the proposed preface to Mary Hays, *Letters and Essays* (London, 1793).

70. Hays, *La Victime du préjugé*, 2 vols (Paris, 1799), vol. 2, pp. 35-8. I have not had access to the original, *The Victim of Prejudice*, 2 vols (London, 1799). Hays knew and admired Holcroft's *Anna St. Ives;* she quotes it in *Memoirs of Emma Courtney*, 2 vols (London, 1796), vol. 1, p. 163, vol. 2, pp. 58, 84.
71. Hays, *Appeal to the Men of Great Britain in behalf of women* (London, 1798), pp. 31-3, 53, 56.
72. Hays, *Appeal*, p. 91.
73. Ibid., Advertisement to the Reader, not paginated.
74. *The Anti-Jacobin*, 7 (1801), p. 376. The same issue includes a favourable review of her *Appeal*, pp. 150-8.
75. For discussion, see Marilyn Butler, *Jane Austen and the War of Ideas* (Oxford: Clarendon Press, 1975).
76. Elwood, *Literary Ladies of England*, vol. 2, p. 150. The best modern biography of Wollstonecraft is Claire Tomalin, *The Life and Death of Mary Wollstonecraft* (London: Weidenfeld and Nicolson, 1974). For other sources on Wollstonecraft's life and writings, see Janet M. Todd, *Mary Wollstonecraft: An Annotated Bibliography* (New York and London: Garland Publishing, Inc., 1976).
77. William Godwin, *Memoirs of the Author of a Vindication of the Rights of Woman*, ed. W. Clark Durant (London: Constable and New York: Greenberg, 1927); Wollstonecraft, *Posthumous Works*, 4 vols (London, 1798).
78. Ibid., vol. 3, Preface, not paginated.
79. Godwin, *Memoirs*, ed. Durant, p. 73.
80. Wollstonecraft, *Letters written during a short residence in Sweden, Norway, and Denmark* (London, 1796), pp. 187-8.
81. Charles Lloyd, 'Lines to Mary Wollstonecraft Godwin', in Charles Lloyd and Charles Lamb, *Blank Verse* (London, 1798), pp. 64-72; Helena Wells Whitford, *Constantia Neville; or the West Indian*, 3 vols (London, 1800), vol. 2, pp. 38-45.
82. *A Defence of the Character and Conduct of the late Mrs Mary Wollstonecraft Godwin* (London, 1803), pp. 50-1.
83. Richard Polwhele, *The Unsex'd Females* (London, 1798), pp. 29-30.
84. See hostile reviews of Godwin's *Memoirs*, in the *Anti-Jacobin Review*, 1 (July 1798), pp. 94-102; *Monthly Review*, 27 (September–December 1798), pp. 321-4; contrast with the favourable review in *Analytical Review*, 27 (January–June 1798), pp. 235-40. For other attacks on Wollstonecraft and on the biography, see Thomas Mathias, *The Shade of Alexander Pope on the Banks of the Thames* (London, 1799), pp. 44-53; Jane West, *Letters addressed to a Young Man*, 3 vols (London, 1801), vol. 3, pp. 344-5. For further bibliography on the response to Godwin's *Memoirs*, see Durant's edn, pp. 335-47.
85. Hamilton, *Memoirs of Modern Philosophers*, 1st edn, vol. 3, pp.

304, 307, 335; Lloyd, *Edmund Oliver*, 2 vols (Bristol, 1798), vol. 2, p. 172.

86. *The Wrongs of Woman* was first published as vols 1 and 2 of Wollstonecraft's *Posthumous Works*. There is a modern edition by James Kinsley and Gary Kelly (Oxford: Oxford University Press, 1976).
87. *Anti-Jacobin Review*, 1 (July, 1798), p. 92.
88. West, *Letters to a Young Lady*, 2nd edn, 3 vols (London, 1806), vol. 1, pp. 231-2.
89. Lawrence, *The Empire of the Nairs*, 4 vols (London, 1811), vol. 4, p. 48.
90. Walker, *The Vagabond*, p. 99.
91. Sappho Search (i.e. John Black), *A Poetical Review of Miss Hannah More's Strictures on Female Education* (London, 1800), p. 23.
92. Hannah More, *Strictures on the Modern System of Female Education*, 2 vols (London, 1799), vol. 1, pp. 45, 134; Mary Berry, *Extracts from the Journal and Correspondence of Miss Berry*, ed. Lady Theresa Lewis, 2nd edn, 3 vols (London, 1866), vol. 2, pp. 91-2.
93. See M.G. Jones, *Hannah More* (Cambridge: Cambridge University Press, 1952).
94. For discussion of this notion, see Nancy F. Cott, *The Bonds of Womanhood: 'Woman's Sphere' in New England, 1780–1835* (New Haven and London: Yale University Press, 1977).
95. More, *Strictures*, vol. 1, pp. 40-1.
96. West, *Letters to a Young Lady*, vol. 1, pp. 369-70.
97. More, *Strictures*, vol. 2, p. 26.
98. Ibid., pp. 43, 45.
99. West, *Letters to a Young Lady*, vol. 2, p. 361.
100. Sophia, *Woman's Superior Excellence over Man*, (London, 1740), p. 81.
101. Terence J. Spencer, *Fair Greece, Sad Relic: Literary Philhellenism from Shakespeare to Byron* (London: Weidenfeld and Nicolson, 1954), pp. 146-70.
102. More, *Strictures*, vol. 2, pp. 28-9.

Bibliography

Primary Sources

Lucy Aikin, *Epistles on Women* (London, 1810).
William Alexander, M.D., *The History of Women, from the Earliest Antiquity to the Present Time*, 2 vols (London, 1779).
Richard Allestree, *The Gentlemans Calling* (London, 1660).
Richard Allestree, *The Ladies Calling* (Oxford, 1673) 2nd imp.
Almeria: or, Parental Advice . . . By a Friend to the Sex, 2nd edn (London, 1775; 1st edn, 1775).
Richard Ames, *Sylvia's Revenge* (London, 1688).
Richard Ames, *Sylvia's Complaint, of her Sexes Unhappiness* (London, 1692).
The Annual Necrology for 1797–8 (London, 1800).
Archibald Arbuthnot, *Memoirs of the Remarkable Life and Surprizing Adventures of Miss Jenny Cameron* (London, 1746).
Antoine Arnauld and Pierre Nicole, *L'Art de penser. La logique de Port-Royal* (Paris, 1662); trans., *Logic; or, the Art of Thinking* (London, 1685).
Mary Astell, *A Serious Proposal to the Ladies* (London, 1694).
Mary Astell, *A Serious Proposal to the Ladies, Part II* (London, 1697).
Mary Astell, *Some Reflections upon Marriage, occasion'd by the Duke and Dutchess Mazarine's Case . . .* (London, 1700).
Mary Astell, *A Fair Way with the Dissenters and their Patrons* (London, 1704).
Mary Astell, *An Impartial Enquiry into the Causes of Rebellion and Civil War in this Kingdom* (London, 1704).
Mary Astell, *Moderation truly Stated* (London, 1704).
Mary Astell, *The Christian Religion as Profess'd by a Daughter of the Church of England* (London, 1705).

Mary Astell, *Reflections upon Marriage*, 3rd edn (London, 1706).

Mary Astell and John Norris, *Letters Concerning the Love of GOD* (London, 1695).

Robert Bage, *Hermsprong*, 2 vols (Dublin, 1796; 1st edn, London, 1796).

George Ballard, *Memoirs of Several Ladies of Great Britain* (Oxford, 1752), ed. Ruth Perry (Detroit: Wayne State University Press, 1985).

Anna Laetitia Barbauld, *The Female Speaker* (London, 1811).

Theodric Romeyn Beck, *Elements of Medical Jurisprudence*, 2nd edn (London, 1825; 1st edn 1823).

Thomas Beddoes, *Hygeia*, 3 vols (Bristol, 1802-3).

Daniel Bellamy, *The Young Ladies Miscellany* (London, 1723).

George Anne Bellamy, *An Apology for the Life of George Anne Bellamy*, 3rd edn, 6 vols (London, 1785; 1st edn, 1785).

Elizabeth Ogilvie Benger, *The Female Geniad* (London, 1791).

Elizabeth Ogilvie Benger, *Memoirs of the late Mrs. Elizabeth Hamilton*, 2 vols (London, 1818).

John Bennett, *Strictures on Female Education* (London, 1788).

John Bennett, *Letters to a Young Lady*, 2nd edn, 2 vols (London, 1795; 1st edn, Warrington, 1789).

Mary Berry, *Extracts from the Journals and Correspondence of Miss Berry*, ed. Lady Theresa Lewis, 2nd edn, 3 vols (London, 1866; 1st edn, 1865).

Isaac Bickerstaffe, *The Sultan* (London, 1787; 1st edn, 1784).

John Black (under pseudonym Sappho Search), *A Poetical Review of Miss Hannah More's Strictures on Female Education* (London, 1800).

Sir William Blackstone, *Commentaries on the Laws of England*, 12th edn, 4 vols (London, 1793–95; 1st edn, Oxford, 1765–69).

James Boswell, *The Life of Samuel Johnson*, ed. George Birkbeck Hill and L.F. Powell, 6 vols (Oxford: Clarendon Press, 1934–50; 1st edn, 1791).

Edmund Burke, *Reflections on the Revolution in France* (London, 1790).

Edmund Burke, *A Letter from Mr. Burke to a Member of the National Assembly* (Paris and London, 1791).

Frances Burney, *Evelina*, ed. Edward A. Bloom (London: Oxford University Press, 1968; 1st edn, 1778).

J. Burton, *Lectures on Female Education and Manners*, 2 vols (Rochester and London, 1793).

William Cadogan, *An Essay upon Nursing, and the Management of Children* (London, 1748).

R. Campbell, *The London Tradesman* (London, 1747).

Marie Jean Antoine Nicolas Caritat, Marquis de Condorcet, 'Lettres d'un bourgeois de New-Haven', in *Oeuvres*, ed. A. Condorcet O'Connor and M.F. Arago, 12 vols (Paris, 1847–49), vol. 9 (1847).

Elizabeth Carter, *A Series of Letters between Mrs. Elizabeth Carter and Miss Catherine Talbot, from the year 1741 to 1770*, ed. Montagu Pennington, 4 vols (London, 1809).

Elizabeth Carter, *Letters from Mrs. Elizabeth Carter to Mrs. Montagu, between the years 1755 and 1800*, ed. Montagu Pennington, 3 vols (London, 1817).

H. Cartwright, *Letters on Female Education* (London, 1787).

Edward Chamberlayne, *Englands Wants* (London, 1667).

Edward Chamberlayne, *An Academy or Colledge . . .* (London, 1671).

Hester Chapone, *Letters on the Improvement of the Mind*, 4th edn, 2 vols (London, 1774; 1st edn, 1773).

Charlotte Charke, *A Narrative of the Life of Mrs. Charlotte Charke . . .* (London, 1755).

J.-L. Chirol, *An Enquiry into the Best System of Female Education* (London, 1809).

Mary, Lady Chudleigh, *The Ladies Defence* (London, 1701).

Mary, Lady Chudleigh, *Poems on Several Occasions*, 2nd edn (London, 1713; 1st edn, 1703).

Mary, Lady Chudleigh, *Essays upon several Subjects in Prose and Verse* (London, 1710).

William Clark, *The Province of Midwives in the Practice of their Art* (Bath, 1751).

John Cleland, *Memoirs of a Woman of Pleasure*, ed. Peter Sabor (Oxford and New York: Oxford University Press (World's Classics), 1985; 1st edn, 1749).

Mary Cockle, *Important Studies for the Female Sex* (London, 1809).

Jane Collier, *An Essay on the Art of Ingeniously Tormenting* (London, 1753).

Jeremy Collier, *A Short View of the Immorality and Profaneness of the English Stage*, 3rd edn (London, 1698; 1st edn, 1698).

George Colman, *Polly Honeycombe*, 4th edn (London, 1778; 1st edn, 1760).

George Colman and Bonnell Thornton (eds.), *Poems by the Most Eminent Ladies of Great-Britain and Ireland . . .*, 2 vols

(London, 1773).

Patrick Colquhoun, *A Treatise on the Police of the Metropolis*, 4th edn (London, 1797; 1st edn, 1796).

The Compleat Servant-Maid, 6th edn (London, 1700; 1st edn, 1677).

Conjugal Duty: set forth in a Collection of Ingenious and Delightful Wedding-Sermons, 2 vols (London, 1732).

Ann Batten Cristall, *Poetical Sketches* (London, 1795).

The Danger and Immodesty of the present too general custom of unnecessarily employing men-midwives, 2nd edn (London, 1772).

Erasmus Darwin, *A Plan for the Conduct of Female Education in Boarding-Schools* (Derby and London, 1797).

The Life and Adventures of Mrs. Christian Davies, The British Amazon (London, 1740).

Daniel Defoe, *An Essay upon Projects* (London, 1697).

Robert Dingley, *Proposals for establishing a public place of reception for penitent prostitutes* (London, 1758).

Robert Dodsley (ed.), *A Collection of Poems*, 6 vols (London, 1763).

William Duff, *Letters on the intellectual and moral characters of women* (Aberdeen, 1807).

John Duncon, *The Returns of Spiritual Comfort and Grief in a Devout Soul . . .* (London, 1649).

E.H. East, *A Treatise of the Pleas of the Crown*, 2 vols (London, 1803).

Sir Frederic Morton Eden, *The State of the Poor*, 3 vols (London, 1797).

Maria Edgeworth, *Letters for Literary Ladies* (London, 1795).

Maria Edgeworth, *Castle Rackrent* (London, 1800).

Elizabeth Elstob, *An English-Saxon Homily on the Birth-Day of St. Gregory* (London, 1709).

Elizabeth Elstob, *The Rudiments of Grammar for the English-Saxon Tongue* (London, 1715).

Catalogue of the Scarce Books and Valuable Manuscripts of the Chevalière D'Éon . . . (London, 1791).

Claude Érard and C. Marguetel de Saint-Denis, Seigneur de Saint-Évremond, *The Arguments of Monsieur Erard, for Monsieur the Duke of Mazarin . . . And the Factum for Madam the Dutchess of Mazarin . . . by Monsieur de St. Evremont* (London, 1699).

An Essay in Defence of the Female Sex (London, 1696).

John Essex, *The Young Ladies Conduct* (London, 1722).

Eugenia, *The Female Advocate* (London, 1700).

The Female Miscellany, 2 vols (Shrewsbury, 1770 – 71).

The Female Protector. Written in the Year 1800, MS., The Fawcett Library, London.

Sarah Fielding, *Remarks on Clarissa* (London, 1749).

William Fleetwood, *The Relative Duties of Parents and Children, Husbands and Wives, Masters and Servants* (London, 1705).

James Fordyce, *Sermons to Young Women*, 3rd edn, 2 vols (London, 1766; 1st edn, 1766).

James Fordyce, *The Character and Conduct of the Female Sex* (London, 1776).

Francis Foster, *Thoughts on the Times, but Chiefly on the Profligacy of our Women*, 2nd edn (London, 1779; 1st edn, 1779).

David Garrick, *Miss in her Teens* (London, 1749).

James Gillray, *The Caricatures of Gillray* (London, 1818).

Thomas Gisborne, *An Enquiry into the Duties of Men in the Higher and Middle Classes of Great Britain* (London, 1794).

Thomas Gisborne, *An Enquiry into the Duties of the Female Sex* (London, 1797).

S. Glasse, *Advice from a Lady of Quality to her Children*, 2 vols (Gloucester, 1778).

William Godwin, *An Enquiry concerning Political Justice*, 2 vols (London, 1793).

William Godwin, *Memoirs of the Author of a Vindication of the Rights of Woman*, ed. W. Clark Durant (London: Constable, and New York: Greenberg, 1927; 1st edn, 1798).

Elizabeth Sarah Villa-Real Gooch, *The Life of Mrs. Gooch, written by herself*, 3 vols (London, 1792).

Robert Gould, *Works*, 2 vols (London, 1709).

Sarah Green, *Mental Improvement for a Young Lady* (London, 1793).

John Gregory, *A Father's Legacy to his Daughters* (London, 1774).

Elizabeth Griffith, *Essays Addressed to Young Married Women* (London, 1782).

Richard Griffith, *The Triumvirate*, 2 vols (London, 1764).

William Griffith, *Eumenes* (Trenton, NJ, 1799).

William A. Guy, *Principles of Forensic Medicine* (London, 1844).

Elizabeth Hamilton, *Translation of the Letters of a Hindoo Rajah*, 2 vols (London, 1796).

Elizabeth Hamilton, *Memoirs of Modern Philosophers*, 3 vols (Bath 1800); 4th edn, 3 vols (Bath, 1804).

Elizabeth Hamilton, *Letters addressed to the Daughter of a Nobleman*, 3rd edn, 2 vols (London, 1814; 1st edn, 1806).

The Hardships of the English Laws in Relation to Wives (London and Dublin, 1735).

S. Hatfield, *Letters on the Importance of the Female Sex* (London, 1803).

Laetitia-Matilda Hawkins, *Letters on the Female Mind, its powers and pursuits*, 2 vols (London, 1793).

Laetitia-Matilda Hawkins, *The Countess and Gertrude*, 2nd edn, 4 vols (London, 1812; 1st edn, 1811).

William Hayley, *A Philosophical, Historical and Moral Essay on Old Maids*, 3 vols (London, 1785).

Mary Hays, *Letters and Essays* (London, 1793).

Mary Hays, *Memoirs of Emma Courtney*, 2 vols (London, 1796).

Mary Hays, *Appeal to the Men of Great Britain in behalf of women* (London, 1798).

Mary Hays, *The Victim of Prejudice*, 2 vols (London, 1799); trans., *La victime du préjugé*, 2 vols (Paris, 1799).

Mary Hays, *Female Biography*, 6 vols (London, 1803).

Anthony Highmore, *Pietas Londinensis*, 2 vols (London, 1810).

Theodor Gottlieb von Hippel, *Über die bürgerliche Verbesserung der Weiber* (Frankfurt and Leipzig, 1794; 1st edn, Berlin, 1792).

Thomas Holcroft, *Anna St. Ives*, ed. Peter Faulkner (London: Oxford University Press, 1970; 1st edn, 1792).

Isabella Howard, Countess Dowager of Carlisle, *Thoughts in the Form of Maxims: Addressed to Young Ladies*, 2nd edn, London, 1790; 1st edn, 1789).

Alexander Jardine, *Letters from Barbary, France, Spain, Portugal, etc.*, 2 vols (London, 1788).

The Lady's Choice of a New Standing Member, A New Ballad (London, 1747).

A Lady, *Female Rights Vindicated; or the Equality of the Sexes Morally and Physically Proved* (London, 1758).

A Lady, *The Unhappy Wife*, 2 vols (London, 1770).

Louis Lapeyre, *An Enquiry into the Merits of these two important Questions: I. Whether Women with Child ought to Prefer the Assistance of their own Sex to that of Men-Midwives? II. Whether the Assistance of Men-Midwives is contrary to Decency?* (London, 1772).

William Law, *A Serious Call to a Devout and Holy Life* (London, 1729).

James Lawrence, *An Essay on the Nair System of Gallantry and*

Inheritance (London, 1800).

James Lawrence, *The Empire of the Nairs: or, the Rights of Women*, 4 vols (London, 1811).

The Laws respecting Women (London, 1777).

Pierre Le Moyne, *La gallerie des femmes fortes* (Paris, 1647).

Launcelot Light and Laetitia Lookabout, *A Sketch of the Rights of Boys and Girls. Part the First.* (London, 1792).

Charles Lloyd, *Edmund Oliver*, 2 vols (Bristol, 1798).

Charles Lloyd and Charles Lamb, *Blank Verse* (London, 1798).

John Locke, *Two Treatises of Government*, ed. Peter Laslett, 2nd edn (Cambridge: Cambridge University Press, 1967).

John Locke, *The Educational Writings*, ed. James L. Axtell (Cambridge: Cambridge University Press, 1968).

Catharine Macaulay, *Letters on Education* (London, 1790).

Henry Mackenzie, *Julia de Roubigné*, 2 vols (London, 1777).

Martin Madan, *Thelyphthora: or, a Treatise on Female Ruin*, 3 vols (London, 1780-81).

Sarah Maese, *The School*, 3 vols (London, 1766).

The Histories of Some of the Penitents in the Magdalen-House, 2 vols (London, 1760).

The Magdalen, or History of the first Penitent received into that charitable asylum (London, 1780).

The Plan of the Magdalen House for the Reception of Penitent Prostitutes (London, 1758).

Bathsua Makin, *An Essay to Revive the Ancient Education of Gentlewomen* (London, 1673).

Damaris, Lady Masham, *A Discourse concerning the Love of God* (London, 1696).

Thomas Mathias, *The Shade of Alexander Pope on the Banks of the Thames* (London, 1799).

Martha Mears, *The Pupil of Nature* (London, 1797).

John Moir, *Female Tuition* (London, 1784).

Elizabeth Montagu, *Letters*, ed. Matthew Montagu, 3rd edn, 4 vols (London, 1810–13; 1st edn, 1809–13).

Lady Mary Wortley Montagu, *Complete Letters*, ed. Robert Halsband, 3 vols (Oxford: Clarendon Press, 1965–67).

Hannah More, *Strictures on the Modern System of Female Education*, 2 vols (London, 1799).

Hannah More, *Coelebs in Search of a Wife*, 2 vols (London, 1808).

James Armstrong Neal, *An Essay on the Education and Genius of the Female Sex* (Philadelphia, 1795).

William Nicholls, *The Duty of Inferiours towards their Superiours*

(London, 1701).

Elizabeth Nihell, *A Treatise on the Art of Midwifery* (London, 1760).

Amelia Opie, *Adeline Mowbray*, 1st US edn, 2 vols (Georgetown, 1808; 1st edn, London, 1805).

William Paley, *The Principles of Moral and Political Philosophy* (London, 1785).

Montagu Pennington, *Memoirs of the Life of Mrs. Elizabeth Carter*, 3rd edn, 2 vols (London, 1816; 1st edn, 1807).

Sarah, Lady Pennington, *A Mother's Advice to her Absent Daughters* (London, 1761).

Philautus, *The Pretty Gentleman: or, Softness of Manners Vindicated from the false Ridicule Exhibited under the Character of William Fribble, Esq.* (London, 1747).

Laetitia Pilkington, *Memoirs*, 3 vols (Dublin, 1748–54).

The Polite Academy; or School of Behaviour for Young Gentlemen and Ladies, 3rd edn (London, 1765; 1st edn, Salisbury, 1762).

Richard Polwhele, *The Unsex'd Females*, (London, 1799).

Alexander Pope, *Epistles to Several Persons*, ed. F.W. Bateson (London: Methuen, and New Haven: Yale University Press, 1951) (vol. III.ii of Twickenham edn of *Poems*).

Portia, *The Polite Lady*, (London, 1760).

François Poulain de la Barre, *De l'excellence des hommes contre l'égalité des deux sexes* (Paris, 1675).

François Poulain de la Barre, *De l'égalité des deux sexes* (Paris, 1673); trans., *The Woman as Good as the Man* (London, 1677).

François Poulain de la Barre, *Dissertation ou discours pour servir de troisième partie au livre de l'égalité des deux sexes* (Paris, 1690).

Mary Ann Radcliffe, *The Female Advocate; or an attempt to recover the Rights of Women from male usurpation* (London, 1799).

Mary Ann Radcliffe, *The Memoirs of Mrs. Mary Ann Radcliffe* (Edinburgh, 1810).

Clara Reeve, *The Progress of Romance*, 2 vols (Colchester and London, 1785).

Clara Reeve, *The School for Widows*, 3 vols (London, 1791).

Clara Reeve, *Plans of Education* (London, 1792).

Samuel Richardson, *Correspondence*, ed. Anna Laetitia Barbauld, 6 vols (London, 1804).

R. Roberts, *Sermons Written by a Lady* (London, 1770).

Mary Robinson, *The False Friend*, 4 vols (London, 1799).

Mary Robinson (under pseudonym Anne Frances Randall), *A Letter to the Women of England, on the Injustice of Mental*

Subordination (London, 1799).

Mary Robinson, *Memoirs*, 2 vols (London, 1801).

Mary Robinson, *Poetical Works*, 3 vols (London, 1806).

Timothy Rogers, *The Character of a Good Woman* (London, 1697).

Archibald Hamilton Rowan, *Autobiography* (Dublin, 1840).

François Salignac de la Mothe Fénelon, *Instructions for the education of a daughter*, trans. George Hickes (London, 1707).

George Savile, Marquis of Halifax, *The Lady's New-Year's Gift: or Advice to a Daughter* (London, 1688).

Anna Maria van Schurman, *Dissertatio de ingenii muliebris ad doctrinam et meliores litteras aptitudine* (Leyden, 1641; trans., *The Learned Maid*, London, 1659).

Anna Maria van Schurman, *Opuscula Hebraea, Graeca, Latina, Gallica*, (2nd edn, Leyden, 1650; 1st edn, 1648).

Anna Maria van Schurman, *Eukleria seu melioris partis electio* (Altona, 1673).

Mary Scott, *The Female Advocate* (London, 1774).

Sarah Scott, *A Description of Millennium Hall*, ed. Walter M. Crittenden (New York: Bookman Associates, 1955; 1st edn, London, 1762).

Sir Walter Scott, *Letters*, ed. H.J.C. Grierson *et al.*, 12 vols (London: Constable, 1932 –37).

Anna Seward, *Llangollen Vale* (London, 1796).

Anna Seward, 'Letter to E. Jerningham', *The Gentleman's Magazine*, 71 (1801), pp. 113-17, 195-7.

Anna Seward, *Poetical Works; with Extracts from her literary Correspondence*, 3 vols (Edinburgh, 1810).

Anna Seward, *Letters*, 6 vols (Edinburgh, 1811).

Thomas Seward, 'The Female Right to Literature', in Robert Dodsley (ed.), *A Collection of Poems*, 6 vols (London, 1763), vol. 2, pp. 294-300.

Thomas Sharp, *The Life of John Sharp, D.D., Lord Archbishop of York*, 2 vols (London, 1825).

William Sherlock, *The Case of the Allegiance due to Soveraign Powers*, 3rd edn (London, 1691; 1st edn, 1691).

Hugh Smith, *Letters to Married Women*, 4th edn (Dublin, 1777; 1st edn, 1767).

The Female Soldier: or the Surprising Life and Adventures of Hannah Snell (London, 1750).

The Society for Bettering the Condition and Increasing the Comforts of the Poor, *Reports*, vol. 2 (London, 1800); vol. 3 (London, 1802); vol. 4 (London, 1805).

The Society for the Suppression of Vice, *Report* (1825).

Sophia, *Man Superior to Woman* (London, 1739).

Sophia, *Woman not Inferior to Man* (London, 1739).

Sophia, *Woman's Superior Excellence over Man* (London, 1740).

John Sprint, *The Bride-Woman's Counsellor* (London, 1699).

Edward Stephens, *A Christian Admonition to the Grecians* (London, 1701).

Sarah Stone, *A Complete Practice of Midwifery* (London, 1737).

Jeremy Taylor, *The Rule and Exercises of Holy Living,* in vol. 3 of *Works,* ed. Reginald Heber and Charles Page Eden, 10 vols (London, 1854; 1st edn of *Holy Living,* 1650).

Jeremy Taylor, *A Discourse of the Measures and Offices of Friendship,* 3rd edn (London, 1662; 1st edn, 1657).

Thomas Taylor, *A Vindication of the Rights of Brutes* (London, 1792).

Elizabeth Thomas, *The Honourable Lovers: Or, the Second and Last Volume of Pylades and Corinna* (London, 1732).

Hester Lynch Thrale, *Thraliana,* ed. Katharine C. Balderston, 2 vols (Oxford: Clarendon Press, 1942).

A Treatise of Feme Coverts: or the Lady's Law (London, 1732).

Sarah Trimmer, *The Oeconomy of Charity* (London, 1787).

Catherine Trotter Cockburn, *A defence of the Essay of human understanding, written by Mr. Lock* (London, 1702).

Sir John Vanbrugh, *Complete Works,* ed. Geoffrey Webb and Bonamy Dobrée, 4 vols (London: Nonesuch Press, 1927–28).

Priscilla Wakefield, *Mental Improvement,* 2 vols (London, 1794).

Priscilla Wakefield, *Reflections on the Present Condition of the Female Sex* (London, 1798).

Priscilla Wakefield, *A Family Tour through the British Empire* (London, 1804).

George Walker, *The Vagabond,* 2nd American edn, from the 4th English edn (Harrisonburg, 1814; 1st edn, 2 vols, London, 1799).

William Walsh, *A Dialogue Concerning Women,* in *Works* (London, 1736).

Edward Ward, *A Compleat and Humorous Account of the Remarkable Clubs and Societies in the Cities of London and Westminster,* (London, 1745; 1st edn, 1709).

Saunders Welch, *A Proposal to render effective a Plan, to remove the Nuisance of Common Prostitutes from the Streets of this Metropolis* (London, 1758).

Helena Wells Whitford, *Letters on subjects of importance to the happiness of young females* (London, 1799).

Helena Wells Whitford, *Constantia Neville; or the West Indian*, 3 vols (London, 1800).

Helena Wells Whitford, *Thoughts and Remarks on Establishing an Institution for the Support and Education of Unportioned Respectable Females* (London, 1809).

Jane West, *Letters addressed to a Young Man*, 3 vols (London, 1801).

Jane West, *Letters to a Young Lady*, 2nd edn, 3 vols (London, 1806; 1st edn, 1806).

Sir George Wheeler, *The Protestant Monastery* (London, 1698).

William Whiston, *A New Theory of the Earth* (London, 1696).

The Whole Duty of a Woman (London, 1700).

The Whole Duty of a Woman (London, 1737).

Wetenhall Wilkes, *A Letter of Genteel and Moral Advice to a Young Lady* (Dublin, 1740).

Helen Maria Williams, *Julia, a Novel*, 2 vols (London, 1790).

Helen Maria Williams, *Letters written in France in the Summer of 1790* (Dublin, 1791).

Helen Maria Williams, *A Residence in France during the years 1792, 1793, 1794 and 1795; described in a series of letters from an English Lady*, 3rd edn, 2 vols (London, 1797).

Harriette Wilson, *Memoirs*, 2nd edn, 4 vols (London, 1825; 1st edn, 1825).

Mary Wollstonecraft, *Collected Letters*, ed. Ralph M. Wardle (Ithaca, NY, and London: Cornell University Press, 1979).

Mary Wollstonecraft, *Thoughts on the Education of Daughters* (London, 1787).

Mary Wollstonecraft (ed. under pseudonym Mr Cresswick), *The Female Reader* (London, 1789).

Mary Wollstonecraft, *A Vindication of the Rights of Men, in a letter to the Right Honourable Edmund Burke* (London, 1790).

Mary Wollstonecraft, *Elements of Morality for the Use of Children*, 2 vols (London, 1790). (Translation of Christian Gotthilf Salzmann, *Moralisches Elementarbuch*, Leipzig, 1782).

Mary Wollstonecraft, *A Vindication of the Rights of Woman*, 2nd edn (London, 1792; 1st edn, 1792).

Mary Wollstonecraft, *An Historical and Moral View of the Progress of the French Revolution* (London, 1794).

Mary Wollstonecraft, *Letters written during a short residence in Sweden, Norway, and Denmark* (London, 1796).

Mary Wollstonecraft, *Mary, and The Wrongs of Woman*, ed. James Kinsley and Gary Kelly (Oxford: Oxford University Press, 1976; 1st edns 1788 and 1798).

Mary Wollstonecraft, *Posthumous Works*, 4 vols (London, 1798).

A Defence of the Character and Conduct of the late Mrs. Mary Wollstonecraft Godwin (London, 1803).

Hannah Woolley, *The Gentlewoman's Companion* (London, 1675).

William Wotton, *Reflections upon Ancient and Modern Learning* (London, 1694).

Mary Wray (ed.), *The Ladies Library*, 3 vols (London, 1714).

Secondary Sources

Jane Abray, 'Feminism in the French Revolution', *American Historical Review* 80 (1975), pp. 43-62.

Richard Acworth, *The Philosophy of John Norris of Bemerton (1657–1712)* (Hildesheim and New York: Georg Olms Verlag, 1979).

George A. Aitken, 'Steele's "Ladies' Library"', *The Athenaeum*, no. 2958 (5 July 1884).

Marc Angenot, *Les Champions des femmes* (Montreal: Les Presses de l'Université du Québec, 1977).

Dudley W.R. Bahlman, *The Moral Revolution of 1688* (London and New Haven: Yale University Press, 1957).

Robert D. Bass, *The Green Dragoon: The Lives of Banastre Tarleton and Mary Robinson* (New York: Henry Holt and Co., 1957).

Una Birch Pope-Hennessy, *Anna Maria van Schurman* (London: Longmans, Green and Co., 1909).

Dorothy Blakey, *The Minerva Press, 1790–1820* (London: for the Bibliographical Society at the University Press, Oxford, 1939).

Reginald Blunt (ed.), *Mrs. Montagu 'Queen of the Blues': Her Letters and Friendships from 1762 to 1800*, 2 vols (London: Constable, 1923).

Paul-Gabriel Boucé (ed.), *Sexuality in Eighteenth-Century Britain* (Manchester: Manchester University Press, and Totowa, NJ: Barnes and Noble, 1982).

James T. Boulton, *The Language of Politics in the Age of Wilkes and Burke* (London: Routledge and Kegan Paul, and

Toronto: University of Toronto Press, 1963).

William C. Braithwaite, *The Beginnings of Quakerism*, 2nd edn (Cambridge: Cambridge University Press, 1955).

William C. Braithwaite, *The Second Period of Quakerism*, 2nd edn (Cambridge: Cambridge University Press, 1955).

George C. Brauer, Jr, *The Education of a Gentleman* (New York: Bookman Associates, 1959).

Alan Bray, *Homosexuality in Renaissance England* (London: Gay Men's Press, 1982).

Renate Bridenthal and Claudia Koonz (eds.), *Becoming Visible: Women in European History* (Boston: Houghton Mifflin Co., 1977).

Ford K. Brown, *Fathers of the Victorians* (Cambridge: Cambridge University Press, 1961).

Pierre Burgelin, 'L' éducation de Sophie', *Annales de la société Jean-Jacques Rousseau*, 35 (1959–62), pp. 113-30.

Marilyn Butler, *Maria Edgeworth: A Literary Biography* (Oxford: Oxford University Press, 1972).

Marilyn Butler, *Jane Austen and the War of Ideas* (Oxford: Clarendon Press, 1975).

John Campbell, *The Lives of the Lord Chancellors*, 5 vols (London, 1845–46).

Terry Castle, 'The Carnivalization of Eighteenth-Century English Narrative', *PMLA* 99 (1984), pp. 903-16.

Terry Castle, 'Eros and Liberty at the English Masquerade, 1710–90', *Eighteenth-Century Studies* 17 (2) (1983–84), pp. 156-76.

Michel de Certeau, *La Fable mystique xvie–xviie siècle* (Paris: Gallimard, 1982).

H.F. B. Compston, *The Magdalen Hospital: The Story of a Great Charity* (London: SPCK, 1917).

Nancy F. Cott, *The Bonds of Womanhood: 'Woman's Sphere' in New England, 1780–1835* (New Haven and London: Yale University Press, 1977).

Lester G. Crocker, 'Julie ou la nouvelle duplicité', *Annales de la société Jean-Jacques Rousseau*, 36 (1963–65), pp. 105-52.

Robert Darnton, *The Great Cat Massacre and Other Episodes in French Cultural History* (New York: Basic Books, 1984).

David Brion Davis, *The Problem of Slavery in Western Culture* (Ithaca, NY: Cornell University Press, 1966).

Natalie Zemon Davis, *Society and Culture in Early Modern France* (London: Duckworth, and Stanford: Stanford University Press, 1975).

Bibliography

Jean Donnison, *Midwives and Medical Men: A History of Inter-Professional Rivalries and Women's Rights* (London: Heinemann, 1977).

Margaret Doody, *A Natural Passion: A Study of the Novels of Samuel Richardson* (Oxford: Clarendon Press, 1974).

Dianne Dugaw, 'Balladry's Female Warriors: Women, Warfare and Disguise in the Eighteenth Century', *Eighteenth Century Life*, 9 (2) n.s. (1985), pp. 1-20.

T.C. Duncan Eaves and Ben Kimpel, *Samuel Richardson: A Biography* (Oxford: Clarendon Press, 1971).

Audrey Eccles, *Obstetrics and Gynaecology in Tudor and Stuart England* (London and Canberra: Croom Helm, 1982).

Zillah R. Eisenstein, *The Radical Future of Liberal Feminism* (New York and London: Longman, 1981).

Anne Katherine Elwood, *Memoirs of the Literary Ladies of England*, 2 vols (London, 1843).

Barbara English and John Savile, *Strict Settlement: A Guide for Historians* (University of Hull Press, 1983) (Hull University Press Occasional Papers in Economic and Social History, no. 10).

Lillian Faderman, *Surpassing the Love of Men* (New York: Morrow, 1981, and London: Junction Books, 1982).

Pierre Fauchery, *La Destinée féminine dans le roman européen du dix-huitième siècle* (Paris: Armand Colin, 1972).

Charlotte Fell-Smith, *Mary Rich, Countess of Warwick* (London: Longmans, Green and Co., 1901).

David Foxon, *Libertine Literature in England 1660–1745* (London: reprinted from *The Book Collector*, 1964).

Paul Fritz and Richard Morton (eds.), *Woman in the Eighteenth Century and other essays* (Toronto and Sarasota: Samuel Stevens Hakkert and Co., 1976) (Publications of the McMaster University Association for Eighteenth-Century Studies, vol. 4).

Elizabeth B. Gasking, *Investigations into Generation 1651–1828* (Baltimore: The Johns Hopkins Press, and London: Hutchinson, 1967).

M. Dorothy George, *London Life in the Eighteenth Century* (London: Penguin, 1966; 1st edn, 1925).

C.H. Hartmann, *The Vagabond Duchess* (London: G. Routledge and Sons, 1926).

J. Jean Hecht, *The Domestic Servant Class in Eighteenth-Century England* (London: Routledge and Kegan Paul, 1956).

Joachim Henrich, *Die Frauenfrage bei Steele und Addison*

(Leipzig: Mayer und Müller, 1930) (*Palaestra* 168).

G. Birkbeck Hill, *Johnsonian Miscellanies*, 2 vols (Oxford, 1897).

Derek Hirst, *The Representative of the People? Voters and Voting in England under the Early Stuarts* (Cambridge: Cambridge University Press, 1975).

Peter C. Hoffer and N.E.H. Hull, *Murdering Mothers: Infanticide in England and New England 1558–1803* (New York and London: New York University Press, 1981) (New York University School of Law Studies in Legal History, 2).

Paul Hoffmann, *La Femme dans la pensée des lumières* (Paris: Éditions Ophrys, 1977).

Lee Holcombe, *Wives and Property: Reform of the Married Women's Property Law in Nineteenth-Century England* (Toronto: University of Toronto Press, 1983).

James K. Hopkins, *A Woman to Deliver Her People: Joanna Southcott and English Millenarianism in an Era of Revolution* (Austin: University of Texas Press, 1982).

Joyce M. Horner, *The English Women Novelists and their Connection with the Feminist Movement (1688–1797)* (Smith College Studies in Modern Languages, XI (1, 2, 3)). (Northampton, Mass., 1929–30).

Wilbur Samuel Howell, *Logic and Rhetoric in England 1500–1700* (Princeton, NJ: Princeton University Press, 1956).

Joyce Irwin, 'Anna Maria van Schurman: From Feminism to Pietism', *Church History*, 46 (1) (1977), pp. 48-62.

R.M. Janes, 'On the Reception of Mary Wollstonecraft's *A Vindication of the Rights of Woman*', *Journal of the History of Ideas*, 39 (2) (April/June 1978), pp. 293-302.

M.G. Jones, *The Charity School Movement: A Study of Eighteenth-Century Puritanism in Action* (Cambridge: Cambridge University Press, 1938; reprinted Hamden, Conn.: Archon Books, 1964).

M.G. Jones, *Hannah More* (Cambridge: Cambridge University Press, 1952).

Josephine Kamm, *Hope Deferred* (London, Methuen, 1965).

Barbara Kanner (ed.), *The Women of England* (Hamden, Conn.: Archon Books, 1979, and London: Mansell, 1980).

Courtney Stanhope Kenny, *The History of the Law of England as to the Effects of Marriage on Property and on the Wife's Legal Capacity* (London, 1879).

Shirley Strum Kenny, 'Marriage in English Comedy 1690–1720', *South Atlantic Quarterly* 78 (1979), pp. 84-106.

Bibliography

J.P. Kenyon, *Revolution Principles: The Politics of Party 1689–1720* (Cambridge: Cambridge University Press, 1977).

Frank J. Klingberg and Sigurd B. Hustvedt (eds.), *The Warning Drum: The British Home Front Faces Napoleon: Broadsides of 1803* (Berkeley and Los Angeles: University of California Press, 1944).

Arnold Lloyd, *Quaker Social History 1669–1738* (London: Longmans, Green, and Co., 1951).

Gina M. Luria, *Mary Hays: A Critical Biography* (Ph.D thesis, New York University, 1972).

B.G. MacCarthy, *The Later Women Novelists 1744–1818* (Cork: Cork University Press, and Oxford: Basil Blackwell, 1947).

Ruth K. McClure, *Coram's Children: The London Foundling Hospital in the Eighteenth Century* (New Haven and London: Yale University Press, 1981).

Robert H. MacDonald, 'The Frightful Consequences of Onanism: Notes on the History of a Delusion', *Journal of the History of Ideas*, 28 (3) (1967), pp. 423-31.

Margaret Eliot MacGregor, *Amelia Alderson Opie: Worldling and Friend* (Northampton, Mass., 1933) (Smith College Studies in Modern Languages, vol. 14, nos. 1-2, October 1932–January 1933).

O.R. McGregor, *Divorce in England* (London: William Heinemann, 1957).

Ian Maclean, *The Renaissance Notion of Woman* (Cambridge: Cambridge University Press, 1980).

Dorothy Marshall, *The English Poor in the Eighteenth Century* (London: George Routledge and Sons Ltd, 1926).

Elizabeth Mavor, *The Ladies of Llangollen* (London: Michael Joseph, 1971).

Samuel Pyatt Menefee, *Wives for Sale* (Oxford: Basil Blackwell, 1981).

Nancy K. Miller, *The Heroine's Text: Readings in the French and English Novel, 1722–1782* (New York: Columbia University Press, 1980).

R.P. Neuman, 'Masturbation, Madness, and the Modern Concepts of Childhood and Adolescence', *Journal of Social History*, 8 (3) (1975), pp. 1-27.

Mary Beth Norton, *Liberty's Daughters: The Revolutionary Experience of American Women, 1750–1800* (Boston and Toronto: Little, Brown and Co., 1980).

Felicity A. Nussbaum, *The Brink of All We Hate: English Satires on Women 1660–1750* (Lexington: University Press of

Kentucky, 1984).

Susan Moller Okin, *Women in Western Political Thought* (Princeton, NJ: Princeton University Press, 1979).

Susan Moller Okin, 'Patriarchy and Married Women's Property in England: Questions on Some Current Views', *Eighteenth-Century Studies*, 17 (2) (Winter 1983-84), pp. 121-38.

Ronald Paulson, *Hogarth's Graphic Works*, revised edn, 2 vols (New Haven and London: Yale University Press, 1970).

Ruth Perry, 'A seventeenth-century feminist poet', *Times Literary Supplement* (20 August 1982), p. 911.

Ruth Perry, *The Celebrated Mary Astell: An Early English Feminist* (Chicago and London: University of Chicago Press, 1986).

Ivy Pinchbeck, *Women Workers and the Industrial Revolution 1750–1850* (London: Routledge, 1930).

Ivy Pinchbeck and Margaret Hewitt, *Children in English Society*, 2 vols (London: Routledge and Kegan Paul, and Toronto: University of Toronto Press, 1969–73).

Mary Poovey, *The Proper Lady and the Woman Writer: Ideology as Style in the Works of Mary Wollstonecraft, Mary Shelley, and Jane Austen* (Chicago and London: University of Chicago Press, 1984).

Maurice J. Quinlan, *Victorian Prelude: A History of English Manners 1700–1850* (New York: Columbia University Press, 1941).

Leon Radzinowicz, *A History of English Criminal Law and its Administration from 1750*, 4 vols (London: Stevens and Sons, 1948–68).

Betsy Rodgers, *Cloak of Charity* (London: Methuen, 1949).

Katharine M. Rogers, *Feminism in Eighteenth-Century England* (Urbana: University of Illinois Press, and Brighton: Harvester Press, 1982).

William Merritt Sale, Jr, *Samuel Richardson: A Bibliographical Record of his Literary Career* (New Haven: Yale University Press, and London: Oxford University Press, 1936).

David M. Schneider and Kathleen Gough, *Matrilineal Kinship* (Berkeley and Los Angeles: University of California Press, 1961).

Barbara Brandon Schnorrenburg, 'Education for Women in Eighteenth Century England: An Annotated Bibliography', *Women and Literature*, 4 (1) (1976), pp. 49-55.

Gordon J. Schochet, *Patriarchalism in Political Thought*

(Oxford: Basil Blackwell, 1975).

Joel Schwartz, *The Sexual Politics of Jean-Jacques Rousseau* (Chicago and London: University of Chicago Press, 1984).

Michael A. Seidel, 'Poulain de la Barre's *The Woman as Good as the Man*', *Journal of the History of Ideas*, 35 (3) (1974), pp. 499-508.

Philippe Séjourné, *Aspects généraux du roman féminin en Angleterre de 1740 à 1800* (Publications des Annales de la Faculté des Lettres, Aix-en-Provence, Nouvelle série no. 52, 1966).

C.A. Seligman, 'Mary Toft – The Rabbit Breeder', *Medical History*, 5 (1961), pp. 349-60.

Edward Shorter, *A History of Women's Bodies* (New York: Basic Books, 1982, and London: Allen Lane, 1983).

Florence M. Smith, *Mary Astell* (New York: Columbia University Press, 1916).

Philip Webster Souers, *The Matchless Orinda* (Cambridge, Mass.: Harvard University Press, 1931).

Patricia Meyer Spacks, 'Ev'ry Woman is at Heart a Rake', *Eighteenth-Century Studies*, 8 (1) (1974), pp. 27-46.

Patricia Meyer Spacks, *Imagining a Self: Autobiography and Novel in Eighteenth-Century England* (Cambridge, Mass. and London: Harvard University Press, 1976).

Terence Spencer, *Fair Greece, Sad Relic: Literary Philhellenism from Shakespeare to Byron* (London: Weidenfeld and Nicolson, 1954).

Donald A. Stauffer, *The Art of Biography in Eighteenth Century England* (Princeton, NJ: Princeton University Press, 1941).

Susan Staves, 'British Seduced Maidens', *Eighteenth-Century Studies*, 14 (2) (1980-81), pp. 109-34.

Lawrence Stone, *The Crisis of the Aristocracy 1558-1641* (Oxford: Clarendon Press, 1965).

Lawrence Stone, *The Family, Sex and Marriage in England 1500-1800* (London: Weidenfeld and Nicolson, 1977).

Wylie Sypher, *Guinea's Captive Kings: British Anti-Slavery Literature of the XVIIIth Century* (Chapel Hill: University of North Carolina Press, 1942).

Keith Thomas, 'The Double Standard', *Journal of the History of Ideas*, 20 (2) (1959), pp. 195-216.

Janet M. Todd, *Mary Wollstonecraft: An Annotated Bibliography* (New York and London: Garland Publishing, Inc., 1976).

Janet M. Todd, *Women's Friendship in Literature* (New York: Columbia University Press, 1980).

Claire Tomalin, *The Life and Death of Mary Wollstonecraft* (London: Weidenfeld and Nicolson, 1974).

Randolph Trumbach,*The Rise of the Egalitarian Family* (New York: Academic Press, 1978).

Susie I. Tucker, *Protean Shape: A Study in Eighteenth-Century Vocabulary and Usage* (London: The Athlone Press, 1967).

James H. Warner, 'Eighteenth-Century English reactions to the *Nouvelle Héloïse', PMLA*, 52 (1937), pp. 802-19.

Miriam Wilford, 'Bentham on the Rights of Women', *Journal of the History of Ideas*, 36 (1) (1975), pp. 167-76.

Guy Williams, *The Age of Agony: The Art of Healing c. 1700 –1800* (London: Constable, 1975).

E.A. Wrigley and R.S. Schofield, *The Population History of England 1541–1871* (London: Edward Arnold, 1981).

Index